Say What Happened

Nick Fraser is the author of *The Voice of Modern Hatred* and *The Importance of Being Eton*. Of French and British parentage, he has lived and worked in the United States, France and Britain. After suffering a stroke in 2017, he has recovered through writing this book. He received the 2017 BAFTA Special Award. He is also a contributing editor of *Harper's Magazine* and frequently writes for the *Observer*. He is the creative director of Docsville.

Say What Happened

A Story of Documentaries

NICK FRASER

FABER & FABER

First published in 2019
by Faber & Faber Limited
Bloomsbury House
74–77 Great Russell Street, London WC1B 3DA

Typeset by Ian Bahrami
Printed in England by CPI Group (UK) Ltd, Croydon CR0 4YY

Excerpt on p. 39 from *Collected Poems* by Robert Lowell. Copyright © 2003 by Harriet
Lowell and Sheridan Lowell. Reprinted by permission of Farrar, Straus and Giroux

Stills from: *The Arbor* (2010) © Clio Barnard (p. xi); *India's Daughter* (2015) © Leslee
Udwin (p. 1); *Man on Wire* (2008) © Philippe Petit (p. 49); *Man with a Movie Camera*
(1929) © BFI (p. 83); *Life on Earth* (1979) © Press Association (p. 115); *Faces Places* (2017)
© Cine Tamaris (p. 145); *Grey Gardens* (1975) © Maysles Films (p. 163); *The Leader, His
Driver and the Driver's Wife* (1991) © Nick Broomfield (p. 199); *Shoah* (1985) © New Yorker
Films (p. 235); *When We Were Kings* (1996) © Authentic Brands Group (p. 263); *Please Vote
for Me* (2007) © Weijun Chen (p. 317); *La Sortie de l'usine Lumière à Lyon* (1895) © BFI
(p. 339); *The English Surgeon* (2007) © Geoffrey Smith (p. 371)

The right of Nick Fraser to be identified as author of this work
has been asserted in accordance with Section 77 of the
Copyright, Designs and Patents Act 1988

A CIP record for this book
is available from the British Library

ISBN 978–0–571–32956–4

2 4 6 8 10 9 7 5 3

To all the film-makers with whom I've worked

Contents

Acknowledgements

I cannot list all the people that I've worked with – there are so many, and so many great films. I am thankful for everyone's help and intelligence, and this book is a testament to all of them. For their contributions over the last year, I must give special mention to Roy Ackerman, Claire Aguilar, Axel Arnö, Adam Benzine, Rudy Buttignol, Mandy Chang, Dan Cogan, Alex Cooke, Heather Croall, Jeremy Cunningham, Rosie Dastgir, Jason Emerton, John Gapper, Alex Gibney, Ann Gollin, Roger Graef, Naomi Gryn, Alan Hayling, Mette Heide, Georgina Hill, Marc Isaacs, Eugene Jarecki, Pete Joy, Margje de Koning, Lewis Lapham, Jo Lapping, Ben Lewis, Sean McAllister, Robert McCrum, Ursula Macfarlane, Charlotte Moore, Veronica Noah, Kevin Pakenham, Brenda Phipps, Ros Sloboda, Mark Thompson, Kate Townsend and Alan Yentob. Special love for my forbearing family: Joanne, Wiz (a great reader/listener) and Charlie, and my sisters Elisabeth and Anne. Special thanks to my colleagues at Docsville, Lawrence Elman and Holly Whiston. India Woods helped complete this book by reading the drafts and making sense of them. Some of its contents are extracted from my pamphlet published by the Reuters Institute for the Study of Journalism in Oxford. John Lloyd first told me to write the book. Thanks to Jane Ferguson and John Mulholland at the *Observer*. My agent Jonny Geller loves documentaries. Walter Donohue and Ian Bahrami at Faber worked with me on the edit. Through the Why

Foundation I have made many films with Mette Hoffmann and Charlotte Meyer that have been shown to millions throughout the world.

This isn't an academic or historical book and I hope that I don't annoy too many fans of documentary films. Thanks to Kevin Macdonald and Mark Cousins, who compiled *Imagining Reality: The Faber Book of Documentary*.

Introduction

Acting out reality: Clio Barnard's *The Arbor* (2010).
Films should make the worst things comprehensible.

This isn't in any way a definitive book about documentary film. Nor can I claim to have written an academic text. I lack the qualifications for such work, so I've tried instead to explain how documentary films began, how they matured and developed; how over past decades they came from the margins to become a significant cultural form and one of the ways in which we understand the world around us. The story remains important to me because that is how I've come to see documentaries. For seventeen years, I supervised the BBC documentary series *Storyville*. I created it with the help of colleagues, and as I watched it mature, I followed the remarkable progress of the films that we created and transmitted. But I was always aware of the limits of documentaries. They often don't reach their audiences, and even when they do, they tend to thrive within the cultures that have grown up with them. I enjoyed this culture, taking part in its rituals, but I always felt like a bit of an outsider. My view was that it would be better if documentaries were seen by more people, even those who objected to what they showed. This is part of the story I tell.

I've been a reporter and I've written books. Writing comes easier to me than sitting watching hours and hours of footage. I suspect that ingrained impatience made my life as an editor easier, but it also made this book harder for me to write. Documentaries describe and recreate slivers of the world we inhabit. At their best, they illuminate our surroundings. Sometimes the beam is fitful and narrow, like an erratic handheld torch or a searchlight swinging in the dark; sometimes everything comes up brightly in plain view. They are often arbitrary in their approach, unsystematic, impermanent. But this means that to write about documentaries, one must try to understand the cultural environment in which they were created and, just as importantly, the media landscape from which they sprang. In writing this book, I have tried to understand a problematic and confusing scene. 'I don't really understand contemporary media,' Mark Thompson, my former boss at the BBC, a supporter of *Storyville* and now the chief executive officer of the New York Times Company, told me. He added that he felt that he had once understood it, but no longer did, so unpredictable and complex had its effects become.

After spending much of my lifetime in proximity to print and film, I concur with this judgement, but acknowledge, too, that it makes it much harder to write about docs. How are they viewed? Do they really change minds? If they were differently conceived, and shown in another way, might they be more effective? These questions are also part of my story. But I've come to feel that there's another dimension to my doubts, looming behind the subject like a giant, ceaselessly moving stage set. I am referring to the current state of the world, and how this affects us all. I do not recall a moment when so many people I know, in so many countries, have appeared so aware that the world has entered a more hazardous phase. We live in peace, to be sure, but we realise that many do not, and most of us would tend to agree that the calamities implied by a planet that is heating up lie before us. In the meantime, a level of confusion about our own institutions seems to fog our vision. The most basic ideas, such as free speech, seem under fire, not just from their traditional enemies – now more powerful than they were even five years ago – but from our own confusions, too.

I don't know how to describe the epidemic of so-called 'fake news'. I would like to think that its development, alongside those outlined above, will reciprocally encourage the traditional truth-telling aspect of documentary culture, but I cannot be sure. We appear to be at the beginning of some giant cultural mutation to which there is no visible end.

Writing this book against such a background, I felt torn in a number of ways. What do people really want to know? So far, the relatively leisurely pace of documentary film-making hasn't been affected by the instantaneity of new media, but that might soon change. If it does, where will that leave us? Film-makers and media executives tend to shy away from such questions, but I couldn't.

Being an editor involves putting your ear to the zeitgeist. One part of me wished to put up fences against contemporary reality, and I found myself drawn to films depicting relatively sheltered spaces where humans enjoyed themselves. At the same time, I found that I needed to immerse myself in many films that spoke of darkness. I've included these in my narrative, trying to judge them. Let me give an example: *Silvered Water, Syria Self-Portrait* (2014) was made from a combination of YouTube footage posted by soldiers of the Syrian army and by jihadis – many of them thwarted executioners finally able to exercise their chosen profession at large, and without restraint – and the video diary of a Kurdish exile who tried to set up a school for young girls in Damascus, but who abandoned her efforts once she'd been warned that they would endanger her life and those of her charges. It's beautiful, but what it shows is appalling, intolerable.

There are no adjectives to describe adequately what it reveals. Watch the film, is all I can say – or don't. I don't know what the future of such films will be, close as they are to what used to be known as 'snuff movies'. Should we watch them? Can we ask people to watch them? *Silvered Water* was made by Ossama Mohammed, a Syrian exile living in France, and was shown very late at night on the French–German channel Arte. At the time, I thought it was too rough for the squeamish BBC. I now feel that I was wrong and that it should have been shown. You can see the film on YouTube, and I recommend it – but with misgivings. I think that it should be seen, even as I abhor what it's saying: that, yes, human beings do such things, not occasionally but daily, and that violence and cruelty are part of the human condition.

Unlike previous writers who spent years in archives, such as the redoubtable Erik Barnouw, I was able to examine docs past and present wherever I wished, often in hotel rooms or planes travelling all over the world. I feel this may give some clue as to the future prospects of documentaries, because you don't have to watch a non-fiction film on a big screen to enjoy it. A theme of my book is the sheer level of pleasure to be experienced in watching documentary films, and I have included a list of a hundred documentaries at the end of the book. They are not the best docs; they are the films I relied on while trying to make sense of my subject, and I hope that people will enjoy them as much as I did.

1 : What Is Truthful?

Leslee Udwin's *India's Daughter* (2015):
protests in Delhi over rape as a daily occurrence.

When you watch a documentary, it's hard to know what you are looking at. The images are real ones, to be sure, but then so are all images: 'real' is what images are said to be, by those who write about films, those who show them or make them, and by the global horde of film buffs, followers, consumers and addicts. Most films have no pretensions to inform us about anything. They are there to entertain. But then many documentaries aren't really informative at all. They aren't full of facts, and if they are, the facts may seem trivial or misleading or not wholly relevant. A good documentary needn't be factually reliable. It needn't contain any facts at all. Documentaries mostly consist of stories, but this isn't really a requirement either: great documentaries have been made without any regard for narrative coherence. We can agree that documentaries must be truthful, but truthful to what? To their own internal standards of truthfulness? Or to something outside them, which corresponds in some way to what we agree to be a standard of truth? I think we'd agree that the answer lies somewhere between the two. Documentaries that adhere only to some external criterion of truthfulness tend to be pedantic or, if the truth is imposed by government fiat, filled with lies. However, documentaries representing only their own internal standards of truthfulness are like people found muttering to themselves on street corners and in doorways: we might pretend to listen to them but we hurry by. What we call 'social media' is full of hurrying by. Documentaries are a radical alternative to this: they make us stay for a bit – the best ones, at least.

'When you film a documentary, life comes barrelling at you like a wild bear, so the filmic equivalent of the fight-or-flight mechanism takes over,' the film-maker Mark Cousins tells me. Things happen, and you try to frame them visually, capture the key words (if there are words), think ethically and keep one eye open beyond the camera – all at once. You're submitting to events, people, tensions, ch-ch-changes. When you're making a doc, you try to be your best self. You are caring on the hoof, judging what matters and what's moving, and – always, somewhere, if you're good – keeping the plate of form spinning. Perhaps the key to documentaries is how like people they are. They are filled with voices or images connected to them. The question of whom we listen to occupies a good portion of our lives, and it's what drives me to documentaries. I tend to judge a documentary film by how much is said and, just as importantly, how much is revealed. People speak about the beauty of film without regard to the fact that in film – in documentaries, especially – the talk counts, too. Perhaps the talk counts most of all. Some time ago, this last observation would have appeared to contradict the notion that every documentary film has an author. Nowadays, I feel that it doesn't. We think of authors differently now. The fact that someone must have arranged a film is obvious to us today. The real question is how it was arranged, to what purpose and with what result. We want reality to be arranged for us. We desire to see what we call, drably, the 'real world', transfigured by human hands. To that end, we're happy to see a film-maker at work on our behalf.

Docs have acquired a certain chic in recent years. No longer the worthy property of public television, they're seen in cinemas and online, at festivals and gala screenings. Nowadays the likes of Sean Penn and Leonardo DiCaprio want to be their executive producers. From a perch at the BBC, I have watched this transformation over the past seventeen-odd years. But the change in my life goes somewhat deeper. I tend to watch at least three non-fiction films a week. Some of them are over two hours long; others clock in at around an hour. In one way or another, they seem to pose a problem of definition. What are they really telling me? What is 'real' about an assembly of pictures and sounds? Without quite knowing how, I suppose that my life has somehow been spoiled by docs. At the very least, I cannot deal any more with most fictional representations – because reality seems too interesting. I tend to notice how many of the best new serials are derived from some minimal degree of documentary truth. Dostoevsky, Vasily Grossman, Flaubert and Richard Yates apart, no novelists quite match up to the hits of reality I get each week.

Am I improved by so much exposure to the lives of others? I couldn't say, but the experience doesn't seem negative to me. Meanwhile, I can say that docs have become an irreplaceable cultural form of our time. They have become an important way in which we talk to each other; they are how we see things. For a media sector always said by its practitioners to be teetering on the edge of insolvency, docs are in rude health. The fact that they are no longer made by broadcasters for a recognisable public means that their scope is far wider. People tend to think of docs as being made uniquely by the Left, but the reality is more interesting. Not long ago I watched a film that featured Carne Ross, a diplomat who quit the Foreign Office. Steely, self-deprecatory, unbudgeable but bizarrely and haltingly modest, Ross, dressed in an old coat that would have been rejected by the props department of

BBC drama, was like a character from John le Carré. He wanted to be a fighter pilot, but he was colour-blind and became a diplomat instead. Having represented Britain at the UN during the period of Iraqi sanctions, Ross quit the game of diplomacy. He became, improbably but wholly convincingly, an anarchist and founded his own NGO, representing the poorest nations on earth. We see him visit the only functioning anarchist state in the world, Kurdish Syria. He says it's a fully realised democratic utopia, like the Barcelona admired by George Orwell during the Spanish Civil War, and tears run down his cheeks when he leaves. Ross isn't a cardboard figure but a flawed human being who grapples every week with the failure of the world. We have essayists galore capable of describing how one can change one's life, but docs alone allow you to see it as it happens.

And what of documentary film-makers? How have their lives changed? I once said in exasperation that film-makers were the mendicant friars of our time, going from one catastrophe to another, tolling their bells. They are still more lugubrious than I care to admit, more obsessed with their own importance than I sometimes feel they should be. But they, too, have come to a form of maturity. Their films now win prizes, and they aren't spurned at posh receptions. But success hasn't, in most cases, brought wealth – unless you're lucky enough to sell your efforts to Netflix or Amazon. It used to be relatively easy to have a career making factual programmes in television, in the US, Britain and throughout Europe, but with the casualisation of labour in television, and the fact that so much money for docs comes from sources other than broadcasters, this is no longer the case. Documentary-makers are, all of them, out in the cold now. They must fend for themselves, and this has turned making documentaries into a high-risk activity: not really a career at all, but an activity that may or may not reward its devotees. Doc-makers are, by and large, a disorderly bunch, raucous and united in their passions, and above all, not affluent. E. M. Forster imagined his fellow authors at a table in the old British Museum, conversing about the art of fiction in genteel tones. I see makers of docs at a party where the booze is free and not always very good, shouting at each other over the din. To an outsider their lives look scrappy, overenthusiastic, but also enviable, and this is what I have found when working with them.

Here's another important fact about the best docs: like their makers, they are inclusive, helplessly democratic. They don't behave as they are expected to. If you accept them, they will cherish you. They could change your life, if you allow them to. To anyone contemplating a life in docs, I'd ask two questions. First, do you mind if you're poor and insecure? Second, do you want to be exposed to the worst as well as the best in humanity? Answer 'no' to the first and 'yes' to the second, and you'll find yourself bent over a camera at all hours, or else glaring hopelessly at hundreds of hours of footage. You won't be rich, but you'll have a good life.

I really hope that there will be a greater number of documentaries by more diverse, non-male film-makers. Throughout this book and my work at *Storyville*, I found great stories that were not solely from privileged white men. Hopefully the BBC will find more money for outreach and education to encourage a greater representation of women and minorities in the films they show.

I can recall the moment I understood what documentary films could do – not just for an audience, but also for myself. It was the autumn of 1969, and I'd just graduated. I'd spent three years sitting looking at texts, wondering why some stories affected me immediately. With my French mother I spent four hours of a sunny afternoon on the Left Bank, in a small, smoke-filled cinema watching a film that described how the French and the Germans had behaved during the wartime occupation. Marcel Ophüls's *The Sorrow and the Pity* (1969) is among Woody Allen's favourite films (it makes a cameo appearance in *Annie Hall* (1977), when Woody, too, insists on spending a fine afternoon in a similarly small, darkened cinema in New York with his girlfriend), and it has stayed with me throughout my life. Although it took another ten years for the film to be shown on French television, I am sure that *The Sorrow and the Pity* came to profoundly affect the way the French thought of their history. It also became a benchmark for anyone attempting to make sense of the past. It told me that films aren't fixed in time, that their history changes as we do. Films do cause events to be viewed differently, though not always in ways that their makers can control.

On that afternoon, however, the message from the darkened cinema was somewhat different. I was struck by how many in the audience were grizzled, the men with hair *en brosse*, straight-backed, the women dowdily looking like my Protestant aunts, teachers or indeed members of the Resistance. These were correct, not very rich French men and women of a certain age, the sort of people who had scraped a life together without complaining. They were not the sort of people one usually saw in movie houses. Then there were the *soixante-huitards*, as they were called, film buffs with notebooks dressed in shiny, tight-fitting suits, frowning at the screen in anticipation, puffing on untipped Bastos. In the first half-hour, we watched a German wedding party in which a plump, cigar-smoking, ex-Wehrmacht father says what a good time he had in France, and how pleasant it had been to come to so quiet and convivial a place from the Eastern Front. I could hear, suddenly, the odd snicker in the audience. The June 1940 collapse of France was described, most convincingly through the eyes of a pharmacist sitting with his glamorous daughters. It was he who gave the film its title, comparing the humiliating campaign to a football match lost by at least thirty goals to nil. It was one thing to lose, he said, but better not to lose by a huge margin. The cinema seemed to heat up when we got to Clermont-Ferrand, a nondescript town famous principally for being in the exact centre of France, where, one after another, participants described their lives. They didn't stint when it came to acknowledging their support for the geriatric Philippe Pétain, who became head of the Vichy puppet state. Many of them were clear about how they had been (or still were) anti-Semites. I could hear around me sharp intakes of breath and very French expostulations. '*Ah non*,' someone close by said. '*Pas possible*.' I think it was the combination of evasiveness and bizarre candour that had got to them, enabling them to restage a version of the national debate in the darkness. By the time we moved on to the role of communists in the Resistance (a theme treated with deference by the film-makers, who were keen to show how only the less well-off had opposed the Germans, and how unlike today's apparatchiks the communists of the 1940s had been), I noticed both loud applause and hissing. Waves of anger circulated around our closed space. We seemed like the characters in Sartre's play *Huis Clos*, destined to share this small cinema for eternity.

Meanwhile, I found myself taken to a new place, somewhere outside the confines of French discourse. There had been, it now seemed to me, so many ways of responding to the French national disgrace. You could become a *résistant*, go to London and join de Gaulle, though this was hard if you had a family to look after. In a variety of ways, ranging from embarrassingly overt support to mild collusion, you could back the regime – or keep quiet. A worse fate awaited those who were kept in captivity or shipped to Germany as labourers in the Reich war industries. I knew nothing about the women whose heads were shaved or the shameful role of the French police in shipping Jewish children to their deaths: at the time, such things weren't yet talked about, or indeed recorded in books. I'd grown up in Britain with the illusion, fostered by movies, that many French people had resisted the presence of the Germans. How else could I respect my French family?

Walking into daylight, blinking at the small, well-stocked shops and bars on the Left Bank, it was clear to me that things hadn't been that simple or glorious. I could understand now why it had been necessary to conceal ugly things in the name of national unity, but the film suggested that such lies had been futile, less than dignified. We should live in truth where history is concerned. Indeed, we should (as some did in the film) apply such criteria to our own lives. My mother, who had spent the war years as a young widow, looking after my two half-sisters in a village in rural Normandy before meeting my British officer father in 1944, was tearful as we came out into the sunlight. 'It was just like that,' she said. 'I'm sorry to see all this again, but it was just like that.'

Unlike the people of my age in the cinema, I wasn't a film buff. At best, I was aware, after so many afternoons spent in Parisian cinemas, of what film could do. Something, however, had changed. While I had bought into the *nouvelle vague*, glimpsing some sort of truth in the work of François Truffaut, Jean-Luc Godard and

Eric Rohmer, I now became aware of how the real could offer bigger and bigger doses of truthfulness. I need to emphasise how profoundly revolutionary this discovery appeared to me. Why bother to make anything up when what you were looking for lay before you? At that moment I felt that I would like some of my life to consist of making documentary films, without quite knowing how I would go about it. I'd reached the Real Zone.

Over the years, I kept in touch with Marcel Ophüls. He was born in Germany, and went with his parents into exile in the 1930s, first in France, then amid the expatriate German Jewish colony of Los Angeles, where his father, Max, was employed as a director. There he met the likes of Bertolt Brecht. In France, he toyed briefly with his father's profession, before wandering into making documentaries. Though he would hate me for saying this, I think of him as a natural reporter: quizzical, truly curious, always on guard against the possibility of discovering something really terrible, yet always ready to do so. Neither French nor German, he's a cosmopolitan and, rarer still, a genuine liberal. In his autobiography – the film he made about his childhood, *Ain't Misbehavin'* (2013) – he presents himself as someone permanently in the shadow of his famous film-maker father. He wishes that he had been richer or more successful. Marcel's trademarks – the bald head in the corner of the screen, an ear periodically scratched to express scepticism – are distinctive and cannot be emulated. He belongs to the historical moment in which he grew up, and has survived on our behalf as an echo of Europe's mid-century horror. In this sense, he is one of the great Europeans left to us. I can't meet Marcel without fearing that I'll somehow fall into the category of those who disappoint. But he is also marvellous company. He interrupts one, as he does those he interviews.

He completes sentences in order to show the ridiculous or misleading direction you are taking. Somewhere in his autobiography he tells you that he received an inadequate education at Pacific College, but the rest is self-taught.

A curiosity of Marcel's long career is how he has always disparaged his own work. He tells us, for instance, that *Hôtel Terminus* (1988), for which he won an Academy Award, wasn't really very good; the Oscar came only as a consolation prize for the fact that *The Sorrow and the Pity* didn't win. He was so depressed when it was being edited that he nearly killed himself. 'Don't go and watch this shit,' was the message he put on his answering machine. But *Hôtel Terminus* is a fine film, shifting artfully between its tragic essence and the comic implications of its appalling subject. Klaus Barbie, a middle-level psychopath, was the son of teachers and, after indoctrination, ascended through the ranks of the SS and found himself in charge of deporting Jewish children and torturing and killing Resistance activists. His most prominent victim was the extraordinary *résistant* Jean Moulin. After the war, American intelligence recruited Barbie because he appeared to know about Soviet and East German spy networks, now staffed by ex-Nazis. When the French authorities came after him, he was allowed to escape to Bolivia along the 'ratlines' established for this purpose. It took forty years for the French authorities to get him deported and finally try him. The film is named after the hotel in which Barbie lived in Lyon. Ophüls follows the long road of iniquity leading from rural Germany to France and to Bolivia and back again. The nihilism and cruelty of Barbie is a given. Most interesting now are the varieties of mainly tarnished humanity on the way to the terminus: the evasive and shifty, the forthright, the cowardly and the very brave. Marcel's interviewing skills are at their peak. At the end of the film, he encounters petite, smiling Esther Kaddouche, who 'stopped growing' in Auschwitz. She recalls a neighbour who tried to wrest her from the hands of the police who'd come to collect her. However, another neighbour who did nothing is still alive, and she watches Kaddouche and Ophüls from a window. This neighbour still thinks she did nothing wrong.

I think of the then forty-nine-year-old Marcel when I sit on a Sunday afternoon watching his greatest film, *The Memory of Justice*. It was commissioned by the BBC in 1976, but after a series of rows it was taken away from him. Ophüls's editor was able to retain a copy of the 'slash print' (used in those distant days for editing). A cut version, disowned by Ophüls, was shown in the late 1970s, but the one I watch now, with fresh subtitles, was finally completed in 2015. At four and a half hours, it is the tightest meditation on the subject of war guilt and responsibility, and in the age of the war in Iraq, drones and Isis – and despite being rooted in the Vietnam War – it remains arrestingly topical. Ophüls's argument that justice is always needed but never, alas, perfect is taken from a book by Telford Taylor, principal prosecutor at Nuremberg and in later years a prominent critic of the Vietnam War. The Nuremberg trials are present throughout, forming a spine for the film, but Ophüls's own past finds its place: the history of post-war Germany, through denazification to semi-amnesia, is artfully described. There's a section, too, on French torture in Algeria. But the real subject of the film is American innocence, defiled by the Vietnam War, and Ophüls's own troubled relationship with his times. There's an inevitability to the way all but the most exceptional humans collude with disgrace and failure, but Marcel wants us to know that if we want, it could end up otherwise. The greatest scene in the film records Marie-Claude Vaillant-Couturier, communist and *résistante*, inmate of Auschwitz, confronting her Nazi tormentors in the dock at Nuremberg. She pauses and looks at them, saying nothing for a long moment, in so doing expressing her utter contempt and the sense of gratefulness that she, at least, survived to tell her story. I think this is how Marcel feels that we should all behave as humans.

After the screening and the questions, I am able to corner Marcel. I tell him that having watched this film, I now understand him a bit better. It must be frustrating to see the best thing you have ever done ruined. But I also try to tell him that in relation to his father's perceived skills, he undervalues the importance of reportage, because it's so dependent on the contingent. Convention suggests that reporters aren't real creators, that they just set things down. I don't agree with this perspective, and I feel that he has fallen into this trap. I try to tell Marcel how much his own work has influenced my own career, and how astonished I was by his film.

I know that we're influenced by stories, but I'm not sure what this means. Why do some stories affect us, and not others? Why do some narratives work for us, and others don't? Does it matter that human beings, faced with a choice between a statement, a piece of analysis and a story, go for the latter? I think about this, without coming to an easy conclusion, and then find myself turning to something else: how many stories, I ask myself, are true? And how many are only partly true? Somehow, within the context of the adversarial relationship we have with any notion of something being wholly true, stories score if not badly, at least not very well. Religion depends on storytelling, so does propaganda, so does any form of distraction. Although we crave 'real' stories, we have somehow got used to the notion that a story belongs to fiction, that it therefore implies the telling of a lie, or at least the elision of truth. Stories are all around us now, and it's been suggested that they contribute to our befuddlement as citizens. Another group – film-makers, mostly – say that all stories are false, and that that is how we communicate anyhow. Instead of fretting about inauthenticity, we should accept it. I don't entirely agree with either of these semi-antagonistic positions, but before I get any further astray, let me try to enter the documentary experience in a different way. It starts with my own inadvertent self-exposure in the course of reacting to a film widely considered to be a masterpiece, Joshua Oppenheimer's *The Act of Killing* (2012).

Oppenheimer's film retraces the circumstances in which more than half a million people were killed in Indonesia in 1965. However, Oppenheimer describes his film not as a literal account, but as 'a documentary of the imagination'. It would be equally accurate to describe it as an essay in what might be thought of as theatrical epistemology – a sustained look at what is revealed in performance. This is achieved through Oppenheimer's collusive restaging of murders with the assistance of sundry perpetrators, most notably the mass murderer Anwar Congo. Most of the film doesn't deal with the massacres directly. We are told nothing about how they were done, where or indeed why they happened, beyond the fact that the victims were communists. There are many lurid sequences in which the perpetrators make their own film justifying what they did. At the end, over the kitsch soundtrack of Matt Monro's 'Born Free', a perpetrator playing someone who was murdered thanks his killers for allowing him to get to heaven.

Many revered the film, which won many prizes. But my own response, having watched it more than once, was less positive. So let me be as upfront as I can: I dislike the aesthetic and moral premise of *The Act of Killing*. Encouraging killers to script and restage their murders for the benefit of a cinema or television audience seems to me to be a bad idea, for a number of reasons. I find the scenes in the film where the killers retell their exploits, often with lip-smacking expressions of satisfaction, upsetting not because they reveal so much, as many allege, but because they tell us so little of importance. Of course murderers, flattered by their impunity, will behave vilely; of course they will reliably supply enlightened folk with a degraded vision of humanity. But it feels wrong. Something has gone missing here. Something not very good is being done.

I was attacked for these views. This didn't bother me, but it led to the discovery that if you criticise anything these days, it will be assumed that you had some ulterior reason for doing so – an interest in a rival film, a grudge or whatever. I knew many people who didn't like *The Act of Killing* and who didn't express their views. Some of them told me that they had been afraid of voicing their opinion.

But this is to get ahead of my own set of reservations, which emerged from the notion that the film was essentially a fiction. Not long ago, I viewed it again in order to see if I agreed with my own judgement. I didn't feel differently. What I did feel was how out of kilter my misgivings had become with many of those who frequented doc festivals. When I was at college, we were encouraged (with certain qualifications) to handle works of literature as if they should, sometimes at least, contain moral statements, or at least display some moral position in relation to what they describe. This isn't fashionable now. *The Act of Killing* was hailed as a form of anti-journalism, bold in its methodology and going where conventional reporting never quite manages to go. In a piece published in the *Columbia Journalism Review* praising the film, Michael Meyer suggests that we've become inured to mass murder through the conventions of journalism, with its predictable good/bad moral judgements. He concludes that one answer to this problem might be the acknowledgement, in the style of *The Act of Killing*, of a 'messy moral universe' in which audiences are left to draw their own conclusions. I still struggle with this position. Yes, you shouldn't overwhelm those for whom your film is destined with insistent moralising. However, as Hugh Greene, the most notable director-general ever to head the BBC, once said, there are subjects in relation to which the sense of neutrality isn't relevant, and may indeed be culpable.

But then I watched Oppenheimer's second film, *The Look of Silence* (2014), a more factual account of the same massacres, which gives voices both to the perpetrators and the families of victims. Its protagonist is Adi, an optician and the brother of Amli, who was hacked to death in 1965. Oppenheimer gave videotapes of the perpetrators to Adi, and then in 2011, after finishing *The Act of Killing*, filmed some of them in Adi's company. (The film resembles *Enemies of the People* (2009), Rob Lemkin and Thet Sambath's film about the Khmer Rouge, seen through the eyes of a journalist whose family were killed in the Cambodian genocide.) In every respect, this is a better film: more poignant, carrying enough detail to allow the viewer to understand the massacres, empathetic with the villagers who can never forget what happened to their families. Yet despite an Oscar nomination, Oppenheimer's second film received less attention. I suspect that this was because it was less sensational than the first film. For me, this is the most important question posed by Oppenheimer's films: does this mean that nowadays films have to shout louder to get a hearing, that their impact-inducing characteristics, the way that they can be covered with hyperbole, counts more than what they say?

I visited Vietnam as a tourist and saw, lost between the greenery and villages, museums filled with the materiel of the Vietnamese and American combatants and remnants of places destroyed by war. But it seemed as though the Vietnamese wanted to forget. It was clear they hated the French imperialists, but they often spoke highly of their American guests. 'Vietnam drove a stake in the heart of this country,' Ken Burns and Lynn Novick say, over images of American bombs dropping and anti-war dissenters marching. Their *Vietnam War* (2017) is a gargantuan ten-part project, running for seventeen and a quarter hours, overflowing with violent news images, gunships and green paddies, but its rock 'n' roll soundtrack somehow evokes nostalgia for a bygone America, a lost empire destroyed by wealth, idealism and arrogance. With around ninety interviews, one can't help empathising with the pain of the disfigured veterans, the stricken families and the survivors. We can now understand the depth of the lies told by the killers in Washington offices and the magnitude of the lists of villagers and soldiers killed. America has never reached closure on the war; the horror of Vietnam is still clear in the country's collective memory.

I didn't like Ken Burns's films about jazz and baseball, but his film about the war in the South China Sea is anti-heroic and dark. *The Vietnam War* is truly an anti-epic that is wholly engrossing and upsetting. The commentary is flattened, not orotund, the script matter-of-fact. Describing the massacre of South

Vietnamese civilians at My Lai in 1968, the word 'murder', which is usually preferred by film-makers when addressing Vietnam, becomes 'killing' ('The killing of civilians has happened in every war'). An editorial adviser, General Merrill McPeak, who went on an astonishing 269 missions, remembered the rock riffs playing as they dropped bombs over the countryside. The word he thought best described it was 'murder', arguing, 'Let's open the kimono – let's tell it all, see it the way it is.' Burns, in the *New Yorker*, defended his change, on the grounds that My Lai continues to have 'a toxic, radioactive effect'. 'Killing' was the better word, he said, 'even though My Lai *is* murder'. *The Vietnam War* isn't a film or a chronicle, but a different form of documentary. In contemporary news reports, there were no battlefields, no hills blasted and destroyed. Burns and Novick have fashioned a Dos Passos-like narrative through their covering of smaller human stories, woven throughout the episodes. Morley Safer and Walter Cronkite created this new film style in the 1960s. Burns and Novick follow the threads of these individual stories to uncover the worst of human violence. The Vietnamese permitted huge numbers of casualties in Saigon and Hue, thus showing American viewers the real face of war. Vietnamese civilians were massacred en masse by both sides. This is how the American empire ended:

> If the film seems like an epic of fiction, it's because it is less engaged in a quest for historical truth than it is in getting closer to some verities about life and death. If there had been a Truth, America would not have been in Vietnam. It went there to obviate the doubt empires cannot endure. The implication is that there may be no purpose we can rely

on – yet purpose is the justification for most of our wars.
Are the witnesses telling us the truth on the oath of a vérité
camera?

Are we aware of present-day Vietnam? Do we (Americans, of
course, but also the imperialist French) understand anything
about the killing? I am not sure. Lynn Novick and Ken Burns
spent ten years and $30 million scouring the footage. They didn't
sit down with the policy wonks, but they found hidden tapes in
the White House revealing the thoughts of JFK, LBJ, McNamara,
Nixon and Kissinger. They were liars and ideologues. They were
politicians. Naive citizens had half believed the official narrative;
now they couldn't. There is a chasm in the understanding of lies.
People of my generation think that journalism and documentaries maintain the lies of the status quo, and Vietnam was the biggest lie. As Ken Burns says in the *New Yorker*:

> 'Documentaries are traditionally advocates: "Here's a big
> problem. Here are the bad guys. Here are the good guys. How
> do we change this?" That's fine. It's like an editorial, and that's
> what editorials do.' He [Burns] described his own films, in
> contrast, as exercises in 'emotional archeology' that aspire to
> be works of art. 'We just happen to work in history,' he said.
> (He sometimes talks of the need to enliven 'the dry dates,
> facts, and events of the past.')

Here are the jokes on the helmets, the ruined, burnt villages.
Here South Vietnamese try to flee, and a million leave in leaky
ships. Here is the room at the politburo in Hanoi and the
smashed tank that destroyed the gates of the palace in Saigon.

The novelist Bảo Ninh killed American soldiers because they had rations and the Vietnamese couldn't eat. He recounts that he didn't see his mother or his apartment, where his family had neighbours whose sons and daughters had perished in Saigon, for years. 'Only a stone would not have been terrified,' he says. Among the Americans, there's Roger Harris, a handsome man who taught at public schools in Boston: wearing a bow tie, he won't talk about 'the dead Marine zone'; Vincent Okamoto, the most highly decorated Japanese American, who became an LA Superior Court judge; John Musgrave, who was badly wounded and became an alcoholic, traumatised and scarred by unhappiness and anger. They recall witnessing the worst horrors anyone could imagine.

The sheer power of docs is indescribable. They have in some respects taken over from written journalism in their power to startle. In 2014, I found myself in Delhi in order to finish a film about a terrible case of rape. Women are raped every day in India, but I got involved in the making of the film because the 2012 murder of Jyoti Singh seemed to affect people in a lasting way. This was partly because of the appalling suffering she experienced at the hands of her aggressors, who raped her in the back of a private bus as it drove along the Delhi streets. But it was also because of what she and her suffering came to represent. Jyoti was a successful intern on the way to a good career in medicine. The daughter of poor parents who were determined that she should be successful, she seemed in her short life to represent a new India. And this is why her story matters to us. Think, for a moment, about what it means to be Jyoti Singh. You're young, you're getting to where you want to be in life. Soon, you'll be able to pay back your parents. And then, on your way home from seeing a movie with a male friend, you ill-advisedly board a bus. And that's when you're assaulted, punished for being the person you wanted to be, raped again and again, thrown out onto the pavement. Amid scenes of national horror, you become a celebrity. In moments of consciousness, you are aware that you won't recover. Hooked up to tubes, still bleeding, that's what you tell your parents. You say you're sorry – sorry that it ended like this, or that you caused trouble, or indeed sorry because you feel ashamed that a culture beset by shame caused your life to end in this way.

I find myself in pre-monsoon Delhi, in June, for four days. I have never encountered heat like this, and as a result I cannot eat the food. I feel utterly lost. Some of the themes I thought were central to the film when I was back in England – for instance, until recently rape hasn't been a preoccupation of Indians outside the cultural elite – seem less important now. I realise not how vast India is, because that would require a lifetime, but how different it is. Nonetheless, the main question of the film – how such an attack could occur on a crowded street of the capital – persists. I don't know the answer. The Indians I interrogate say they, too, don't know.

Docs are edited in odd, improvised places these days. We're holed up in a guesthouse overlooking a taxi rank, a wall and a mass of greenery over which black birds cluster and alight. I periodically leave the over-chilled room to stand on the balcony, which is by now flecked with raindrops. I can't get any release from the small screens. The film is close to completion, but it has developed its own distinctive set of problems. (Films don't adhere to Tolstoy's famous formulation about families. Some of the least successful ones are happy, and all but a few present problems of an unpredictable nature.) Leslee Udwin, the producer and director, once an actor and now a campaigner, has spent weeks here with the Indian editor, Anuradha, and Dibang, the Indian reporter who is executive producer. As we make each cut, we discuss the film, technically, as most documentary people do, but also as a subject we've entered. The editor tells me that since working on this film, she's afraid to walk home at night. Leslee says she wants to create a global campaign against gender inequality – that, and not the story of Jyoti, is why she came to India. I feel I have a more basic attachment, which comes from what I see as the astonishing fortitude of Jyoti's parents. They have given a lengthy interview, but they haven't seen the film. Will they approve? Would I like it, if my own daughter's death were described in the way the film has described Jyoti's?

I am here to see Jyoti's parents, bearing a letter. Through intermediaries, they respond politely that they are not sure they want to meet me. I don't always want to meet people who appear in films, but I sense that this film is somewhat different. They say yes, then they say no, then they say maybe. When we walk around the streets, people approach Dibang for selfies. Where I come from it's a struggle to wrest viewers from their absorption in fictions, and I envy Dibang his fame and his ability to reach millions with his stories. I look at the girls posing with him and think of their families. What must they think of Jyoti's story? At night, I watch the World Cup with Dibang. I sense that he, too, is upset by the story of Jyoti, but as professionals we don't talk about this. We watch goals being scored.

It was Dibang who interviewed one of the young men on the bus. Convicted and sentenced to death, he awaits the outcome of an appeal. Dibang tells me that he must have hoped that by giving the interview, he would appear in a more sympathetic light, and thus be spared death. (The death penalty is rare in India, carried out only in exceptional circumstances.) The lawyers whom we consult in India aren't sure whether the film can be shown before the Supreme Court has decided whether he should be hanged or not. To be sure, nothing in the film could influence the Supreme Court justices, or indeed India's president, who makes the final decision where the death penalty is concerned. And yet some think the lawyers for the accused will seize on the film in an attempt to somehow reopen the case, casting doubt on the culpability of the rapists. I don't see how this could be the case, but feel obliged to defer to local opinion. Meanwhile, I watch as these suave, well-dressed, middle-aged defence lawyers, some of whom have daughters of their own, say that Jyoti's death was her own doing, that she should never have been out at night with a friend. I find myself hopelessly emotionally split between wanting everyone to know that there are people who cherish such opinions and wondering whether allowing them expression will make it all worse or – and this would be just as bad – make no difference at all.

In between viewings, driving around Delhi with Dibang or hanging out on the top floor of his villa, I think of the world of docs in which I have by chance lived so long, never wholly an inhabitant and yet never able to leave or let go. In the old days, the relative scarcity of docs gave them a cachet, but it also enabled film-makers to hide behind their professed identity. Those who made docs seemed to be superior to humble hacks. Gifted with the power of imagery, they were free (in ways that no news editor on a newspaper would have tolerated) to indulge in metaphor. And, I suppose, they were to some degree freed from the obligation to consider the consequences of their actions as film-makers, because their films were, relatively speaking, unwatched.

It would be foolish to regret the passing of this era, just as it would be insane not to think of the sudden, back-from-oblivion global life of docs as a good thing. But where, precisely, this leaves docs and their makers isn't clear. Do we want to spend our time thinking about what can or should happen to films? Isn't it enough that they should simply be available to us, to find and to watch if we choose? I wonder whether, amid the competitive flow of contradictory messages, docs achieve anything. Decades ago, the Fabian Society journalist and pamphleteer Leonard Woolf declared dolefully that all print journalism (and thus everything he had written in his long career of defending good liberal-left causes) ended up wrapping fish and chips the day after it was published. These days, it is so easy for messages to be lost. Good films and good reportage get neglected or ignored. But some do break through. And when they do, the impact is very different to the reception given to *The Sorrow and the Pity*. They become part of the news cycle. Their impact is brief and meteor-like. I won't say that they are forgotten, but the slow cultural burn of *The Sorrow and the Pity* isn't possible any more. People like myself who want to see things remembered and considered must be happy with speed.

A few months later, the parents watch *India's Daughter* (2015) and they like it. The lawyers now believe that the ruminations of the Supreme Court, still with no outcome, present no obstacle to showing the film. We can now arrange a global showing. I wonder about the ultimate fate of the film. Will it really achieve anything at all? Of the many, many films I've helped launch into the world, some have significantly underperformed. No reliable means of predicting the success or impact of a film exists. You can blow money on an outreach programme and get nowhere.

25

Alternatively, you can assume that a film doesn't require promotion, that it will somehow catch on anyhow, and be proved completely wrong. You don't need luck, cleverness or cunning to know that Jyoti's story will attract viewers in India and elsewhere, I tell myself in London. There's a wave of global indignation. People want to put a stop to such terrible events. They are angry. But I am not prepared for what is about to happen.

Just before it is due to be shown throughout Europe, the Indian government halts the showing in India. The reasons seem to me to be complex and contradictory. They hinge around the question of whether Leslee got permission to film, which she did; also whether the interview with the rapist dishonours women (it does not, plainly) and whether it might impede justice (it does not, because there is no jury in an appeal, and the rapists have been found guilty). We show the film at once on the BBC. Our version leaks via YouTube into India. And then the perfect media storm envelops us.

I struggle for words to describe what must be among the most extreme experiences of my career. One explosion follows another in quick succession. We cannot control the way the film is discussed. We cannot anticipate what feature of the film will be attacked next. We can't rely on being defended, though this does happen. All we can really do is watch and periodically intervene, often ineffectually.

Sitting in London, I try not to panic. I call Dibang in Delhi every day. Leslee has left India, and she travels through London, giving interviews, on the way to a launch in the US with Meryl Streep. There are furious campaigns around the film, pro and con. Its methodology is picked over; its appropriateness is questioned. Should there have been an interview with a convicted

rapist? The ethics and motives of Dibang and Leslee are endlessly examined. Of course, the BBC's motives are impugned.
However, in the midst of all this, one can find voices of reason. I
am impressed by the news that two groups of twenty-something
Delhi law students are petitioning the Supreme Court to over-
turn the ban. I like best a long-considered online critique from
an Indian feminist, who takes apart the contradictory views of
the film's opponents and then says how much she likes the film,
while criticising it.

My own reaction is troubled as well as exhilarated. I worry
for the parents, for Leslee and Dibang, and for the editor of the
film, some of whom have had to leave India. I panic at the idea
that something within our meticulously ordered procedures may
not have been done, rendering us all vulnerable; I reflect that no
project can be rendered wholly bombproof. But a deeper sense
of disquiet affects me, and it comes down to something about
the way in which we read social narratives. Do we really absorb
them at all? Don't we just half notice what they say, and react to
shortened versions of them, with the way in which it is presumed
we should react built into them? Isn't that what social media
does to any kind of long-form attention? Isn't real attention to
things on its way out? It strikes me as odd that most of the endless Twitter feeds aren't about the film at all, which most people
in India can't have seen. There are, it is true, posts about why the
film was banned, or whether it was appropriate to make it and
interview the rapist. However, most people simply say that they
hate the film and don't want it; or, on the other side, that they
applaud it. They have fixed positions. They don't seem to enter
into the arguments. I had hoped that the film might provoke
discussion about how rape could be more easily prosecuted, or

indeed how rapists might be identified. Should one focus on the police and the non-reporting of rapes? Or make the court system less degrading for victims? How, in a country as big as India, does one know where to start? For the moment at least, such a debate isn't forthcoming, and I wonder what this tells me.

There are gains, too, from the messy, uncategorisable zeitgeist in which documentaries now exist. If, as I argue, docs have morphed into contemporary essays, becoming a form whereby we get to experience highly provisional stabs at reality, then that can only be good for us. Docs do transform reality, but, far more than fictions, which are usually finished and fixed in their own reality, they are also transformed by it. *When We Were Kings* (1996) started life as a music doc, but you can watch it now for the portrait of Muhammad Ali in his prime. It has also come to seem like a homage to Africanness: not the Africa of the awful, leopard-skin-obsessed dictator, but the crowds of African children and adults who revere Ali as their own idol, come from another planet, speaking, walking, fighting, ultimately alive for them.

The best docs celebrate a sense of the accidental. And they matter. Like unknowable bits of the universe, they come into existence when a collision occurs. The collision needn't be violent; it can be contrived. Good docs appear to wrest a degree of coherence from the contingent mess of life, but when we finally leave them, we must be aware that the ordering was wholly provisional. That's the only real way to make a documentary film – by setting out what you believe to be true, or beautiful, and destroying any certainty by implying that, yes, it could have been described in a myriad of other ways. This comes down to having a strategy for life, while being prepared to abandon it. What other way is there of staying alive?

This is the conclusion I've come to after sitting watching doc after doc. The films I like are irremediably hybrid: a mixture of authorial personality, cod epistemology, appropriated or created history and whatever seems current and interesting. Sometimes they are polemical, sometimes they are tinged with fictional contrivance. The only rule is that they should have no rules. They should *be*, rather than tell. They should make the worst things comprehensible. No documentary should be without some aesthetic bliss, even if it is tamped down, minimal, barely noticeable.

The BBC is now fact-obsessed. For many years, I worked within the mild tyranny of facts, vetting films according to periodically strict criteria. I've come to enjoy hybrid, complex takes on our world. Among them is the remarkable *The Arbor* (2010). Clio Barnard's masterpiece is, on the surface, an account of the brief career and early death of Andrea Dunbar, who lived in the Buttershaw estate in Bradford. Dunbar wrote an early play, *The Arbor*, before *Rita, Sue and Bob Too*, which was a hit in London and was then made into a film. But Dunbar was an alcoholic, and by the time she died at the age of twenty-nine she had already suffered the consequences of fame. She left behind three children. Out of the existing archive, Barnard recreates Dunbar's troubled, astonishing talent. The scenes from *The Arbor* shot in the open, among a crowd of Buttershaw residents, are heartbreakingly intense. But Barnard has bigger ambitions here. She came to film after working in performance art, and hit on the idea of using actors to play Dunbar's children, acquaintances, lovers and neighbours – but lip-synching the real voices. The actors memorised these interviews, vocalising them while listening to them. 'I used this technique to draw attention to the fact that documentary narratives are as constructed as fictional ones,' Barnard explains. These devices are her own way of penetrating Dunbar's tragic world. But Barnard, as it turns out, isn't interested just in Dunbar's brief life. The latter part of the film recounts, in heart-rending detail, the life story of her addict daughter Lorraine, the death of Lorraine's own son and her consequent trial for manslaughter. We get to see, over three generations, the scarring caused by poverty, drugs and abandonment – and the struggle to survive, too. Each time I watch the film I tell myself that fiction, even Dunbar's, often can't do this, but *The Arbor* does.

Anyone sitting at an editing table encounters the dilemma of truthfulness hourly. If you strive to be more 'real' (i.e. less stodgy, less bound to dull things such as 'facts' and 'objectivity'), does that make you more or less truthful? Some of the people who make docs are, by their own account, great fibbers; others see themselves as meticulous recorders of literal truths. My sense is that many of the best docs come to life within this often-crossed divide, enriching our perceptions of both by creating bridges between the two. War films don't usually begin with a pack of feral dogs, but *Waltz with Bashir*, Ari Folman's 2008 animated film about his own experiences as a nineteen-year-old soldier in the 1982 Israeli invasion of Lebanon, owes more to novels such as *Catch-22* and *Slaughterhouse-Five* than to films. But this is, nonetheless, a documentary. Folman reconstructs his nightmares, along with his visits to shrinks. Most of the interviews with his fellow veterans are real. 'Memory fills the holes with things that never happened,' a psychologist tells him, but 'memory takes us where we need to go'.

The film is ravishing as well as scary: dark, dark scenes, punctuated by Israeli military heavy metal. Folman can't recall what happened to him in Beirut, and what he uncovers first is the fact that war is never wholly real or understandable to the participants. As he comes closer to his own past, the film focuses on the ill-fated Israeli siege of Beirut. Israeli forces were stationed for three days at the perimeter of the Sabra and Shatila refugee camps, while Christian Phalangist militias avenged the death of their leader, Bashir Gemayel, by massacring Palestinians – children as well as adults – on the grounds that they were terrorists. Israeli collusion was acknowledged after the event, but Folman wants to know how far his own responsibility went. He launched flares over the camp, placing himself in a 'second circle' of those who knew but didn't help or impede. Folman is the son of Auschwitz survivors, and to him this makes his offence against humanity worse. The film ends with real-life shots of dead Palestinians. This was much criticised, on aesthetic grounds as well as those of taste, but it seems wholly right to remind viewers that the animation they are watching is, in Folman's sense, 'real'. 'Nothing is objective in film-making,' Folman says. 'Is a drawing done by a talented artist somehow less real than a photographic image composed of pixels, et cetera?'

There are crossovers, too, in another film that taught me to love the sheer power of mixed-up categories. In *Stories We Tell* (2012), Sarah Polley appears to give a straightforward account of her mother, Diane, a vivacious and scatty actress and agent who died when Polley was eleven, and Diane's relationship with the two sets of children from her marriages. Unexpectedly, however, the story is told by Polley's father, Michael, who has also written a memoir, which he reads out, often prompted by his stern, perfectionist daughter. Polley is a successful actor and director herself, and to begin with it's possible to feel that this is just a very good home movie. But there have always been family rumours that Polley isn't Michael's daughter, and the main revelation of the film is that they are true. Her mother had an affair with the film producer Harry Gulkin, and DNA testing reveals him to be Polley's biological father. But Diane had been married before, and the Canadian court puritanically censured her, denying her full access to her children because she had left her husband for Michael. This second discovery allows Polley to speculate that insecurity may have meant that her mother didn't leave Michael for Harry – though the film, on this, as on other matters, disdains any fake sense of certainty.

Polley is interested in what these discoveries mean, in how people do or don't talk to each other. She quotes from the writer Joan Didion: 'Stories are what we tell to keep ourselves alive.' Her own sharpness and steeliness stop the film from ever slipping into schmaltz. When Harry wants to publish his own account of the affair that led to her birth, she stops him. He claims to know about her mother exclusively, but she'd rather have a more nuanced depiction dependent on the thoughts of others – and one, of course, marshalled by herself. Instead, she chooses the ageing Michael as the narrator for her story – because he was her 'real' father, but also because his own very partial and incomplete view reflects the way she wants to tell her own equally incomplete story. *Stories We Tell* is as complex and layered as the best fiction, but also, like the very best documentaries, truth-obsessed, questing. Polley has a cold eye as well as a loving heart. Her own blog, published when the film came out, does justice to her rigorous family interrogation. 'Anything I want to say myself about this part of my life is said in the film,' she writes. 'It's a search still, a search for meaning, truth, for whether there can ever be a truth. I have spent five years deciding, frame by frame and word by word, how to tell this story in this film. I'd hate to see my inability to think before I speak wipe out years of work with one stupid comment that I haven't thought through.'

Among the most baffling aspects of docs is their privileged social position in what Marshall McLuhan described fifty years ago as the 'global village'. From the status of pariahs, they have come to occupy a privileged place. They are the poor but interesting relations, kept around the powerful to give lustre or to remind the rich cousins of what might, in a different world, be important. Some are indeed less poor now, due to the sudden intense presence of the likes of Netflix and Amazon. Documentaries began as a casual experiment in seeing what happened when you pointed a camera at the things around you. They never caught on in cinemas and were displaced by fiction. Nowadays, it's common to hear documentary film described as the new rock 'n' roll.

I thought of this while watching Noah Baumbach's *While We're Young* (2014). The real subject of the film is encroaching age, and what it feels like to be up against the perceived capability of younger people to change arbitrarily and fecklessly. But the film's pitch-perfect evocation of three generations of people known in New York as 'documentarians' gives ballast to the plot, as well as allowing the film-maker to riff perceptively and inconclusively on what, if anything, separates what is entertaining from what is truthful. Grumpy old Leslie Breitbart (played by Charles Grodin) is a 1960s literalist full of earnest clichés about what we can learn from the impoverished African Americans whose images he appropriates, and which are now screened at galas celebrating his work. His son-in-law Josh (played by Ben Stiller) is stuck with an excruciating six-hour essay ('It's seven hours too long,' Leslie tells him cruelly) on the subject of the US Constitution, featuring a garrulous historian. A young film-maker, Jamie (played by Adam Driver), makes use of these doc elders in order to gain cred and backing for a not-so-real Facebook-derived exploration of post-traumatic stress, in which he and his floppy hat are the ultimate focus of attention. A decade ago, these characters would have been writing narrative scripts, and two decades ago they would more probably have been wrestling with the Great American Novel. Now, simply and naturally, they make docs out of their own lives. I was interested to see how much New York film-makers appeared to dislike Baumbach's film.

Among film festivals, Sundance occupies a special place. It's keenly cutting-edge, a bit recherché, and it has a record of having been right about the direction taken by film culture. People talk about documentary films now at lavishly funded parties. They tend not to say how much money these films are about to make. Instead, they tell each other how good the docs are, how much better than the fictional offerings. Films that only a few years ago would have been restricted to the smallest audiences are now keenly sought out. They're received rapturously, and audiences are reluctant to let their makers leave the Q&A sessions afterwards.

It was a documentary that saved Al Gore from political oblivion, winning him an Oscar. Few Hollywood directors have actually made documentaries (Martin Scorsese is an exception, though Werner Herzog has been able once again to make fictions as a consequence of his successful documentaries), but it has become commonplace to see the names of Brad Pitt, Leonardo DiCaprio or Sam Mendes attached to films as executive producers. Patrons such as the Ford Foundation, George Soros, Robert Redford's

Sundance Institute, Gucci and Puma lend their blessing, giving funds to film-makers.

I wonder sometimes about the celebritisation of docs, even as I find myself sucked into it. Seated beside him on a panel at Sundance, it was flattering to be called Nicky by Robert Redford. I enjoyed, too, sitting behind the heiress and kidnap victim Patty Hearst as she watched a film about her abduction. Who could resist the mix of gloss, wealth and social concern? But something seemed lost among the Mountain Time trimmings, and I came to see the festival as an annual encounter with the rich liberal minority culture bubble of the US. I talked about these things with Sheila Nevins, who'd worked for more than thirty years at HBO. We met the day after the killing of forty-nine people in a gay club in Florida. Glamorous, persistent, eloquent from her training at Yale School of Drama, Sheila regards films as 'dramas about ordinary people'. She always says that one can learn from ordinary people. 'No one is truly uninteresting,' she says. 'That's why documentaries are so good.' Sheila was among the most stubborn and accomplished backers of difficult subjects, until she left HBO in 2017. She also liked winning prizes. But I can empathise with her core survival instincts.

I told Sheila how hard it was to adjust to the darkness of our times, how so much of American liberalism was too sunny for me, how I found the compulsive optimism of places like Sundance not always helpful when it came to describing what the world was really like. She criticised me not for pessimism, but for my refusal to see good within the darkness. She didn't like making films about politics ('So boring to me ... Why make a film about the Capitol?'). She always found some light, even if she didn't know where to look. I drew a different message from

Sheila's words. In America, freely expressed sunniness was the entry price you paid for reality. If you signed up to human self-amelioration, you could do pretty much what you wanted. Given the opportunity, that's what I'd do in a second life spent creating documentaries. In the meantime, I had to match film-making with the darkness of the world, I needed to avoid plunging audiences into that darkness around us. I wondered whether, if she were starting out now, she'd find the task easier or more difficult. She said she couldn't answer the question. 'People always find a way,' she said wistfully, but with conviction. 'In the worst things, they always do.'

I'm not writing a history of docs here – not because the history isn't interesting, but because I want people to see docs in the present for which they were made. All docs exist in the permanent present that they create. This isn't an attempt to create a canon; one of the things that attracts me about docs is that they cannot be reduced to something as formal as a canon. But I do have a practical reason for writing this book, and that's because no one knows about the best docs; indeed, no one knows where to find them. So many come with extraordinary stories attached to them, and the story of such films is worth telling. It took Claude Lanzmann more than ten years to make *Shoah* (1985). How did the Maysles brothers come across Big Edie and Little Edie, the wayward stars of *Grey Gardens* (1975)? Who funded it? Who watched it? There are great documentaries about the making of films, such as *Hearts of Darkness: A Filmmaker's Apocalypse* (1991), which is about Francis Ford Coppola's *Apocalypse Now* (1979). And then there are miracle films like *The Gatekeepers* (2012), in which elite Israeli spies appear in a film to repudiate the policy they had administered for the past forty-odd years. *Please*

Vote for Me (1997), which tells how nine-year-old Chinese children behave in a classroom election once the idea of democracy is explained to them, is used in seminars in American universities. It has become a bootleg sensation in China.

Films such as these are big, bold attempts to describe pieces of the world. I want people to know about them and watch them. Not long ago, I gave a talk at Oxford University about a series of films on global poverty on which I had worked. Someone asked me what had been most difficult about the venture, and I paused. I could have talked about the problems with money, or the fact that a gulf separates even the best-intentioned from the lives of the really poor. These factors and others had led to immense difficulties. Instead, I told the audience how difficult it had been to keep the stories out of the hands of NGOs. Not that I disagreed with their aims or felt that they shouldn't use film to project their messages, but for me some sort of line separated film-making and advocacy. You could make a film that became a campaign, but that wasn't the same as making a film that was part of a campaign. And these problems of definition were becoming more acute. No easy answers were to hand, and high intentions were often fatal. One of the least acknowledged problems of the present day is the prevalence of good intentions. Alas, saving the world isn't the same as telling the truth. After the talk I encountered Theodore Zeldin, a professor whose seminars on Proust I had attended, an ironist, someone I had thought touched by genius. He'd become bored with fictions, too. 'It's hard to tell the truth about anything,' he said to me. He didn't just mean that people wouldn't thank me for doing this; he wanted to tell me, putting it as simply as he could, that it was hard. Why should it be easy?

I talked about truth with the film-maker Stephen Frears, as we walked together around Notting Hill. Like most British directors, Stephen got his start in docs. He made one film in the 1960s about the ripping out of a slum neighbourhood in Nottingham and its replacement by tower blocks. Back then, this was thought to be part of the progressive zeitgeist, but Stephen had worked with the journalist Ray Gosling, who told him that people loved their imperfect, overused slums. Years later, he returned in order to view the film with its participants, and realised that Gosling had indeed been correct – they had in fact preferred where they were, and being moved had proved to be a loss. 'I get more and more scripts based on truth,' Stephen said. 'Are they really true?' I asked. 'Well, sort of . . . but everything nowadays is "sort of". Real is only sort of real.'

'Documentary,' says the dictionary. 'Noun. Based on or re-creating an actual event, era, life story, that purports to be factually accurate and contains no fictional elements.' This is useful, so far as it goes, but excessively minimal. Why shouldn't non-fiction contain elements of fiction? And why should something only 'purport' to be factually accurate? When you describe anything, it is altered. The act of seeing modifies what is seen. It isn't necessary to be a visionary to understand this. The photographic record-ing of actuality complicates things. 'I am a camera,' Christopher Isherwood's famous formulation, isn't in the least convincing. We may own or use photographic means of reproduction, but we aren't cameras. Yet the discussion of documentaries has been dogged, perhaps understandably, by photographic literalism.

In a late, elegiac work, the poet Robert Lowell comes close to recreating the act of description:

Yet why not say what happened?
Pray for the grace of accuracy
Vermeer gave to the sun's illumination
Stealing like the tide across a map
To his girl solid with yearning.
We are poor passing facts,
Warned by that to give
Each figure in the photograph
His living name.

Lowell died a year after writing this poem, in the back of a New York taxi, clutching a Lucian Freud portrait of his estranged girlfriend. He was only sixty, and his life had been marred by the grotesque deformations of reality caused by a severe bipolar affliction, resulting in the loss of his home and multiple lawsuits. I like these sad end-of-life lines because they show that there's no real conflict between the desire for accuracy and the spirit of illumination. You might think that saying exactly what happened (simply facts) is a lowly, banal activity. No, Lowell is saying, it isn't, it's far from being banal. Indeed, it is so important that one must pray for it. It does represent a kind of grace, though not in any religious sense. There is no single reliable way of capturing anything. We cannot rely on anything, let alone sight or a machine as fallible as a camera. Most likely, we can but hope for the best, repudiating both literalism and the excessive use of metaphors. Let's be honest, drudgery is part of it, and rote, as well as obsessiveness. But nothing, as Lowell insists, should rightly be excluded. How else will the names come alive?

Why fret about the future of a lowly form widely considered to be on a par with the other offerings of television? Why attempt to elevate what is no more than the cunning assembly of sound and images into more-or-less plausible narratives? Documentaries have for a long time occupied a humble position in the television economy, securing reliable audiences for a relatively low cost. Many people, year after year, are comforted by the experience of watching slices of life carved out of familiar material for their distraction. Do we need to investigate the relationship between documentaries and reality? My reply to such observations is that the widespread uncritical acceptance of documentaries damaged them. Cultural snobbery still surrounds documentaries. Primarily, they've been regarded as filler; alternatively, as a form of agitprop – and they are still condescended to, by journalists and film critics, even by those who make documentaries.

Do documentaries matter? Why do they matter? These are big questions, easily posed yet difficult to answer. I believe they do matter. Before saying why this is the case, however, it seems appropriate to detail some of the ways in which they have been undermined, both by their successes and their failures.

Take an extreme example of the degree to which the depiction of reality in film has been prejudiced by its associations with the state. In 1997, I went to St Petersburg in order to work with the film-maker Viktor Kossakovsky on *Wednesday* (1997), a film in which he rendered in counterpoint the day of his own birth – 19 July 1961 – with the lives of others born on the same day in the city that was then part of the Soviet Union and known as Leningrad. Under communism, everyone was supposed to be equal and, therefore, enjoy a similar life. Viktor's efforts were directed at demonstrating how the contrary had happened. A few of those he found had got rich, but most were poor – some alcoholics or drug addicts – and the film showed signs of slipping into a contemporary vision of St Petersburg's lower depths. We needed to show what had been dreamt of in the days of identical ambitions, egalitarian cribs and Pioneer rallies. So Viktor and I went to Lenfilm, the old communist archives, located in a crumbling Stalin-era building, and watched archive films for a day. The machinery seemed out of Orwell, meticulously preserved, like the rolls and rolls of film preserved for posterity. We found footage of identical white beds in which small, newborn Soviet citizens nestled silently. We also saw samples of lavishly produced weekly accounts of life in which nothing significant happened. The big event was the visit of a surprisingly svelte Fidel Castro, or Nikita Khrushchev's bulky form, sighted at a Ukrainian dairy farm. And it was in this respect that our visit proved to be useful: as a revelation of how much of what was filmed was wholly impersonal, dictated by forgotten needs. There was no idea of any independently acquired truth here, no sense that one could go out with a camera, as one might bear a pad and a pencil, and simply describe what was happening. Everything was prearranged, controlled from the top.

A milder form of such attitudes was pervasive among British TV broadcasters. They were obliged to serve mass audiences, so it became part of the job of television executives to vet product, ensuring its acceptability. Many bland series were made as a consequence of such obligations. Lifeboats were recurrent subjects, as well as veterinary surgeries. It would be futile, as well as snobbish, to dismiss such artefacts because they gave many people much pleasure.

In response to such material, and as a revolt against mass culture, experimental films were highly prized. Briefly, in the 1970s and 1980s, it became fashionable within academies to speak of the death of the author. Was it possible to be original? Could one even purport to tell the truth? Observers of the cultural scene would reply with a shrug or a nod implying that the question was a stupid one. Forget about individuals, they said, in one dogmatic article after another. All that matters are the patterns on the carpet.

I was never interested in such ideas, and they still leave me cold. Postmodernism is mercifully out of fashion now, but among film critics the view that documentaries do or should resemble narrative fictions remains widespread. A recent crop of films mixing fact with fiction prompted these thoughts from Nigel Andrews, film critic of the *Financial Times*:

> Think about it. Do we still buy, if we ever did, the notion
> that non-fiction on-screen is anything other than an artefact?
> That it is not shot through with point-of-view, with the
> cultural perspectives and prejudices of the day? That it is not
> as storied and subjective, in its way, as a narrative feature film?

The claims made on behalf of the documentary as artefact seem exaggerated to me. Any representation of reality, in any medium, can reasonably be described as an artefact. But that doesn't mean that all representations are false, or that the ability to distinguish between fact and fiction isn't important. In particular, the argument that people perform in front of cameras, and that this makes all docs 'fictional', strikes me as absurd. Some do perform, and some do not. But it's not hard, if you are patient and cunning, to make people forget they are in a film.

Film-makers themselves are concerned with the 'hows' of their trade – practical things like access, visas, lenses and suchlike. They may talk about why they were attracted to certain narratives, but they are reluctant to say why one set of circumstances rather than another might make for a better, more involving, more lasting film. For a long time, pressed to explain the impact of their films, film-makers would reply in the idiom of John Grierson, the founding father of British documentary. Grierson, in his left-wing Calvinist way, believed that films should raise spirits through their ability to depict good lives, or at least lives in which people strove for humanity. Viewing such singular, ordinary lives, audiences would experience a degree of solidarity. Nowadays, with so many channels and the reluctance of television executives to admit to any large-scale educative function of the medium, the idea of the documentary as a binding force in society, viewed by large numbers of people and attesting to cultural solidarity, is in decline. It has been replaced by the idea that documentaries can be linked to campaigns and made to change the world.

On occasions, perhaps they can and do have such an effect, but no evidence exists to suggest that film is especially good at social mobilisation. Nor is it evident that film-makers will be well served by seeing their films bundled into social movements and used to further the interests of NGOs. This is an idea deemed suitable for an age in which many people believe that the world, unless fixed rapidly, will come to grief. The continuous transformation of media has become what any world citizen must now expect. Among so many inventions, however, some things don't easily change. When Ted Turner instituted twenty-four-hour satellite news, spreading his network globally in the 1980s, he didn't imagine that this might be a means whereby people might more easily enter each other's lives. But, to a degree, Turner's dream hasn't endured. The horizons of world news have shrunk, even as powerful governments have created their own news services. CNN, Turner's creation, is less ambitious now, though its non-US service supplies global news with a strong American slant. BBC World News remains hobbled by a lack of funds. Al-Jazeera, paid for by the emir of Qatar but relatively independent, covers many African and Asian stories neglected in the West. To its credit, it has become the voice of progressive Arab nationalism, giving air-time to democrats throughout the Middle East. Many of Russia Today's programmes, however, would not have seemed out of place in Soviet times, and the same is true of China's global services. Meanwhile, France 24 occupies an uneasy space between modern global reporting and the traditional French desire to export cultural values.

One can get stuck somewhere between the cacophony of the Internet and such officially sponsored views. And it is in this context that documentaries reveal their true utility. In the end, all non-fiction may be dissolved online, becoming part of an endless chain of cause and effect. For the moment, however, we can agree that narratives do exist, and that some are more truthful than others. And it is in this space that the best documentaries survive. I was attracted to docs because I liked them. I still do. I also like the fact that no serious theoretical basis exists to legitimise them. They have come to subsist, precariously, at a crossroads in contemporary culture, somewhere between journalism, film narrative and television entertainment. They appear to thrive on contradictions: between the stubborn reality they purport to capture and their necessarily limited means; between the impositions of storytelling and the desire to interpret or analyse. They aren't fictional, ever, but their attractiveness can make them appear more real than reality. Ultimately, they remain provisional, snapshot-like. In fact, they appear to be doomed to remain on or outside the perimeters of the cultural world, which accounts both for their freshness and the relative poverty of those who make them.

It is this special quality of being both at the edge and at the centre of things that makes them matter most of all. They can evoke what the evolutionary biologist Steven Pinker describes as 'the widening circle of human sympathy'. They let us see humans as individuals. And they accomplish this superlatively, not as a matter of routine but because their makers have taken great care to allow us to share this vision.

No one should be able to dictate what a documentary is or should be. It doesn't seem right to fence in the form, excluding the force fields – dramatic fictions, news, agitprop – that surround it. Nonetheless, here are some ways of characterising the good ones.

First, they should be provisional. You shouldn't know where you are going when you start. Second, somewhere – not in a script, perhaps, or by means of a reportorial presence, but through the lens, through editing, through what they are – there must be some notion of an author, or at least that the film was guided by an individual hand or an association of individually motivated hands. Third, they must represent some sort of creative collision with the received idea of how anything can or should be depicted. Also – and this is rare – they should be occasionally funny. Most documentaries aren't. This is a mistake, because the shock of the real isn't without its own humorous aspects.

And most importantly, those who watch documentaries, as well as those who make them, should realise that anything goes. There are traditions of film-making, to be sure. But the vitality of the documentary resides in the fact that it thrives at a series of crossroads scarred by accidents. You can arrive at the idea of documentary through tabloid journalism or philosophy, out of a desire to change the world, or merely because there is a story you wish to tell. What you really want to do is say what happened.

In his compendium of the contemporary cultural scene, *Cultural Amnesia*, Clive James makes the point that for those only moderately ingenious, never has it been easier to access the totality of world culture. You don't need much money to find out about things. It is easier these days to discover things about our fellow inhabitants of the planet. If we so desire, we can find out many more. This remains the simplest definition of why documentaries matter, and we should ensure that not just great docs, but also good ones continue to be created and shown throughout the world.

But let me go back to why we should cherish documentaries. Of the current manifestations of contemporary culture, which would you choose to conserve? I suspect that documentaries wouldn't make it. They have no real cultural recognition. They inhabit, creatively, a nowhereness, always somewhere between other things; but that's a very good place from which to observe the contradictions and horrors of our times. They may be hard to find, but you would miss them if they disappeared. You might even miss them very much. I've watched documentaries in editing rooms, at festivals, on rubbish TV sets and laptops. I see the endless versions they go through, with so much pain taken and given before they're finished. I like to watch them with audiences and at home. I'll watch them anytime I am bored, and if I am not bored, too. No one will ever be able to tell me definitively what a documentary does or how it affects people, any more than I can say for sure what the cumulative effect of a newspaper report, a sonnet, a Shakespeare tragedy or *Madame Bovary* is. But I do know that documentaries, taken individually, resemble a group of old and new friends. If the species became extinct, I am convinced that this would be a more than small loss for humanity.

2 : How to Make a Doc

James Marsh's *Man on Wire* (2008): Philippe Petit, an ant-like figure between the Twin Towers, when the two buildings defined New York City.

All good docs involve a struggle between the materials at one's disposal and the recalcitrant, fleeting aspects of reality. But a secondary struggle takes place in the making of every film, and that involves those who make them. The battles are often comically self-important, but they are of consequence, too, because films that might have been better are sunk by them, because really excellent films emerge from such struggles: through technology, the milieu of doc-makers, their politics, the institutions in which they thrived or (more usually) didn't. Running alongside this story, however, is the equally important one of thousands and thousands of hours spent typing outlines, arguing, filming, editing and re-editing, and finally finishing. How a film is made determines what it becomes, and there are many ways of making them.

Although I never tried to make films, I'm aware that people do want to make docs, but I don't want to say that without help films cannot be made – the help does exist. Looking around at the mass of cables, files, huge assemblies and edits, the simpler you can keep your space, the better. Documentaries are always messy. I've seen great films emerge from terrible messes, but there are many half-finished docs.

Sometime in 2005, a young producer came into my office. Simon Chinn had a book by Philippe Petit in his hands and wanted to tell me about Petit's appearance on the venerable

BBC radio programme *Desert Island Discs*. Petit was the French high-wire walker who on one clear morning in 1974 had walked between the Twin Towers, affording those in the streets an unequalled view of an ant-like figure with a horizontal bar perched astonishingly on a cable, though in reality in motion and making his own trail to compete with the jet stream. I had been in New York at the time, and I remembered the episode as an urban fairy tale in which the citizens of a near-bankrupt city could for a few hours dream about what it might be like to come close to one of humanity's oldest dreams: becoming a bird and flying. Of course, the towers had since been reduced to rubble. That a *funambule* such as Petit would do such a thing was, as he would have said with a caricatural shrug, *impensable*, ridiculous. These days, you'd be in jail – not just, as Petit was, detained for a few hours at the behest of a proud, indulgent mayor and the police. You wouldn't be able to walk between two towers, because the world in which such things could be countenanced, planned and brought to fruition doesn't exist any more. It had taken Petit and his co-workers more than a year to pull off this feat. How had they lived during that time? How had they bought the cable they needed? How had the cable been smuggled into the towers? This was a heist movie, but it would also be one that would recount all that we lost on 9/11. You wouldn't see the towers going down. Instead, you'd discover why they were built, how resistant New Yorkers had been to their upended-Kleenex-box appearance. I hoped their existence in the film would take away some of the horror surrounding their loss. I also hoped that the sheer boldness and beauty of Petit's ridiculous act of heroism might chase away the images of apocalypse thoughtlessly deployed in every media depiction of the troubles of our age.

I suppose I was seeking a degree of consolation, even as I wanted people to understand exactly what had been lost.

I liked the way Petit spoke English, because his accent was as thick as Maurice Chevalier's. I knew that I wanted James Marsh to direct the film. Marsh had made films that didn't look like BBC films: not just *Wisconsin Death Trip* (1999), based on photographs of violent crime from the nineteenth century, but also *The Burger and the King* (1995), an account of Elvis's last troubled days that detailed the astonishing amount of calories he'd consumed, a film that was at once dark and funny and yet still respectful towards the King. Marsh lived in Brooklyn with his Danish wife – he would have had a grandstand perspective of the falling towers – and was finding that it was difficult to survive in the highly commercial US environment.

I've worked with many exceptionally talented human beings, and James Marsh is one of them. He remains captivating to me, in ways that I still find hard to describe. He is smallish, slight, with piercing greenish eyes and slightly off-red hair. He has a soft manner, not so much diffident, but working his own sentences as they come to him. He often starts in mid-sentence, and they come tumbling out. Nonetheless, they are very ordered. James talks as if he were creating sequences in films out of stories and lives, but he is always careful to place meaning in these narratives. I could never see him plundering life for his own work, and this, I think, made him so attractive to me. After a meeting with him, I'd always feel much richer, because he knew things that I didn't know and because, in a way that I could never wholly character-ise, he would have told me something.

I'd scraped together enough money to help James make a film about the New York homeless soccer team. I was not sure that this was a terrifically good idea. No one was excessively interested in soccer in the US at that moment, and it seemed that no one was very interested in the homeless. Few European broadcasters were interested in the tournament, which was staged with provincial hoopla in Austria. James was interested in how these dysfunctional lives were altered by playing together. Some of his subjects would never return to what we thought of as real life, but at least they could play football – or, rather, just about play – and that was a kind of victory.

I am not certain why I always felt that James would make a film about Philippe and the Twin Towers that would win an Oscar, but quite early on this became an *idée fixe*. One film I'd commissioned, *One Day in September* (1999), had won an Oscar five years previously. Nobody was telling me to go out and win Oscars; I just felt making such a film would be a good idea. But it was instantly apparent to me that the success of *Man on Wire* meant something special. When it was shown at Sundance, those near me in the audience were crying. People thanked James for giving them back what they had lost. When I watched it again recently, however, I responded to different things in the film. I wanted to reapproach it in a different way.

If you attend film school in the US, you may well be told that documentary films should be constructed like fictional narratives. You will hear about 'narrative arcs' or 'three-act structures'. During proposals – and sometimes when discussing their films during the process of editing – people do actually talk like this. I've never been certain that this is the right way to think of documentaries. It seems unorganic, artificial, neglectful of the fact that docs do come from life. Each film I've worked on has, in my view, required a different approach. Some have worked better than others, but as I looked at *Man on Wire* I found I understood better how these problems might be resolved – in other words, how you might think of making a film, and if that didn't work, how you might change course, experiment, try again until it was right. So my own *Man on Wire* experience stands here not as a template or a masterclass, but as a series of markers or lines in the sand.

What makes a good idea? Docs swim in shoals, and the first thing to figure out is whether you want to be part of the shoal. With docs there's no easy relationship between supply and demand. I've never figured out why so many films about Plains Indians or Australian Aboriginals were made. Then came dolphins, honking, having sex, smiling. Ancient Rome – CGI, Christians thrown to lions, trumpets, ill-fitting togas and suspiciously plastic-looking swords – was also a winner, superseded only by the pharaohs. The shoal mentality accounts for much that is banally repetitive about television. Do we need always to be telling people what they already know? Well, yes, we do. You can wonder, as you pass through an airport, whether the world needs quite so many shops selling upmarket handbags. Isn't there a limit to what the market can bear? The best ideas I have encountered came as accidents. I was once walking through a vast Mao-era former furniture store in Guangzhou, now turned into a restaurant. Floor after floor of diners were bent over their dumpling soup, slurping audibly. I thought of a world of slurpers – how many litres of stock consumed, how many eviscerated ducks, how many dogs in ovens, how much getting and spending and eating. It was clear that for many Chinese, whose ancestors had starved through the centuries, food approximated to life. It was what brought families together. For those enamoured of ordinary life, I told myself, China is the place. I enjoyed this brief epiphany while it lasted. Then I confronted a small pen filled with medium-sized alligators climbing over each other. Even as I wondered what was going on, a member of the kitchen staff bent over and grasped one of them by the tail, yanking the specimen out and then decapitating it. At that moment, I thought it would be a good idea to make a series about the biggest Chinese restaurant in the world. Not a gastro-investigation, to be sure, but an account of how such places came to exist.

One of my bosses, Jeremy Isaacs, once said that he defined his own job as a television executive in terms of being unable to describe to his mother what he did. Many people these days are known as commissioning editors, but depending on which part of the media vineyard they labour in, they perform very different tasks. I tended to tell people that I looked after docs. Yes, I'd say, this was one of my docs. Sometimes I worked like a producer, making detailed decisions. I was often involved in seeking cash, an onerous activity. I travelled the seven seas in the company of other commissioning editors, visiting the growing number of documentary festivals, to which pitching sessions were increasingly attached, attended by producers obliged to hawk their own programmes in order to find money.

I was frequently summoned to a production that showed signs of derailing. I couldn't have worked as I did without the store of talent at the BBC. Early on I realised how important it was to allow one's truly bad ideas to be overruled, thus avoiding the wastage of time, money and talent that characterises media life. I got better at this. More important was the continuous half-attention I paid to ideas, though I was always aware that this didn't look like work. I got a reputation for being tough, but I never thought this was deserved. All good books, articles or films begin with subjects or ideas. If the project was wrongly conceived, it would be badly executed. I suppose there were people who didn't think like this, but I couldn't think in any other way. Sometimes I felt thin-skinned when people referred to me as being arrogant, and I wondered whether I would have been treated in this way in another career – working as the editor of a newspaper, for instance. Then the film I'd been working on would turn out well, and I'd forget about the criticisms.

Look and read, read and look. I read reflexively, like a scavenger. I want film-makers to be like magpies, always looking for what is unexpectedly shiny. For a long time, I was tormented by certain ideas; it would occur to me that such-and-such a subject merited attention. Then I found out that this wasn't the way to talk to film-makers. If I did talk about subjects – globalisation, gender alteration – we'd either have a good conversation or not, but we'd never have a film. It was a bit better if we talked about stories, but not much – because the stories seemed to dangle in a void, lacking any meaning or *raison d'être*. I tried to explain how many films have failed because their makers had taken a subject and glued characters onto the surface, as if it were something in a classroom; or how many appeared to just go from one damn thing to another, never really finding any reason for their existence. Projects not only featured people, they also resembled them. They were, to quote the title of one of my favourite films, the lives of others. So I evolved pseudo-Socratic methods that were often baffling to my interlocutors. 'Why is this story good?' I'd ask, or 'Why are you interested in this subject?' Frequently, they didn't have an answer to the question, but I found that posing it was useful. As I write this, however, I feel like adding a qualification. I didn't emphatically require answers to these questions. Often the fact that there was no discernible answer was a good thing, not because I wanted films with no answers, but because asking the question seemed desirable. And this is how I became involved with many excellent projects. It was in my living room that Eugene Jarecki talked to me about the last speech President Eisenhower made before his retirement, on the military–industrial–congressional complex, in which he predicted a dire fate for the American republic if the influence of commerce over the arms trade was allowed to increase. I recall being baffled by the speech, which was delivered haltingly, as if Ike was nervous to be raising such a subject. But like Eugene I thought that the final testament of a war hero best known for his games of golf would get us somewhere, and out of this shared insight – via the works of Frank Capra, the burning towers of 9/11 and numerous arms fairs at which lethal weapons were sold as if they were fashion accessories – came Eugene's essay *Why We Fight* (2005).

I went with such subjects because I was curious and wanted to learn. I feel that many of the best film-makers exist in a state of permanent curiosity. I will never know enough about the now extinct, often horrifying century in which I was born. I was always intimidated by the mayhem of the twentieth century and the attention it received. How could I find new ways into so much that was known in outline? One day, I got a call out of the blue from the international lawyer Philippe Sands, who had read a piece of mine and liked it. Philippe said he had some footage to show me. It depicted two seventy-somethings, Austrian and German, arguing in ill-tempered, Muppet-like style over the respective responsibilities of their fathers for mass murder. One of them, Niklas Frank, had spent his life incriminating his

Nazi father, and carried a photograph of the hanged man around with him. The other, Horst von Wächter, still insisted, despite evidence to the contrary, that his own father was a hero. As we watched, Philippe explained his own connection to their story. This wound through a city once called Lemberg, in the Habsburg empire, then Lvov, in interwar Poland, and now Lviv, in contemporary Ukraine. He'd gone there in search of his own family, many of whom were murdered by agents of the fathers of these two squabbling old men. But he was also interested in the origins of his own profession. Why had both Hersch Lauterpacht, author of much of the Nuremberg trials charge sheet and creator of the idea that 'crimes against humanity' could be punished, and Raphael Lemkin, who had first formulated the legal concept of genocide, been educated at the law school in Lemberg/Lvov/Lviv? What was so special about having come from this squabbled-over piece of central European real estate? It was this, rather than the guilt of the two fathers, that interested me, but I could see that one could only approach this larger theme through the story of the fathers. We embarked on *What Our Fathers Did: A Nazi Legacy* (2015), which did indeed turn out to be an account of Philippe's quest, and much else besides.

Now comes the most difficult question in the making of any doc: why do some narratives fly and others don't? It would be simplest to say that certain film-makers understand narrative and others don't. Some films wrestle themselves painfully into storyhood, without ever quite getting there. Others make it seem all so easy, when it isn't. James Marsh wrote a sixty-page outline for *Man on Wire*. For his next film, *Project Nim* (2011), he came up with a somewhat simpler account of a 1970s experiment in which a chimpanzee was brought up as a human: breastfed, kitted out with diapers and, once grown, taught to decipher letters and then words. James explained that he wasn't making a nature film; he wasn't interested in the theory or practice of animal rights. Instead, he wanted to know why the experiment had been abandoned by the professor whose idea it had been. Poor Nim had been passed from one set of humans to another, in the manner of a foundling in a Dickens novel. At one point, he had been cosseted and dressed in a red pullover, appearing in PBS programmes for children. Some of his human playmates took part in sexual games with him. When he was consigned to an animal experimentation centre, things got really bad. What James discovered was much worse than he had initially thought, and he created a parable expressing the inability of humans to comprehend animals without treating them as their own property. Nim wasn't encouraged to be an animal, and he couldn't become a human. The only human gift he received proved to be a tragic life, and in this respect the experiment was horribly successful. Nim got to hate his erratic guardians, attacking them. The only human he got on with was a non-scientist who liked him for what he was, letting him run where he wished.

James's film was admired, but I felt that the admiration was shadowed by disapprobation. Humans will watch shows about the loss of our remaining wilderness; these television ventures have become the way we lament the progressive destruction of nature. But James had something different to say, and it wasn't popular. He wasn't delivering a message. All he wanted to say was that it would be better if we didn't treat animals in the way Nim had been treated. I liked *Project Nim* as much as *Man on Wire*. In some respects, I found it a more challenging film. But I also realised that we had only been able to make it because of James's success with *Man on Wire*. Would there have been a way of telling poor Nim's story in a different, more human-friendly way? To do that we would have had to make a film with a more recognisable message. We would have had to tell Nim's story from the point of view of humans – not, to be sure, in order to say that he had been treated well, but so that he became a case history. There have been very different films pointing out the abuse of animals, watched by many millions. *Blackfish* (2013) tells the story of Tilikum, an orca driven to attacking his keepers because he had been imprisoned for life in an aquarium. The film is a brilliant piece of investigative journalism, showing the indifference of the aquarium operators to the animals in their charge, and the cruelty, inadvertent or not, of placing large mammals capable of swimming hundreds of miles and communicating in complex languages in confined spaces. The film had a big impact, not just in the US, where most of it was filmed, but globally. It uncovered that these animals would be sold by the Americans to Chinese companies. But it didn't do what James had tried to achieve: to tell us about humans from the point of view of an animal.

Another film about animals and humans, *Unlocking the Cage* (2016), explored the Nim experience from the vantage point of the animal rights lawyer Steven Wise, who had spent twenty years attempting to bring a case in which an animal was a plaintiff to court. This was an examination of the legal 'personhood' or otherwise of great apes. Expressed as a legal conundrum, the issue of humans' treatment of animals was more easily approached; the comically, endearingly persistent aspects of Wise's efforts, in conjunction with the evident interest on the part of the New York judges in addressing the question of animal personhood, made the film much easier to watch.

Often films are the consequence of a carefully nursed and cherished obsession. In 2006, Malik Bendjelloul, a young Swedish director, took leave from his television job and travelled around the world. In Cape Town, he visited a store and fell into conversation with the owner. This is how he came across the story of Sixto Rodriguez, a singer from Dearborn, Detroit, who made two unsuccessful albums in the late 1960s and early 1970s, and then disappeared. Old copies of Rodriguez's albums were still available in South Africa, however, where they had sold well. There was a rumour there that Rodriguez had killed himself onstage; in reality, he was working as a demolition handyman in Detroit. After a South African journalist ascertained that he was alive, he came on tour to Cape Town. Told in this way, *Searching for Sugar Man* (2012) would seem to be a banal story worthy of no more than cursory attention, one that carried the standard moral about what it means to fail in American showbiz. But Rodriguez had a special talent, which Bendjelloul, perhaps being an outsider himself, was quick to recognise. There was also something special about the veneration heaped on him by his white Afrikaner fans: improbably, they saw in the Latino singer an image of their own struggles (Rodriguez had no following among South African blacks).

Bendjelloul made a short film out of the Rodriguez story, and got some money to make a feature-length version. He fell out with his producer, but persisted, contacting Simon Chinn, who had just won an Oscar for *Man on Wire*. Bendjelloul told Chinn he had a film that would win another. Extensively recut, *Searching for Sugar Man* did deservedly win its Oscar, but watching the film one can see how narrow the space between success and failure in docs is. It would have been easy to make a dull film about Rodriguez, who wasn't cooperative and didn't really want to revisit his past. Luckily, his daughters are clever and warm, and they tell the story of willed obscurity with passionate regard for their father. Contributing most to the film's success, however, is its structure, which, according to Chinn, came late, entailing a wholesale revision based on viewings of *Citizen Kane*.

The film starts in Cape Town, and after a nod to the dereliction of post-1960s Detroit, moves back there again. Forty-five minutes elapse before we're told that Rodriguez's death by setting fire to himself onstage was a fantasy of his fans. He lived in the same house for thirty years. The story of South African music journalists searching for him could have been somewhat dull, but the film is saved by a clever evocation of the wholly lost world of South African whites. There's a brilliantly telling interview with a radio censor, who tells how the more risqué tracks of Rodriguez's albums were scratched so they couldn't be played. Nobody cares much about white South Africa now, just as nobody cared much about Rodriguez; but we are asked to care, and we do. Rodriguez was discovered earlier by Australian fans, who were less isolated from the music world than South Africans, and he died there. Many people find this omission from the doc not wholly honest, but it seems legitimate to me, because the film is focused on South Africa. Revealing that Rodriguez was never quite lost to the world would have spoilt the story. His neglect by agents and record-company people in the US, artfully revealed by a persistent Bendjelloul, does seem outrageous. The best lines of the film come from his demolition mate Emmerson, who sees Rodriguez as a working-class genius, suffering for his art and touchingly indifferent to anything like celebrity. It's this wholly unfashionable aspect of the Rodriguez story that lingers after each viewing.

In 2014, Malik Bendjelloul jumped in front of a train in Stockholm, killing himself. He had seemed happy, but some of his friends said he worried about never again finding a story to which he could give as much as he had to Rodriguez. But Bendjelloul's own ending somehow mirrors the dark side of his story. One can feel indignant that a man who in part rescued another man couldn't rescue himself, yet still not be wholly surprised by this real-life ending.

I can see that films take on the lives of those who make them. I met Bendjelloul only briefly, and he seemed as sweet and attentive as his film. A Swedish journalist told me that Bendjelloul suffered from serious bipolar disorder, struggling to stay off the drugs prescribed by his doctors. 'His death had nothing to do with the film,' he told me. I hope this is true, but at the risk of banality, I'd counsel against over-absorption. I'd say that replacing your own life with the lives of others is a bad idea.

There is no accepted way to make a documentary film. How you work depends not just on your own temperament, but on the subject matter. There are theories about this, and they've evolved over the decades, as I'll show later. What hasn't changed, and never will, is the element of risk attached to each venture into the real. It really is impossible to know what the outcome of a film will be when you start. This means that you go through a long period of wondering not just whether your film will be any good, but whether you have a film at all or just a collection of not very interesting interviews and images. Of course, the process of filming is cheaper now, but someone has to pay the film-maker. I think that this is where support from the likes of the BBC is important. Someone has to bet on the story. It's not fair to ask film-makers to shoulder all the burden. They have to be reassured that if things go wrong, either something can be salvaged or, in the worst case, someone other than the film-maker can absorb the loss. But these days broadcasters are reluctant to act as patrons. With shrinking budgets, they have become more cautious. This is also happening in what remains of print journalism, but the rush to caution is greater in documentaries. I did hate squandering the BBC's precious public money, but it happened only rarely. I think that this was because, like any print editor, I developed a sense of the person and the subject, and how they would work for each other. Or maybe I just felt that it was good to be reckless. But this was not something I could communicate easily to my colleagues, and there were many battles: 'How do you know this will work?' I would tell them that we should take the risk anyhow.

I like films where the risk factor is most intense. I enjoy working on them, and they give me the most satisfaction because they've been stress-tested, run through some kind of fire, surviving intact. Each one of them is a prototype, an experiment in life. In *The English Surgeon* (2007), you can imagine the debonair, ironical, mischievous Henry Marsh being played by Alec Guinness in an Ealing comedy. Henry had starred in a BBC series, but it was the prospect of going to Kiev, in Ukraine, with him that appealed. He frets constantly about the bureaucracy of Britain's NHS, but what really bothers him is the exercising of moral choice in medical interventions, and what happens if, and when, you guess wrong or make mistakes. In Geoffrey Smith's film, we see him encountering them day by day, as they happen. Henry was a would-be Sovietologist before he dumped the study of politics and turned to brain surgery. Each year he went from London to Kiev, where he worked with his friend Igor; they rented space from the former KGB, creating a hospital. In the

UK, a 'perforator' (something that opens skulls) costs £80 and is used once; Igor uses them again and again – drilling skulls in Ukraine is performed with a domestic-quality Bosch appliance. The centrepiece of the film, unrehearsed, comic and terrifying, is a long, hazardous, noisy, bloody (and ultimately successful) operation performed on Marian, whose tumour has caused epilepsy. Henry gives a running commentary, pausing only to ask the still-awake Marian how he feels. 'Surgery's a blood sport,' he tells us, geeing himself up while displaying a touching degree of stage fright. Marian's brain has 'the consistency of very thick cream cheese'. There are deeper insights, too. 'I can't really comprehend that this [the brain] is thought,' he says, peering into Marian's open skull. 'But that's what it is. Thought is a physical process. We are our brain.' Henry visits the home of a girl, Tanya, whose operation went wrong, causing paralysis and, ultimately, death. He loves being in Ukraine. It is clear that Tanya's parents love Henry, and he pauses at her grave in reflection, expressing himself without his reflexive English irony. 'What are we if we don't try to help others?' he asks us. 'Nothing. Nothing at all.' A critic at the *Guardian* praised the film by wondering how it had ever got made, and it was easy to see where they were coming from.

The same might have been said about absolutist Iran, after Kim Longinotto's *Divorce Iranian Style* (1998). In 1997, after lengthy negotiations, Longinotto and Ziba Mir-Hosseini were given permission to film inside a Tehran divorce court. They settled on the proceedings overseen by Judge Deldar. These involved cases in which the terms of the divorce weren't resolved, and the judge's role, in the light of the conservative ethos, was to persuade couples to stick together. But the judge proved to be a kindly figure, alert to the predicament of the women crowding his courtroom. I sat down with Longinotto recently and asked her how she made her films. Wasn't filming in Iran terrifying, when she didn't understand the language or the legal system? She said that it had been one of her easier films, because the courtroom was like theatre. 'I could tell it was interesting,' she said. 'There's always a long moment when you just don't know what you have. The fear never goes away. You ask yourself each night: "Do I really have anything here?" And slowly you begin to believe in the people and the scenes, and feel that it's going to be all right. But the fear never goes away. I always think it's a miracle that I can make films.' No one could have foreseen what Longinotto would find in Tehran, but in those days Channel 4 had the will and the money to see her through. Backers are reassured by the known, but that isn't the way to make great films. Doesn't every documentary film imply the exercising of risk?

Slight, soft-spoken, ridiculously modest, awesomely stubborn, Longinotto has been all over the world making films for the past thirty years. She was interested in gender before this became fashionable. Each of her films reveals a stubborn contest between the ideals of feminism and equality and the recalcitrance of mankind. She also has an eye for humour and irony. In her Iranian masterpiece, she reveals herself to be among the greatest directors, capable of understanding the misery of women trapped in marriages as teenagers and unable either to reclaim the sum of money spent as dowry by their parents or to keep hold of their children. However, she empathises, too, with the stiff-necked, humiliated, now-unwanted men pleading to retain their wives, as if this were a means of achieving dignity. Longinotto is also fascinated by the sheer otherness of human lives, and her film is a tribute to the human powers of survival and recuperation.

In this respect, she has a truly feminist sensibility. In the most heart-rending scene, an eighteen-year-old tells how she has been married twice. When sexually assaulted by her stepfather, her mother tried to beat her. But she nonetheless agrees to reconcile with her mother and try again. Some of the women do emerge from the courtroom with a small portion of the freedom or the support they need. Meanwhile, the judge's assistant's ten-year-old daughter comes into the courtroom and pretends she's the judge, sitting in the chair. Not everything in the Islamic Republic of Iran is about repression.

Roger Graef, who was born in the US, really understands understated British culture. He has made great films about the police (*Police*, 1982) and the serious failings of the British Communist Party (*Decision: British Communism*, 1978). In their low-key way, British film-makers have always been good at taking risks. Never self-conscious enough to designate themselves as a school, they share a degree of what might be termed 'attitude'. Whereas the Americans, Danes and French like to talk about their method, Brits burrow into their own films with a degree of surprise that they were ever made at all. The great British subject is how you wrest something from failure; this may be said to define their non- or anti-method. This is most true of the oeuvre of Sean McAllister, who was born in Hull and acquired a film education after working in a pea-canning factory. Sean shoots his own films, and he appears in them, representing quintessentially, sometimes comically, the principle of immersive film-making. You have to imagine him arriving with the rest of the media in a hellhole. They'll go in one direction, herding each other, and Sean will take the other route. Then he will disappear, often for months. The odd email or blog will recount how the story he was following came to nothing. In the end, however, something will get done. In Iraq, Sean made *The Liberace of Baghdad* (2005), a film about the family life of a fang-toothed ex-classical pianist reduced to making a living by playing for visiting hacks. In Japan, I'd wanted him to make a film about the vanishing Japanese 'salaryman', whose job had been destroyed by the slump. Instead, he lived with a couple in their closet-sized apartment. I forget how his best film came into existence, but Sean reminds me that this, too, was an accident. He had wanted to cover the Arab Spring because the news coverage seemed so predictable and boring. Somehow, he found himself in Yemen, making a film about a man unable to make a living by introducing tourism. In the meantime, however, he had made friends with a Syrian couple opposed to Assad's rule, and began to film with them in Damascus. His activities were interrupted when he was arrested and thrown into prison briefly. Amer and Raghda, meanwhile, were obliged to flee Syria because they featured in Sean's film, which was seized by the police. So Sean's film followed the couple and their children as they went into exile, from Damascus to Lebanon, and then to France.

Doc-makers need to deal with the question of how to treat their subjects. My own feeling is that this isn't complicated. If you involve your subjects in your film – if they appear outside the conventions of journalism, giving over portions of their own lives – then they must surely be allowed to approve of what you did with them. At festivals where *A Syrian Love Story* (2015) was discussed, audiences expressed incredulity (and some reservations) at the degree of intimacy Sean had achieved. And yet Amer and Raghda never complained. They liked having Sean around, especially in their darkest moments. Family life is the theme of this five-year story, but friendship, too. Raghda hasn't been broken by incarceration in Syria, but she goes on suffering. Sometimes Amer shouts at her. He resents how politicised she has become. 'You can't be both Che Guevara and a mother,' he shouts at her. They become older, more drawn, and in the end they give up on the marriage, remaining friends. But their children grow up and seem ready to fulfil so much promise. As a little boy, Kaka is asked about the Assad tyranny. 'Does it make you want to leave?' He answers: 'No, fight.' As a teenager in France his views are very different. Meanwhile, Amer paints and gardens, in a spirit of half-contented resignation. Raghda goes to Turkey in order to work towards a democratic Syria. Beyond the sufferings of war and exile, the film is a raw, astonishingly accomplished portrait of a marriage breaking up, in which the participants, seen at their most vulnerable and damaged, are never less than heroic. One can watch it and comprehend a small portion of the suffering endured by Syrians, isolated in their catastrophe. It's also a lesson in the strange endurance and capacity for love of human beings.

Jean Chen is among the best editors I know. She works from the small house she inhabits with her mother in Queens. I like to walk with her, either in the suburbs of Taipei, where she was born, or in Manhattan's Lower East Side. She takes me to Chinese street stalls and the sort of Chinese restaurants where the waiters slosh soup around with abandon, staining the table-cloth. She has worked with the Taiwanese director Ang Lee; now she'll only work with those whom she really likes. If a film-maker has faked sequences, telling interviewees what to say or making them cry on camera, Jean will be offended, but you will have to ask someone else exactly what was so offensive about the film-maker's behaviour. Mention Jean to anyone with whom she has worked, and you'll get a succession of superlatives. She is a diviner, alert to the proximity of spirits, and she practises reiki, healing trapped nerves. But it's next to impossible to talk to Jean about what she does with a film. You can only watch her working at an editing table, absorbed. She works too fast for one to be able to comprehend what she is doing. Sometimes it's possible to see how she has removed one portion of material from a long-discarded version, placing it in a new narrative, but this is a minor part of what she does. Jean wants film-makers to let her do things, and becomes annoyed when they don't. I recall one film that was too long, clogged with detail that the film-makers couldn't bear to abandon. Jean took the film from them for a weekend. I've spent much of my life fixing narratives, but what she had done appeared different in kind. It was the same film, to be sure, with the same narrative sequences, but everything was different. The film made sense now as it moved from scene to scene. It was also clear what the film-makers had always meant to do with the story. I wasn't sure exactly how this had happened.

Danish editor Stig Bilde's job was to cut films that were usually ninety minutes long in half, so that they could be shown on news channels at forty minutes. I might send Stig notes, but what I wrote bore no real relation to what he did to the film. These films had often won prizes, but they had changed in Stig's hands. Sequences that never really belonged in the film had vanished, and this meant that other sequences that had gone unnoticed now appeared to be more significant. One film, *Girl Model* (2011), was about the shipment of teenagers from Siberia to the Japanese fashion market. Its real subject was the abuse of these teenagers, who either failed to make enough money and went home to their bewildered Russian parents or were forced into prostitution. But the film, for a variety of reasons, legal or otherwise, could only suggest that this was going on. In Stig's version, the film came closer to being a statement. Now you knew what was happening. You could become angry because you understood.

From the beginning of documentary film, editors have performed an ambiguous role. They work in the shadows, behind grandstanding directors. Sometimes they merely do what these directors want, but more often they shape the films. By and large they don't complain about directors, though you can gauge their frustration through the white knuckles, twiddled fingers, hit keyboards or odd items of their craft banged on editing desks. They are the people who recall the piece of narrative jettisoned months ago and know where to find it. They know how to discard dud suggestions. As Fred Wiseman, who edits his own films, has observed, the process of editing docs is the opposite of the one adopted in fictions. With a fiction, you have a script and material that illustrates the script. In a documentary there is no script, so you have to create one. Beneath the story constructed out of observed reality, a film is made up of thousands of small decisions. When it is finished, these decisions are forgotten. In the old days, when films were assembled by hand, the pain of making a film was physically evident in the celluloid of what was called the 'cutting copy': hundreds of marks around the tape gluing together the endlessly assembled and disassembled film. Editors handled the recalcitrant film; under pressure, they resembled wound-up children's toys, rushing from one half-completed job to another in a frenzied effort to overcome the limits imposed by time.

When I first came to the BBC, I found editors intimidating. I'm still baffled by the sight of an editor sifting through a mass of material conserved on hard drives. I can see how a film is constructed second by second by looking at the diagrammatic patterns of the various software programs editors use. The actual process of compiling a film, from bits and pieces to a finished artefact, is still opaque to me. When I look through hours of rushes, it's remarkable to me that anyone can create a finished film.

Often films seem like they will never reach a completed state, and then, suddenly, they do. There are weeks when a film will go back and forth, seeming to find its centre, only to lose it again. The editor, director and producer will sit around wondering what has gone wrong. Quite often films mysteriously fail at this point, and no one can figure out why. You can be impatient in such circumstances, but this isn't always effective. Or you can leave people to their struggle, with equally bad results.

How is it possible to help a film towards completion? I adopted a method I'd found in the best print editors. They'd leave the line-by-line alterations until very late. Instead, they'd try to ascertain where the real centre of the piece lay. This came down to an attempt to locate the sweet spot of the narrative. At what point did one become aware of what the film was really trying to say? Was it early enough in the story? Did it ever happen? If it didn't, what was preventing it from happening? One television reporter told me that TV was simple. 'You say what the story is about at the beginning,' he said. 'Then you repeat it in the middle. And then you repeat it again at the end.' Docs can be more indirect than this. They can even be elliptical. But I always felt that they required some level of clarity. There are many who don't agree with this view. I've tried to watch allusive, hyper-elliptical docs, but I find they don't do much for me. I wonder how much people really like films that are primarily absorbed in their own construction. At the same time, I don't enjoy docs where the script is over-emphatic. I have no views, one way or another, on the use of scripts, though I never enjoyed writing them. They are the easiest way of imposing a point of view on images. In the 1970s, there were many good television scripts. The best was in the series *The World at War* (1973–4), delivered sonorously by Sir Laurence Olivier. These days many scripts are used to achieve emphasis, or out of a terror that audiences won't stick with what they are seeing. But they remain part of the standard kit of television documentaries.

There are also directors whose work makes sense only right at the end of the process, often long after everyone has given up. Or there are perfectionists, never happy to abandon the process of tinkering with a narrative. The most talented (and most testing) that I have encountered was Norma Percy, who has worked with Brian Lapping for more than twenty years on series that chronicle the great crises of our time. Norma is slight in appearance, hesitant, with a halting, elliptical manner of speaking. There are people whose fascination drives out speculation, such as Norma and Brian. They are habitually marketed as people who frequent the 'corridors of power', but I feel that this isn't the most important aspect of their exhaustively researched work. They look at what really happened. Given a subject, they will go over it again and again, until they are satisfied that what they have is an approximation of the truth. If getting at the truth proved to be difficult, they won't bother to tell you. Instead, they will assume that you should know.

I once asked Norma whether her films were objective, which broadcast journalism is supposed to be, and she paused before replying. 'We look at things from various points of view,' she said. I think she meant that her own point of view was constructed out of the points of view of others. It didn't have to be called 'objective'.

She works with acolytes – younger directors, busy learning – and her interviews often last for hours. She pre-interviews subjects. When she did this with Slobodan Milošević, who at the time was still ruling Serbia, he asked where the camera was; when approached again for the real thing, he initially declined.

I worked with Norma on her series about Yugoslavia when I'd just arrived at the BBC. I did want to understand Balkan politics. Working with Brian and Norma was like attending the seminars of two determined, cranky LSE professors of political science determined to instil the principles of empiricism into their students. I was grateful for the opportunity to continue my education in an area that I had hitherto avoided. Nonetheless, I felt anxious. There were many interviews with Balkan politicians. Their names and their grey suits appeared interchangeable. Strongman Milošević aside, I could recall only one of them at viewings, and that was because he wore a pink Lacoste polo shirt. For some reason, I could recall that he was from Montenegro and that his name was Momčilo Cemović. Whenever we discussed the unravelling of the republics that had composed the now defunct Yugoslavia, I gritted my teeth and thought of tiny Montenegro and the vast, soothing pinkness of Cemović's breast. Where had he acquired a XXXXL polo shirt? Did they make them specially for politicians from small republics?

It was around this time that Silvio Berlusconi mixed up Slovakia with Slovenia, allowing the confusion to persist on his channels for many years. I became anxious on behalf of the BBC audience hunkered down at home. How much of this would they ever understand? At one point, I suggested that it might be good to record at least one long interview with a commentator capable of bringing clarity to the Balkans. This is a method that I've often urged on film-makers, and it does work, but Norma refused the suggestion sternly. She and Brian only interviewed participants. I wrote a long note to them, expressing my views and urging simplicity. Stupidly, I used the word 'rebarbative'. The next time I arrived to view the film, I saw that they'd pasted my letter on the wall, surrounding the offending word with a circle and exclamation marks. 'We didn't know what it meant and had to look it up,' they told me.

I've watched the series *The Death of Yugoslavia* (1995) several times since it was shown more than twenty years ago. When I went to Sarajevo after the war had ended, I met a young CBS correspondent who told me that she couldn't understand what the conflict had been about. I told her to root around her office and see if there were any video cassettes of *The Death of Yugoslavia*. The next day, she said that she had found them and now understood it. Years later, I met Richard Holbrooke, the American diplomat who had brokered the deals that led to the Dayton Agreement, which finally ended the war. I told him I recalled his many appearances in the series with pleasure. Holbrooke was a big man, physical and emphatic, and he hugged me. 'No!' he said. 'You were involved with that series?' He began to reel off a list of revelations that he could recall. He told me that every diplomat posted to the Balkans had been required to watch the series. 'The best factual series I've ever seen on TV,' he said. I agree, and it has become part of my education. But I now view it in a different light to the one cast twenty years ago. The films record the enduring power of nationalisms, big and small. It's clear that the Yugoslav wars, far from marking a last gasp of ethnic passions in Europe, were, in reality, a precursor of a larger revival that is now tearing asunder the rest of Europe. It recalls the folly that my ultimate hero, John Maynard Keynes, saw at the Versailles Peace Conference in 1919, when he observed how humans could know that what they were doing would have terrible consequences, but went ahead and did it anyhow. Thanks, in part, to Brian and Norma, I now look at the world in this tragic context. I'm not sure that this was what they intended, but I am sure that they would not mind my highly 'unobjective' interpretation.

I never cared as much as I should have done about the aesthetic of docs. There has always been a tug between a perceived obligation to be literal and a desire to embellish. Often music has been used to hide the limitations imposed by mediocre footage or a fundamental lack of belief in the narrative. It was used in the early days of docs to make it seem as if the film was much the same as a fiction, with highs, lows, climaxes and spaces between. To be sure, there's a school of film-making that abhors music on principled grounds, but I can't go there. What irritates me is the rote use of sound. At one point, American docs were filled with brass noises, all sounding like Aaron Copland's *Fanfare for the Common Man*. Next came an outbreak of wind music, often paired with laments about the fate of the Plains Indians. And then came the era of Philip Glass, whose minimalism supplied the circular movement on which docs seem to thrive. But it was rare to find directors, like James Marsh, who thought hard about music. The mixture of Erik Satie's *Gymnopédies* and Michael Nyman's music proved to be perfect for *Man on Wire*. It was illustrative in its jauntiness, and yet it added a layer of parody. There's something incredulous about Nyman's minimalism, as if the composer were always asking himself how it was possible to achieve effects with so little, and this seemed to be an aural equivalent of Philippe's exploits.

Nyman is a documentary fanatic, and his rescoring of Dziga Vertov's *Man with a Movie Camera* (1929) is both a homage and an extraordinary improvement on the original 1920s score. When I met him years later, he was working on his own film about World War I, *War Work* (2014). In the opening scene, a doctor and a nurse place a mask on the horrifyingly disfigured face of a soldier dressed in uniform. What's the work of war? The real work? Well, it consists of moving sheep, pigs and cattle to the slaughter, as well as humans. Millions and millions of litres of bad wine will be swilled by those who will die shortly. There are baroque, absurd-looking weapons to try out, and varieties of ill-fitting uniforms fit only for vagrants. Outsize beards are fashionable, though stubble is more common. Some men seem so weary that they cannot walk any longer, and many will never walk again. Somewhere, amid the scarred valleys and the piled-up corpses, we find time for bereaved families, though they must stay quiet, without protest. And yes, a generation of fatherless, ill-fed children will grow up in the streets, with toy guns and planes. We know that they will be sent out to be killed in a few years' time. Would it be better if they knew?

Look for no lasting spirit of consolation in *War Work*. What it offers instead is a brilliant mix of discomfiture and compassion. In this country, the celebration of mass carnage has always been elegiac and apologetic. World War I is coloured by the aestheticised red of poppies. There is a British *Heimat* in the poems we still love, in Siegfried Sassoon and Robert Graves, even in the most savage insights of Wilfred Owen. Modernism and its offshoots, such as Vorticism in Britain and Italian Futurism, were created out of a notion that humanity would be incorporated willy-nilly within machine culture. How would humans survive this transition? The best of Vorticism – Jacob Epstein's *Rock Drill* or Wyndham Lewis's stick humanoids – contrives to warn us even as it exalts raw power. Insights such as these are largely lost to us, in the same way that war has become distant and sanitised. But atrocity remains wholly vivid for Nyman, who loves this aberrant streak in modernism and has reclaimed it for our time. The words don't soften the images or diminish the soaring, plunging, always restless music. But it isn't all darkness in this war, and just occasionally, among the ruined faces, something softer can be sighted. In a medical context, away from the guns and bombast, the pursuit of genuine knowledge is permitted. Aged puppeteers making false limbs or faces are absorbed in their actions, while young nurses and doctors dressed in white try to steady their wrecked, frenzied charges. Working hard at war is what they're doing.

The last thing to say about all the work in progress: at some moment, it is finished. After so many viewings, tinkerings with sound or pictures, so many second and third thoughts about whether such-and-such a sequence does or doesn't belong, someone calls a halt. In desperate circumstances, this might be the backers or an impatient broadcasting exec. These are the disastrous films – the ones somehow blocked or mired in indecision. Among the most important qualities required in making a documentary film is knowing when to stop. Some film-makers make radical decisions about films long after they have actually been finished – indeed, after they have been screened at festivals. Unless you are very wealthy, this is a bad idea. I can recall screaming at film-makers that they must cease their indecision. No aspect of film-making, no matter how important the subject, how complex the effects, justifies so many tenth thoughts. The options in narrative, albeit infinite in theory, are bounded in practice. One decision has to lead to a better outcome than another. So let me evoke the state of mind prevalent among those reaching the end of a truly exhausting film. Let's assume thirty-six weeks have been spent editing. Amid the debris of transcripts are paper cups and pizza boxes. The atmosphere is close and tense with anti-climax. It is by now impossible to know whether the film is any good, even after the positive views of so many visitors. Someone sighs, and the rest of us suppress giggles. There's an editor who needs to cycle home; an Uber car has come and awaits the star of the commentary. And the numerous execs, hangers-on, relatives and advisers wish to go for a drink. And I tell myself, 'This film won't be the last word.' Last words no longer come with films, whether we like it or not.

In the old days, a doc went to what was called post-production, was transferred to a master tape vetted by television execs, and was scheduled and promoted in the way any other television programme was. When I wrote a media column, there was still a basement room at the BBC where journalists gathered each week to look at films. The reviewers were either very young, starting out on a career, or older and on the way to finishing one. Reviewing films is a serious activity, because it is the only coherent account of a film, and for film-makers and executives alike it is the way films are remembered. As a young producer, I can recall papering the walls of my office with good reviews. Awards were dished out each year for political reasons. In those distant days, it was really hard to watch documentaries. The first head of Channel 4, Jeremy Isaacs, was notorious for watching piles of VHS cassettes in bed. When Erik Barnouw, author of a highly regarded history of documentary film, wanted to view films, he was obliged to

take a year viewing them in national television archives throughout the world.

Nowadays, anyone can view a doc with one or two clicks. In
1992, a cargo ship spilt a container of yellow rubber ducks into
the water, with the result that the ducks drifted off, thus telling
oceanographers a lot about the state of the world's currents. This
is now the fate of documentaries. Some are carried to the right
shoreline and get noticed; others just float around until they
reach the most obscure beach; one, or more, may acquire fame
or notoriety. There are ways to prevent the lost-duck experience:
you can hire publicists or construct ad campaigns. My own view
is that by this stage, it's too late to be engineering success. You
would have had to create the film in your head months, even
years before. I often wonder who will watch a film, whether it
will say anything to people. A Chinese producer asked me about
this recently. He'd been talking about the huge interest in docs
among the information-hungry Chinese. Would it be possible to
make films that served such passions, taking people outside the
blandness of heavily censored Chinese television? I told him that
I often knew when a film would be successful. This had been the
case with *Man on Wire*. It was much harder to gauge its commercial success. Maybe it was best to think of what he wanted to
watch, because it pleased him or told him something. He looked
puzzled while the words were being translated, and then nodded,
as if to say yes. A documentary must tell a story.

3 : Pioneers and Propagandists

Dziga Vertov's *Man with a Movie Camera* (1929): 'Now they have perfected the cine camera to penetrate more deeply into the visible world.' Can the same be said of now?

The first documentary depicted Thomas Edison's assistant pretending to sneeze. Early contributions from the Lumière brothers reveal workers leaving the Lumière factory, glaring at the camera. In another Lumière film someone is building a shed, and a bourgeois family are around a table, drinking coffee. All this is being done for the first time, and this is the purpose of documentary film – to show what is happening. 'The films were not an illusion, or a performance, but a grey, flickering mirror of a past reality,' Mark Cousins and Kevin Macdonald inform us in their survey of writings about documentary film. 'The cinema, unlike any previous art form, was able to represent the spontaneous – the very essence of life itself.' Early documentaries were popular with audiences, but the novelty of being able to see what happened wore off once fiction films adopted more sophisticated techniques. So began the long struggle of documentary to find its place in the sun. Was it a new form capable of great originality, destined to compete with manufactured cinematic artifice? Or was it filler for harassed exhibitors who required something to show before the main feature?

For a long time, the slow development of technology appeared to condemn docs to the margins, as did the sheer problem of getting them distributed. Fits and starts characterise documentary history. There is a sense that their protagonists are similarly afflicted – by the passion to describe things, to be sure, but also by a need to work against the grain, creating work in the most improbable circumstances. Those who have written about the history of documentaries are quick to identify the struggle against the odds. But it's also possible to discern the persistence of subjects and, more importantly, of purposes. You can identify the sort of people who made the earliest documentaries. It's possible to think of them shouting at each other that they know how to make a great film. The subject matter of documentaries and the degree to which formal experimentation would be a given of the new form were established early on. At the onset of the Boer War in 1899, cameras were so heavy that they had to be lashed to the decks for the outward voyage to South Africa. War footage was much in demand, and much of it was faked for the benefit of early newsreels. The enhancement of reality would also be a staple of the new form, not because reality was invariably dull, but because audiences were habituated to dramatic refinements by then. The most commercially successful early documentary was *Lawrence of Arabia* (1920). This was assembled from mostly staged footage shot by the American lecturer and cultural entrepreneur Lowell Thomas. Lawrence was a minor figure until his exploits, as recorded by Thomas, gave him cult status. To begin with, Thomas had hoped to interest audiences in the footage he had accumulated of General Allenby conquering the Holy Land. The audiences wanted Lawrence. They wanted a simple story of heroism that might compensate for so much that was hard to comprehend – the apparently meaningless carnage. At the Royal Opera House in Covent Garden, Thomas addressed the royal family, Lloyd George and Winston Churchill, and even, on one occasion, Lawrence himself. 'I saw your show last night,' Lawrence wrote to Thomas. 'Thank God the lights were out.'

But it would be a mistake to think that the first docs are only of historical interest. They let you see how it was deemed appropriate to depict reality so many years ago, but their reach also extends into the present. *Nanook of the North* (1922), the first commercially released documentary, starts with a rambling account of the difficulties incurred by film-maker Robert Flaherty, who had an adventurer's love of the Inuit and the cold Canadian wilderness. Then we get an introduction to the somewhat idealised Nanook – bold, steadfast, a great hunter. We meet his family and his dogs. Most of the film consists of tactfully shot family business, but there are two great set pieces, in which a walrus and a seal are successfully dispatched. It's easy to spot and mock the many artifices employed by the over-eager Flaherty, and the film certainly navigates the perils of condescension badly (the scene in which Nanook's family listen to a gramophone recording and try to eat the shellac discs is truly cringe-making). As many have pointed out, the skins worn by the family are deluxe items, supplied by the production, and the Inuit hadn't hunted for some generations in the style forced on them by Flaherty. There's also the issue of the film-maker fathering a son while making the doc. But, by and large, both he and the film were admired by the Inuit, and *Nanook* was never supposed to be a literal account. Flaherty got his Inuit subjects to build a special igloo that was missing a portion of wall in order to accommodate the camera. At best, this can be called a collaborative version of reality, but it is what generations of 'anthropological' film-makers did in concert with their primitive subjects, even as the process of destruction was hastened. But Flaherty hadn't any elevated purpose in *Nanook*, and that is what saves the film. It does give a sense of lives lived in near-total isolation, family solidarity wrestled from a permanent state of adversity. The same is true of *Man of Aran* (1934), Flaherty's second man-and-sea epic. Here the prey is a giant, clumsy basking shark, and the enemy is the Atlantic Ocean raging around the island. Skip the Aran longueurs and go to the last fifteen minutes. Never mind the contrivances, this is film at its most involving and scary. Placing a camera in the presence of death: none, including Werner Herzog, have done this better than Flaherty.

Flaherty had explored the Inuit lands on behalf of a trading and mining company. He brought his own developing room on location and showed footage to the Inuit, provoking a response somewhere between curiosity and rapture. Back in New York, exhibitors were less enamoured, and the film received mixed notices. It played better in London, Paris and Rome, where it was shown in art-house cinemas. Flaherty was an extravagant, impulsive, outsize figure, a big drinker who spent his wife's money on his expeditions. Editors complained about his lack of discipline, noting that he seemed immune to what became the rules of film-making in his search for the wholly 'real' shot. He was persistent and, it would seem, utterly persuasive. It is apparent that he did believe that modern man had lost something in the catastrophe of what was called 'progress'. His role was to restore humanity to itself – a wistful, half-defensive attitude wholly characteristic of those who try to get documentaries shown to wide audiences.

The rise of the documentary proved to be haphazard. It became clear that film-makers in search of the means to record reality would have to find sources of patronage outside the increasingly profit-oriented, formula-bound system of film production centred in Hollywood. In the absence of private investors, they turned to the other major contemporary source of funding: the twentieth-century state. Here they found ready backers, but they were required to sign up to the ideologies of the time.

Man with a Movie Camera (1929), Dziga Vertov's frenzied constructivist homage to the camera lens, still polls near the top in any ranking by doc-buff theorists. Born David Abelevich Kaufman in Poland in 1896, his first films were made and screened aboard the agitprop trains set in motion during the Russian civil war; they were called *Kino-Pravda* ('Cinema Truth'). Vertov, as he came to call himself, became more interested in how films could capture reality than in grinding out newsreels. In his 'Provisional Instructions to Kino-Eye Groups' (1926), Vertov said: 'Our eyes see very little and very badly – so people dreamed up the microscope to let them see invisible phenomena; they invented the telescope. Now they have perfected the cine-camera to penetrate more deeply into the visible world, to explore and record visual phenomena so that what is happening now, which will have to be taken account of in the future, is not forgotten.' He thrived in the brief utopian 1920s moment of the Russian avant-garde, but by the time he made *Man with a Movie Camera*, his livelihood was being threatened. The film is built out of one dazzlingly edited scene after another, with the cameraman striding from one improbable location to the next. Vertov wished to marry his utopian theories of perception to a depiction of Soviet Man (and, most appealingly, Woman), but it's hard to watch the film now without reading into it the subsequent collapse of the Soviet dream. He made the film in Ukraine, after being sacked from his job in Moscow. Just a few years later, Stalin destroyed the Ukrainian economy, starving millions of peasants in his efforts to break any resistance to Soviet rule. If they weren't party members, many of the ebullient crowds seen on beaches in the film would have been pauperised.

Michael Nyman's beautiful 1997 score of the movie captures some of the underlying melancholy of the Vertov utopia. It also foregrounds Vertov's real achievement as a film-maker: not so much the constructivist obsession with technique as the pre-revolutionary exhilaration of mankind so casually and fleetingly captured. Vertov did create a real laboratory, leaving behind enough ideas to keep documentary film-makers busy for the next few decades. Not long after the completion of *Movie Camera*, he was reduced to editing propagandistic newsreels celebrating the glories of Stalinism. He died in 1954.

Outside the odd, vagrant masterpieces of Flaherty or Vertov, however, it remains hard to resist the sheer backwardness of docs in the pre-sound era. In some respects, the problems arose from the limitations of the technology. Robert Capa's great war photographs were taken with a Leica, a small, elegantly designed object not so different from contemporary cameras. For the most part, movie cameras were bulkier and unwieldy, ill-suited to capturing reality. Synchronous sound was recorded on discs with machinery that fitted neatly into a medium-sized truck. But the clamp placed on the form by ideology proved to be just as important. It shouldn't be surprising that docs were quickly marginalised by the offerings of fiction. But another development was apparent, and it straddled the categories of fiction and non-fiction, in some respects superseding them. In his novel *Hollywood*, Gore Vidal dates the triumph of fiction to a moment in World War I. His characters talk about the creation of an alternate fictional reality. The judgement comes from a society Frenchwoman turned actor, who becomes studio head once transplanted to Los Angeles:

> Caroline suddenly realised that she – and everyone else – had been approaching this game from the wrong direction. Movies were there not just to reflect life or tell stories but to exist in their own autonomous way and to look, as it were, at those who made them and who watched them. They had used the movies to demonize national enemies. Now why not use them to alter the viewer's perception of himself and the world?

Vidal, in his acute, counter-intuitive way, wants to tell us that Hollywood became the propagandistic arm not of the American state, but of itself, claiming to represent a 'real' world more accurately than peripheral activities such as journalism.

Propaganda on a vast, convincing scale had been influential during what was now called the Great War. It was the British who had pioneered its use, herding young men to the recruiting office and, thus, mass slaughter by establishing in the minds of the public throughout the British Empire and the US that the Germans were the exclusive practitioners of atrocities throughout the war and into the 1920s and 1930s. 'Propaganda' wasn't a dirty word in every context. Among the gurus of the day there was a collective worry about the prospects of democracy, as a consequence of the Russian Revolution, the new fascist regime in Italy and the various groups that clustered around the brief, hectic life of the post-war regime in Germany. Although claims would be made associating the future with democracy, they appeared hollow to many. It was felt that the new mass electorates required guidance. They needed a form of education. To some, such as the right-wing polemicist and media theorist Wyndham Lewis, this came down to learning 'the art of being governed'. Others tried to understand how an improved level of democracy could be achieved. This proved to be the lifelong work of Walter Lippmann, the most influential journalist of his time. Lippmann had advised the American president Woodrow Wilson, helping draft the Fourteen Points that the latter introduced in order, he hoped, to create a lasting peace. When Wilson's efforts ended in failure, Lippmann placed much of the blame on public ignorance. In his book *Public Opinion* (1922), Lippmann went back to Plato, concluding that electorates only understood the world through what he called 'stereotypes'. To deal with this, he recommended what he referred to as 'the manufacture of consent'. The phrase was later given a highly pejorative sense by Noam Chomsky, but Lippmann wanted journalism as well as popular culture to be conscripted in the service of illumination. If that didn't happen, he believed that democracy wouldn't survive:

A revolution is taking place, infinitely more significant than any shifting of economic power ... Under the impact of propaganda, not necessarily in the sinister meaning of the word alone, the old constants of our thinking have become variables. It is no longer possible, for example, to believe in the original dogma of democracy; that the knowledge needed for the management of human affairs comes up spontaneously from the human heart. Where we act on that theory we expose ourselves to self-deception, and to forms of persuasion that we cannot verify. It has been demonstrated that we cannot rely upon intuition, conscience, or the accidents of casual opinion if we are to deal with the world beyond our reach.

He ended by demanding the circulation of ideas via a select group of the highly educated. They might exist in the new think tanks that Lippmann and his generation conjured into existence, which would, he believed, be capable of generating policy in the interest of the masses.

How effective was this bold new linkage of propagandistic aims and methods with film? The most distinctive propaganda came from the new regime in Germany, and consideration of it involves the oeuvre of the redoubtable and appalling Leni Riefenstahl. In his thorough and wholly revealing biography *Leni* (2007), Steven Bach shows her to have been a liar and a narcissist of epic proportions. She made many enemies on her way from Alpine cheesecake starlet to her position as one of the only women, aside from Eva Braun, with whom the Führer could entertain the briefest chat. Later, of course, she downplayed her commitment to Nazism and lied about the fact that she made use of prisoners as extras. As remarkable as what a documentary called her 'wonderful, horrible' life is her mastery of the varieties of propaganda. Both *Triumph of the Will* (1935) and *Olympia* (1938) are classics, but they approach the question of persuasion in very different ways. *Triumph of the Will* begins with a plane, presumably bearing the Führer, coming through the clouds on its way to the medieval city of Nuremberg. The film's footage, taken at different rallies and enhanced by sequences shot on a set, depicts the quasi-mystical connection between the Führer and his adoring devotees. It is principally interesting now because of the range of buckles, insignia and folk costumes on display, the homoerotic joshing of young Nazis (carefully observed by a nosy Riefenstahl, always with an eye for any sexual action) and Albert Speer's cathedral of light, to the accompaniment of drums. The

Führer had wanted the film made in order to establish his total pre-eminence after he had disposed of Ernst Röhm and the SA, and the Wehrmacht were too cowed to complain that they had been left out of the story. Riefenstahl has some idea of Hitler's warped charisma, beginning with his slightly camp version of the salute. It's easy to understand why crowds flocked to see *Triumph of the Will* – they were told to go. As a film, though, it remains on a par with the official propaganda of the time, from the Left as well as the Right, which Orwell parodied so adroitly in *1984*: ninety minutes of love and hate, with the strangely inert howling and screaming protagonist at its heart.

In the 1970s, the New York critic Susan Sontag cautioned against the re-annexation of Nazi chic for commercial purposes. Both David Bowie and, of course, Madonna made use of the leather of Nazi über-kitsch. But Riefenstahl's talents were somewhat larger. She and Joseph Goebbels, Hitler's minister for propaganda, quarrelled over money and were in fundamental disagreement. Goebbels admired Hollywood; his favourite film was *Gone with the Wind* (1939). He concocted endless sugary comedies to ensure that national morale remained stable and was keen to ensure that the regime retained its claim to be cutting-edge modern. *Olympia*, Riefenstahl's two-hour account of the 1936 Berlin Olympic Games, reflects the Nazi obsession with being modern. It may begin with the famous kitsch sequence of ruins and a Greek discus thrower (seduced without much ado by Riefenstahl, then abandoned), but the film morphs rapidly into a sustained essay on the possibilities of long and short lenses, minute-plus tracking shots and astonishingly revealing close-ups of athletes doing the real business of high-performance sport. No sporting film has equalled Riefenstahl's first effort in conveying exertion. This is partly because of the many miles of film she was able to shoot with an almost unlimited budget, but it also reflects her own very Nazi determination to counter the unappealing image of fascism. Goebbels told Riefenstahl to stress the individuality of the athletes, and this she did. The film was to be the first effort at wholly direct (i.e. locally recorded) sound, but the quality wasn't good enough for Riefenstahl, and the sound had to be reconstructed second by second in a studio, which took months. Athletes are rigorously identified with the countries they represent, and the claques of supporters who had come to Berlin are shown, something that has since become a stock feature of sports films. (In the German announcer's commentary, heavy emphasis is placed on nationality, as in *'der Englander'*. But black American athletes such as Jesse Owens are emphatically called *'der Neger Amerikaner'*.) For foreign versions, images of a grinning, unathletic Hitler dressed military-style and applauding each German victory were removed from the film. Riefenstahl went around the US in an attempt to sell it, but her trip coincided with the 1938 trashing of Jewish businesses and the internment of Jews after Kristallnacht. Goebbels was furious that the film was never shown in the US or Britain, but he can hardly have been surprised. As much as it highlights the collective success achieved by nations in sport, Riefenstahl's film remains a chronicle of individual efforts. Its stylistic tics have been taken up by generations of commercial film-makers. It was conceived as a gigantic, non-overt, non-explicit commercial for the new Germany, and that is how it should be seen.

I like to imagine attending a progressive film club in the 1930s to see its perspective. The people I would meet would be antecedents of those who go to documentary film festivals or cinema screenings today. Some would be tastefully, if austerely, dressed in tweeds or greys; others would be scruffier, in homage to the proletariat. They'd be familiar with the catastrophes shortly to engulf their world, but confident that somehow, with the help of good intentions, these might be averted. I'd expect to find the yellow covers of the Left Book Club sticking out from coat pockets, and we could discuss what was going on in Europe with some erudition. Almost the same crowd, I expect, could have been found watching docs in Greenwich Village, Los Angeles and Tokyo. In the 1930s, along with radio, docs were the most up-to-date form of communication capable of being the greatest influence for good. No notion of 'independent' film existed yet. Film was at the service of commercial interests or so-called public ones. It was up to film-makers to decide how they used their skills and, implicitly, how they allowed themselves to be used. Many became propagandists, espousing the causes of the day. It would be too simple to conclude that they did this merely to raise money for their films, though this was often the case. Many of them believed in the causes they espoused.

The most impassioned believer was the Dutch film-maker Joris Ivens. 'I don't need doubt,' he explained in his memoirs. 'I need my certainties to be able to live.' 'A militant documentary film has to reach further,' he said on another occasion, after rejecting Hemingway's observation that writers should aim to tell the truth. 'After informing and moving audiences, it should agitate – mobilize them to be active in connection with the problems shown in the film.' Few communist governments failed to receive his earnest support. Ivens was a complex figure who cared about film, a brilliant assembler of material and an observer with an eye that was the equal of his contemporaries

Robert Capa and Henri Cartier-Bresson. His peers described him as remote and unknowable – 'the tall Dutchman', as Hemingway called him. 'You can see all the history of docs in the work of Ivens,' the historian Brian Winston says. 'He would have been really famous globally if he hadn't been Dutch and a commie.'

Ivens came from a well-to-do family; his father had a photographic business in Nijmegen. His first film, *Rain* (1929), was self-funded and took three years to make. Its exquisite blacks and greys depict Amsterdam as it usually is – half under water. Here are drains with water, canals overflowing, bicycles, rain and more rain. Ivens was influenced by German and Russian constructivist models, and he much admired Vertov. But his own sensibility is already on display – removed, a bit cold, heartless in the pursuit of the best shot, conscious of his time. Nowadays, such a film, with its studiedly avant-garde air and fashionable music, would play well at festivals or performance spaces. But Ivens was restless and attuned to the chaos of his time. After making progressive industrial films for the hi-tech firm Philips – and founding a cinema club dedicated to progressivism – he went to the Soviet Union. There he experienced an instant conversion to the idea of collectivism. When he returned to Amsterdam and friends tasked him with explaining the horrors of the Soviet Union, he brushed them aside. 'I'm a film-maker,' he said. 'I don't need to go into these things.'

Ivens's films are interesting nowadays for their combination of astounding technical sophistication and political naivety. He accepted the obligation to hide portions of the truth, from the persecutions and famines of the 1930s through to the vengeful actions against class enemies in the 1940s. He found ways of excusing all of Mao's catastrophic errors, from the famines of the Great Leap Forward to the horrors of the Cultural Revolution. It would be wrong to call him a fellow traveller, so totally did he identify with the global cause of socialism. Many held these views but weren't as overt as Ivens. This was perhaps because Ivens, being Dutch and coming from a comfortable democracy, was protected from the consequences of his views. But he did live like a political hippy, decamping from country to country, cause to cause, woman to woman. On his first visit to the Soviet Union, he was told that his avant-garde style was bourgeois and unsuitable for the depiction of the great socialist upheaval. He agreed with the commissars, setting out to include reconstructions of proletarian life in his depictions of oppression. After making a film about the locking out of coal miners in a depressed part of Belgium, in which reconstructed scenes are artfully mixed with newsreel footage, he travelled east once more. *Song of Heroes* (1932) was his attempt to toe the new ideological line. Shot in the new steel town of Magnitogorsk, his film includes many astounding shots of blast furnaces being built from nothing on the steppe. The scenes with workers, recruited from the local agitprop company or working on the city's trams, are fragmentary. This may have been because Ivens had never directed people, preferring to film objects, but it probably also reflected a perception that artifice in documentaries, although justifiable as a means of persuasion, was best kept to a minimum. The scenes he shot could have come from the work of Ken Loach. They seem real; indeed, they may have been. But they weren't popular with the commissars in Moscow. They weren't faked enough to meet the norms of social realism now installed by Stalin. There were limits, however, to the degree of truth that Ivens chose to accommodate. Not far away from the new blast furnaces lived thirty thousand deported kulaks, victims of Stalin's uprooting of potential class enemies. 'I cursed them now and then, as one curses weeds in the garden,' Ivens says in his memoirs. 'In the day they dug, in the night they committed sabotage.' He didn't film these rejects. Instead, he recorded the Stakhanovite efforts of the Komsomol youth brigades as they worked night and day to exceed American norms of production.

A subtler level of concealment affects Ivens's best-known film, *The Spanish Earth* (1937). This was made to alert international audiences to the plight of the Spanish Republican cause, and it was shown to Eleanor and Franklin Roosevelt in the White House. The list of those involved – Ernest Hemingway, Lilian Hellman, John Dos Passos, Marc Blitzstein, Aaron Copland, Archibald MacLeish – reads like a roster of Hollywood and Manhattan progressives. Its surface story is a somewhat trite and contrived account of the efforts of villagers behind the lines attempting to grow more food in order to supply a besieged Madrid. The Hemingway commentary (read out by Orson Welles) is laboured and worthy. Food was short, to be sure, but that wasn't the real reason for the destruction of the Republican forces, which were annihilated because of the superior armaments supplied to the Nationalists by Germany, while the neutrality of Britain and France came with an arms embargo, none of which is mentioned in the film.

But the pace quickens, and the film becomes involving when we are taken to Madrid, and the sequences of bombed-out, terrified civilians and shattered buildings are as good as anything by Capa. There's a visit to a political meeting and footage of the defenders of Spain, including Dolores (La Pasionaria) Ibárruri.

We're told that these people are the real Spain. What we are not told is that by the time they were filmed, they were not merely supported by the Soviet Union, but had colluded or helped insti-gate the 'liquidation' of the non-Stalinist, Trotskyist or anarchist militias (POUM) in Barcelona. Of course, this wasn't widely reported at the time, and we owe our understanding to George Orwell, whose book *Homage to Catalonia* (1938) recounts the uneven struggle from a personal point of view and who was obliged to flee with his wife to avoid being killed. But it's clear that Ivens knew what had happened in Barcelona and chose to suppress it. He and his progressive followers would most likely have thought that all this was too complex, too doubt-instilling. In bad times one must keep things simple, and the same lesson was drawn by the comrades in Britain, who trashed Orwell's book or simply refused to acknowledge its existence. It would be nice to think that Franklin and Eleanor Roosevelt might have been acquainted with the true face of Stalinism, but the truthfulness of Ivens's film wasn't called into question at the time. In the *New York Times*, a critic praised him for his aes-thetic sense, but felt that the film departed too easily from its poetic context, slipping into propaganda. It was, of course, seen by Ivens and those who worked with him as propaganda. And as propaganda, accompanied by Orson Welles, it is a pretty good model to follow.

There are, today, many film-makers like Ivens, though per-haps not many who are quite so habituated to propaganda. In his declining years, Ivens was invited back to China sometime in the midst of the Cultural Revolution, and he came back with what was, at 763 minutes, the longest documentary made up to that point, *How Yukong Moved the Mountains* (1976). It would be an exaggeration to say that it doesn't contain a true scene. Just as important, however, is the fact that all documentaries require funding, and funders – whether socialist governments, corporations, NGOs or public television stations – have their own views about what they want to see. Ivens only too successfully internalised the views of his Soviet and, later, Eastern Bloc patrons. The same is true, to a lesser degree, of those who worked in 1930s Britain and the US, and later in Canada.

The films of the time were conceived generically, as a means of winning over hearts and minds, and for that reason it's best to pick through the smallish mass of what came to be called, in the 1930s, the British Movement in documentary film. First, you become aware of men labouring. They often look underfed, and usually they are middle-aged. The clothes they wear – shirts with rolled-up sleeves, studded boots, black trousers with braces holding them up – speak of days long gone. There are many of these men. Sometimes they are on pitching seas, looking for shoals of herring and dumping nets over the side of antiquated trawlers, as in John Grierson's first film, *Drifters* (1929). They are an army in Paul Rotha's *Shipyard* (1935), which recounts the construction of the vast steel hulk of ship no. 697, a liner-to-be, christened the *Orion* and destined for the passage to Australia and back. In the film the young, leftish Rotha is enamoured of the modernist shape of the liner. He spent months in Barrow-in-Furness, shooting the construction of two identical hulls. He loves the way the enormous ships-to-be seem to dwarf the modest two-up two-downs of the workers. He admires how neatly dressed the workers are and follows them to their favourite sport of dog racing on Sunday mornings. In the last lingering shots of the film, however, he reminds us that once the ship is built, there may not be another one. These men may go on the dole. This is the truth of the 1930s Depression in Britain.

Similar men are seen packing and unpacking mail, sorting it during the course of an overnight journey, sending off and receiving bags at prearranged trackside points in the best-known film of the time, *Night Mail* (1936). The experience of viewing these films now is astonishing because of the sheer distance from what they convey. Not all of this vanished world is recorded in a patronising way. These are indeed real people and they have real lives – narrower and more cramped, but in some respects more real because of the pervasive need to work. The films take this as a given, unsentimentally.

And yet look more closely, and it becomes clear that another set of messages is being conveyed. Some of these films, like *Shipyard*, are made for commercial interests: the shipbuilders Vickers, for instance, who still exist, or the shipping line about to take possession of no. 697, which disappeared many years ago. In *Night Mail*, of course, the patron is the GPO, Britain's publicly owned postal service, which was keen to show off its employees and demonstrate how mail from anywhere in England can arrive in Scotland the next morning. But the film-makers found something else. In *Night Mail*, the intervention is more spectacular because it is more sudden. Film-maker Alberto Cavalcanti is a Brazilian among these British tyros, an avowed continental, knowledgeable about experimentation. When the train gets north of the border, it gathers speed, and so does the editing. Then we get the poem from W. H. Auden, young, left-wing, busy finding ways of smuggling love, survival, community and isolation into verse that seemed as simple as it was intricate and highly patterned:

Asleep in working Glasgow, asleep in well-set Edinburgh,
Asleep in granite Aberdeen,
They continue their dreams,
But shall wake soon and hope for letters,
And none will hear the postman's knock
Without a quickening of the heart,
For who can bear to feel himself forgotten?

These are among the best of Auden's words, though they tend not to appear in the poet's many revised collections of his work. They are distinctively British and of their time, a conjuring of a small portion of utopia out of the everyday and the wholly banal. But they reflect, too, what these young leftists wished to achieve in their films. They wanted no one to be forgotten. In the war, much had been culpably overlooked. On the other side of the Atlantic, in a country stricken by the Great Depression, it was commonplace to speak of forgotten men. In their own art everyone, not just the burghers awaiting the postman's knock, should receive the right messages.

To an astonishing degree, the existence of these messages was determined by the activities of one man. John Grierson has a mixed press these days. For the historian Brian Winston, he's 'something of a snake-oil salesman'. Winston reproaches him for never really coming clean about the implications of government and corporate sponsorship. 'He always acted as if the presence of these funders somehow enhanced the films. It's as if the fact that he had found the money somehow made it cleaner.' For the filmmaker Mark Cousins, however, some aspects of the Grierson achievement remain. Half scolding Grierson for his fixed, somewhat dogmatic views, Cousins nonetheless ends by praising him.

My own views lie somewhere between these two points. I can respect his huge achievement, while wondering why the Grierson cult lasted for so many decades. It's surely possible to admire his tenacity and the risks he took inventing a new form, while wondering whether he couldn't have been a bit less dogmatic.

Grierson, as he often told people, was like John Reith, whom he resembled in his belief in high public purpose and in his astonishing stubbornness. A 'son of the manse', he believed that film should tell people things. He wasn't a communist or a fellow traveller, but he insisted that the future lay with the Left. At the University of Chicago, he met Walter Lippmann and fell under his spell. But the lesson Grierson drew from Lippmann's scepticism about democracy was a somewhat different one. He would enlist film in the clichéd raising of public consciousness, which he called 'civic education'. Smallish, pawky, speaking in firm Scottish prose, Grierson was a good constructor of phrases. Every paragraph that he wrote carried the same message. Documentary, as he called it, is good for you because it is good for society:

Documentary represented a reaction from the early and middle 20s – Bloomsbury, Left Bank, T. S. Eliot, Clive Bell and all – by people with every reason to know it well. Likewise, if it was a return to 'reality', it was a return not unconnected with Clydeside movements, the Independent Labour Party, the Great Depression, not to mention Lord Keynes, the LSE P.L.P. and such. Documentary was born and nurtured on the bandwagon of uprising social democracy everywhere – that is to say, it had an uprising majority social movement, which is to say a logical sponsorship of public money, behind it . . .

Half apparatchik, half entrepreneur, Grierson didn't really believe in individual freedoms. 'I am not going to pretend that I do not understand how "totalitarian" some of my conclusions seem,' he told a Canadian audience. 'You can be "totalitarian" for evil and you can also be "totalitarian" for good. Some of us came out of a highly disciplined religion and see no reason to fear discipline and denial.' Grierson may not quite have worshipped power, but he found the posture of worshipping power convenient, because it helped with the collection plate. In the creation of such parastatal organisations as the Crown Film Unit or working with the GPO or the Empire Marketing Board, Grierson brought films into existence. He did get things done. And he became a cult figure of sorts. It didn't seem absurd during the 1930s to say that 'Grierson and his boys' were the leading lights of British progressive culture.

People worked outside the commercial system for Grierson, and in this respect he was a true begetter of documentaries. Paul Rotha, in his book *Documentary Film* (1936), says that the EMB was at one time based at the bottom of Soho's Wardour Street, 'in an eight-foot-square room, where all cutting and office work was done, including projecting onto a lavatory wall with a hand-turn projector'. Grierson looked after those who worked for him, and he did the same in wartime Canada, through his greatest bureaucratic creation, the National Film Board of Canada. 'There was no question where one's duty lay,' he explained. 'There was no question that it started out in a political conception, a political, social conception.'

Grierson was convinced that the future lay in the non-commercial public exhibition of films. In Canada, he created a network of community screenings in village or town halls. In the name of reaching people, and then indoctrinating them, he paid his dues to the spirit of extreme literalism. ('There's nothing like the camera for getting around,' he explained helpfully. 'That's what makes it unique, the fact that it can travel from place to place.') Most damaging, perhaps, were the compromises with his paymasters over the question of how his subjects should be depicted. Prudently, in order to survive within the British cultural establishment, Grierson decided that films should reflect the 'interdependence' of humans. This meant that his school shied away from overt class-war propaganda. But it also perpetuated a woozy propagandist worldview in which poor people were patronised, somewhat in the style of contemporary 'one world' social commentary, with its obsessional focus on the 'flatness' of the world at the expense of human differences. In the 1930s, companies like Shell funded documentaries; they could prove surprisingly open-minded when it came to the question of whether they should impose their will on film-makers eager to make their own films. But it is hard to regard these early corporate docs as a genuine advance of the documentary form. At their best they anticipate the films of our day that are funded by NGOs or companies. They bear the same resemblance to film-making as the most sophisticated PR handouts do to independent reportage.

Was there a means of extending non-fiction films beyond minority film club screenings? Grierson dreamt of his own public network, but there were others who felt that there was another way. The earliest effort to take documentaries out of specialist film clubs into the developing mass media came from Henry Luce's news magazine *Time*. Luce, the son of missionaries in China and educated at Yale, was a consummate marketer of good ideas. He bet on the desire of the new American middle classes to want to know about the rest of the world, as well as to enjoy and revere their own society. Luce is most famous for his 1942 article evoking the arrival of the American society. Later, his magazines appeared to rehash stale cold war ideas, but in his early career he was able to upend the conventions of journalism, making commentary anew by erasing the borders between dreary factual accounts and interpretations considered to be risqué or tendentious. He had the idea of extending his own popular print format into film, and employed a team to create films that could be shown before the main feature but which were longer than newsreels. Luce didn't make the additional fortune he had hoped for from *The March of Time* (1935–51), but the films were successful as a marketing device, reaching twenty million Americans each week.

The March of Time films can be viewed online nowadays, through the Time Warner archive. Once one gets used to the crashing music and the pompous corporate voice, many of them feel surprisingly fresh. Luce had toyed with the European dictators, in a spurt of admiration for Mussolini and his punctual trains, and for a while was attracted to the isolationism of the time, reflecting on his own views in the columns of *Time* magazine. But *The March of Time* takes a more robust view of the perils that encircled the 1930s. It would seem hard to better the twenty-five-minute edition devoted to Hitler's Germany in 1938, which skilfully mixes propaganda footage with shocking images of the persecution of German Jews. Luce's men convey the essence of totalitarianism simply but effectively, lingering on the capacity for total control at the regime's disposal. Luce, a liberal Republican, didn't like what he saw as FDR's attempts to increase the power of the American state in his New Deal programmes, but unlike many of his fellow Republicans, he never confused what was going on in Great Depression America with the threats to world order in Europe. An edition from 1939 adroitly takes a sympathetic view of the British policy of appeasement, while applauding its extinction. Unlike the American ambassador Joseph Kennedy, who believed that Britain wouldn't have the stomach to resist Hitler, *The March of Time* understood that the British would resist. But the piece is also savvy enough to depict – not uncritically – the vast British propaganda movement under way, in which the identity of British and American interests was foregrounded.

Writing in the *Guardian*, Alistair Cooke referred to the London premiere of *The March of Time* as 'far and away the most important thing that has happened for years'. Critics did complain of the sensationalism of the series, observing that content was usually subordinated to narrative requirements. But significantly, in the 1930s, it was Luce's apparent lack of ideological bias that appeared offensive to liberal commentators such as Frank Crowninshield, the founding editor of *Vanity Fair*. Less apparent at the time was the frequent use of amateur actors in reconstructions. Haile Selassie was played by a *Time* office boy. For *Inside Nazi Germany* (1938), the film-makers went to German neighbourhoods in Hoboken, New Jersey, using American streets to depict German cities in which Jewish stores and residences had been defaced with daubed swastikas. Innovations such as these – which, for better or worse, have come to define much of contemporary broadcast journalism – were introduced without fuss or prior consultation. It would seem that nobody complained.

During World War II, newsreels were shown weekly to vast audiences, but many of these resembled the weekly hate-speech moments commemorated in *1984*: they were artefacts concocted for fixed purposes – to elicit hate or appreciation, to educate in the least-defined way or to convey propaganda. Documentaries were somewhat rarer, but were expected to join in the task of raising morale. Films from the Grierson school did just this, and the interdependence ethos fitted easily with the one-size-fits-all wartime cultural egalitarianism voiced at the time by Orwell in *The Lion and the Unicorn* (1941). The most interesting ventures of the time, however, are those of Humphrey Jennings, a Cambridge aesthete and poet. *A Diary for Timothy* (1945) is one of the few films to explain, through the device of a diary kept on behalf of a newborn, scripted by E. M. Forster, what post-war Britain should be like. Not through statistics or assertion, but poetically, with wide-eyed wonder, Jennings raises the possibility that through social democracy people might learn to look after each other. But there were limitations to his approach. It was Forster who complained about the patronising, class-based aspects of the draft script submitted to him. ('Tim,' he fussed, 'must be someone, and why shouldn't he be born in a rectory and have a lovely choral baptism instead of being an industrialist [*sic*] baby at a registry office?') In the final version, Michael Redgrave's plummy condescension appears to smother poor Timothy in his NHS cot: 'Are you going to have greed for money and power ousting decency from the world, as they have in the past? Or are you going to make the world a different place – you and all the other babies?' Little Timothy's first days are set against the dreary last winter of the war. It's clear that there will be no Jerusalem ahead, only bad weather and rationing. Timothy's mum sounds and looks like the bored, dutiful Celia Johnson in Noël Coward's *Brief Encounter*, and his father is still in the Middle East, doing something unwarlike in khaki. There's enough fire in the grate of the rectory at Henley-on-Thames, but that's the only good thing you can say about the khaki British present.

Tim's future obligations are laid out at the end of Jennings's cycle of patriotic masterpieces. A talented artist, Jennings's surrealist paintings display a fine, perhaps slightly fey sensibility. It comes as no surprise that Grierson didn't approve of him. The war gave him his real subject, which was an intuitive, non-ideological understanding of what bound people together in bad times. One can call these films propagandistic, but that involves stretching the term somewhat. Jennings was finding a way of reaching out of propaganda into something much more interesting. *Fires Were Started* (1943) focuses on firemen, recreating in detail their efforts – ultimately successful – to put out a fire in the London docks. The blaze is terrifying, lasting long enough, in what seems like real time, to give a sense of how hard it was to turn each London blaze into ashes and hulks of buildings. The firemen seem what they are: wholly real, truly modest, without the panto deference that blights so many contemporary depictions of the so-called 'ordinary'. The dialogue, for once, sounds totally authentic, though it was, of course, added after shooting. Then there is the equally astonishing *Listen to Britain* (1942), in which wartime Britain, with its Spitfires, dancing couples, air raids and bad canteen food, is set to music.

Jennings, Cambridge-educated, a surrealist painter, a talker and experimenter via socialist-leaning projects such as Mass-Observation, was, as his great admirer Lindsay Anderson observed, a maker of films about war where 'the feeling is never, or almost never, warlike'. You can watch these films again and again, while seeing fresh connections. 'All art is propaganda,' Orwell explained. With their surface simplicity, they seem as dense and pertinent as an Orwell essay, speaking to us across the decades. Jennings was, as Anderson suggested, writing in 1955, 'the only real poet the British cinema has yet produced', but his work has animated generations of film-makers in search of the quirky individuality and profound sense of solidarity of the British people. How about the National Health Service, binding together the wounded pilot, and the Welsh miner we see nearly getting killed in an accident? British socialism is yet to come – but it will do. Forster hopes that it will be somehow reconciled with his own individualism, and we tell ourselves that freedom will indeed triumph – just about, anyhow. But all these developments are presented not as an attractive prospect, but as what should be due to a battered, victorious nation.

Another wartime innovation was to prove more significant, and that was the alarm of state patrons in the army or civil service when confronted by material likely to upset or destabilise audiences or powerful bosses. Much of the most explicit wartime coverage from the 1940s wasn't shown until many years later, and this proved to be the fate of *German Concentration Camps Factual Survey*, the film that Sidney Bernstein shot in 1945, after the liberation of Belsen. The showing of John Huston's *The Battle of San Pietro* (1945), which gives an unvarnished, wrenching account of the carnage involved in taking a small Italian town, was delayed for a year as his army patrons pondered its negative message. His next film, *Let There Be Light* (1946), for which he spent three months in the veterans' ward of the Mason General Hospital, shooting 375,000 feet of film, now seems to be a wholly honest depiction of trauma, but it was never shown, though it is available.

Factual films were useful, and thus desirable, but it was thought that they should stay within certain limits. But this aspect of the Grierson tradition began to quickly go stale, as peacetime crowds required more than what appeared to be dull viewing in what was a grey time. Denis Forman, who began his career at the Orwellian-named COI (Central Office of Information), later becoming the inspiration behind Granada Television's factual programmes, captures the cod-liver-oil atmosphere:

> Many of the film-makers . . . were fellow-travellers or communist sympathisers . . . As a result they would throw in morsels of left-wing propaganda which had nothing to do with the topic in hand. For instance, a film on the history of domestic architecture paused when it reached a servants' bedroom in a great town house to deliver a homily on the wretched way in which the aristocracy had treated the lower classes.

How would documentaries be viewed? Could they be enlisted in efforts to change the world? Ambitions notwithstanding, documentaries were viewed by pitifully small audiences, usually consisting of the already engaged.

The delusion survives to this day, in the notion that films made for a small left-wing audience can somehow change the world. It has given birth to the proposition, never fully discussed, that documentary is inherently a left-wing or social-democratic form, based on the idea that they are collective enterprises and somehow, Grierson-style, lend themselves to the promotion of collective effort. In the 1930s, there was no commercial market for factual film, so the financing of documentary film required the support of public bodies. These might be government information services, bodies set up to support the making of documentaries, television stations or networks given public obligations. Whichever the case, documentaries became anchored in a culture of well-meaning, left-of-centre pedagogy. They were not meant to change the world exactly – that would have seemed too ambitious – but to act as a conscience. At their most ambitious, they were seen as warning signs giving notice of what might go wrong. 'Problems' or 'issues' were the fittest subjects for documentaries, most safely within such contemporary preoccupations as housing, health, education, etc. Those who made docs wrestled with this orthodoxy, but they accepted it, too. But they also acquired a significant degree of freedom. It became customary for film-makers to define their work in opposition to the ostensibly value-free news bulletins shown each night. Authorship of documentaries was thus defined in the most conservative left-wing style: you were an author to the degree that your work succeeded in pressing the correct social buttons, thus arousing the faithful. It's still possible to applaud screenings where a large handful of believers – maybe interspersed with some who can be converted – watch a film as they did in the 1930s and 1940s, for mutually conveyed illumination. Proponents of such a view of the role of factual film would argue that this is appropriate. But halfway through the century, documentaries were about to find a new place for themselves in the growing medium of television.

4 : On the Box

David Attenborough among gorillas in the BBC's *Life on Earth* (1979):
'There is more meaning and mutual understanding in exchanging a
glance with a gorilla than with any other animal I know.'

In 1964, teams from the commercially funded television station Granada began filming interviews with young Britons. With its leftish, 1960s outlook, Granada went looking for class division. The first black-and-white images seem to come from another country. 'Startlingly different backgrounds,' is how the know-all voice describes the context in which we get to meet a selection of British seven-year-olds. Here are the well-off males, at what the Brits still called pre-prep school; a female at what appears to be an academy for young ladies; here, too, are the male middling classes (located in a suburb of Liverpool), as well as those already branded with the mark of Cain at a state boarding school after being dumped by, or prised from, their parents. The commentary sounds like a cross between Dickens's Dotheboys Hall and *Lord of the Flies*. 'Give me a child for the first seven years,' the remote voice intones, echoing the Jesuit maxim, before explaining how the children have been taken to meet each other at the zoo and then left to play in an adventure playground – surely a Scandinavian import of the period. The children do play, but awkwardly, with the sense that they don't belong together. This still seems to be an important moment, not just in the history of television, but in that of Britain, too.

Class divisions, permanent greyness, social imprisonment – this is how the world felt to the leftish producers of Granada in the supposedly egalitarian mid-1960s. They make us fear for the future of these diffident guinea pigs. However, over the years these investigations change in tone, as their subjects evolve in less than totally predictable directions, growing up and sometimes out of class stereotypes – or at least giving us a sense of how one needn't be wholly imprisoned by an environment that one can never entirely escape. It would be tempting to conclude that British society is less grimly susceptible to prediction, and this is certainly the case: the subjects of what must be the best format ever devised for factual television evolve in different ways. The most calm-seeming goes off the rails, becoming a borderline vagrant, and the roughest, having tried to be a jockey, drives cabs and then becomes a successful businessman. But the snobbily precocious, *Financial Times*-reading boy–adults do slow down. They become less entrenched in privilege, despite their somewhat conventional fates. Even the abrupt, chippy farmer's son turned physicist becomes calmer, tamed by divorce and remarriage.

From its *7 Up* beginnings in 1964 to *56 Up*, shown in 2012, the world followed these lives. There has never been a televisual experience like *Up* and, most likely, there will never be another. It has been imitated over the world – in the US, South Africa, Russia and throughout Europe. Some of its success may have to do with the skills of Michael Apted, who produced all but the first series. It may also be due to the fact that these lives (with the exception of one subject – bizarrely, a documentary film-maker) remain on public display. The subjects must have learnt over the years how to be on television, but something important, too, transpires as a result of England's changes. So rigid, class-structured a place did loosen up, not in the way Granada anticipated, but no longer condemning its citizens to the social level they were once doomed to occupy. *Up* follows its original structure to the letter, and this can seem irritating. You can admire the endeavour but still ask why the questions and the editing have to be so predictable. You may, as the participants tell us at their reunions, simply want to know a bit more than what television seems capable of telling us. But Apted, who did get out of Britain, becoming a successful Hollywood director, followed these lives without imposing much of his own worldview. Television is best when it appears neutral, affording a view of the goldfish bowl. It is only rarely comfortable with attitude or tragedy. On television it's best to be warm and to satisfy curiosity. That remains the great achievement of the *Up* experiment, and that is what it still tells us about the great age of broadcast television, which purported to be a medium belonging to everyone – and *Up* fulfilled this promise.

For those over forty, broadcast television has become a lost utopia. We recall the first programmes we watched, and this is subsumed into a cosy, self-sustaining view of how things used to be. But for those who managed television, or thought about its funding, broadcasting represented something else. As the historian of the BBC Jean Seaton demonstrates, right up until the 1980s television was regarded as being like national glue. In most broadcasts, it did whet the public's appetite, but it did not inquire into topics such as Israel or South Africa. It was as biased as North Korea. It was what kept people together. More importantly, it afforded a path to self-education. It created the illusion that an educated citizenry living in a democracy would always survive. Many of these claims have half vanished in the tidal wash of new media, but they are powerful and, indeed, viable. Millions still watch documentaries on broadcast television. From their Griersonian or agitprop origins, docs became mainstream, which is what, in some instances, they remain. Throughout northern Europe and in Canada you can still watch documentaries every night. They document social issues, they nag at injustice. These aren't chic docs, but they are what many people watch and rely on.

I'd grown up watching documentaries, but I didn't understand the utopian, educative claims of the proponents of public television until I was asked to produce a lecture given by the dramatist and polemicist Dennis Potter. He was dying of cancer, and most of my efforts consisted of fetching him bottles of the bitter, vile-tasting Italian liqueur Fernet-Branca. Potter came from the grammar-school-educated post-war elite and didn't fail to let one know about the class differences identified by the Granada producers. He was also able to quote verse after verse of English poetry, gasping with pain or half animated with morphine. He talked about television, with an affection bordering on reverence, as a 'palace of varieties in the corner of the room' and told me how he'd never wanted to write for any other medium. Working in Hollywood gave him the capability to handle audiences, but that, he insisted, was nothing compared with the possibility of educating people. Like most people working in the medium, he had bad memories of the television elite. ('A croak-voiced Dalek,' was how he described the then head of the BBC.) But this went with a redemptive degree of generosity that was made more convincing because of his constant pain. At one point, before his psoriasis set in and incapacitated him, Potter had wanted to be a politician. He had little interest in politics now, though of course he hated Mrs Thatcher. But when we talked about the BBC over the Fernet-Branca, it was the series *The Great War* (1964) to which he would return. 'There wasn't anything like it,' he said. 'It changed everything. It was marvellous how it affected people's lives. I really thought: "This is what the BBC is for."'

For a long time, it was hard to watch *The Great War*. You had to go to the BBC vaults. Low-level conspiracy theories flourished as a means of explaining why the BBC wouldn't share its gem with outsiders. It was possible to view the twenty-six black-and-white episodes preserved on one-inch tape, which is what I did before screening them again on the BBC's newish cultural channel. I was not overwhelmed by the experience. It was a vast achievement, to be sure, and I could see why it seemed in 1964 to define not just the potential of historical documentaries, but also the function of the BBC itself as the guardian of the national culture. I couldn't avoid being moved by its evocation of folly and suffering. When I watched each episode aged sixteen, I was starting to read seriously. Like most of my generation, I read the war poets and the books that had started to appear in which, from the perspective of the 1960s, the war could be dismissed as a futile recourse to mass murder. As I went through the series – from the Somme to Passchendaele, pausing at Verdun (where my grandfather had been wounded) and the collapse of imperial Russia – watching it as a teenager came back to me. But I found that I didn't quite experience the moment. It wasn't the omissions that bothered me, though even at twenty-six episodes the series had skimped on certain aspects. Nor was it the over-ripe narration from Sir Michael Redgrave. Nor, emphatically, was it the fact that so much of the archive material either came from miles behind the front or was used incorrectly.

What was the ultimate purpose of *The Great War*? Its function was to commemorate rather than say what happened. Explanation wasn't really required. One can accept that this was a requirement of the time, governed by the fiftieth anniversary of the war and the trauma in British and Commonwealth memory that it still represents. But its status as a memorial does affect its historical credentials. It now seems like a portion of the memory of the war rather than a study of it. A clue to the mild sense of discomfiture it now induces comes at once, with the masterly opening titles, in which a camera moves down from a cross to a soldier in profile to a skull staring artfully out of a posed or Photoshop-like cadaver in uniform, and then a close-up, now celebrated, of a soldier at the Somme in pain, looking at whoever recorded this moment. This was a montage, of course, though the audience were most likely not aware of this fact. The image of the staring soldier is astonishingly well chosen, but it had been taken out of its context of a line of otherwise happier soldiers. In the BBC's hands it performed a good service, assuming a level of celebrity equalled only by Ropert Capa's loyalist Spanish soldier being killed or Don McCullin's blank-eyed Vietnam GI staring at the camera. No one found out the identity of the soldier, and no one knew whether he'd died or not. But he became a television Unknown Soldier, seeming to stand for the experience of the entire war, defining the series. This was the intention of the film-makers behind the series, if not of the experts they consulted. In the BBC archive, much is made of the artifice of these titles, the images 'tilting down into blackness'. One can see how successful the series was in eliciting a sense of horror from the letters unearthed by historian Emma Hanna in the BBC archives:

If one looks deep and long into this picture – into this abyss of hell – a whole galaxy of the horrors of war are revealed. Once a quiet sort of chap really, quite content to go home to his wife and kids after a hard day's work, eyes that held nothing but love for his family. But now after training to kill or be killed, are eyes that seem to burn and accuse us, the eyes seem filled with shock – hatred – disgust – despair – loneliness, and the pleading questions of why – for what – to what end – for whom . . . yes, it's all there even a look of pity, like forgive them for they know not what they do . . .

The producer, Tony Essex, had said he wished to create 'a story as great as that of the Bible', and in press coverage the series was hailed as 'The Intelligent Man's Guide to Armageddon'. Something, however, was lost in transition to the box. *The Great War* displayed little of the intelligent scepticism I found in the 1960s books I encountered, such as Barbara Tuchman's frequently counterfactual *The Guns of August*. Its scriptwriter, John Terraine, claimed that the series was successful in its emotional impact. 'I am sick to death of being told how good it was by people who know nothing of the subject, but were "moved" by it,' he wrote. 'Where for example was any analysis of the leading characters of the War, military or civil? How could there be, in that style?'

But the series had another function partly entombed within its commemorative form: recollection. Many of the interviews with survivors were recorded in the spring of 1964. These were rehearsed, but the consciousness of performing is important to protagonists. No one at that time had been asked to give an account of themselves 'for history'. The interviews could be used only in short snatches, and they seemed to be drowned out by the apparatus of crashing chords and portentous vowels. Now they come back to us with an astonishing directness. Here is someone who was a young officer during the war describing spending close to twenty-four hours in a shell hole after a botched attack, fearing he would crack up. Here's a signals operator telling you what happens when you do crack up, ask your pals not to save you and wake up on a stretcher. A mill-worker from Manchester describes the moment when, eight months pregnant, she got a letter saying her husband had been killed. And here is a British intelligence officer recording, for the benefit of the prime minister, the state of insurrection of almost the entire French army in 1917, details of which remain suppressed to this day. David Lloyd George asked his emissary to swear on his own honour 'as an officer and a general', as the French army would, 'and then I walked out'. These interviews are far more revealing than the series in which they were ultimately embedded. At first sight they seem to come from the long-gone Britain of stiffened lips, but I suspect that this is an illusion. I watched them shortly after finishing *Censored Voices* (2015), in which the young kibbutznik warriors of 1967 told of what they had seen. (Their detailed observations were censored by the Israeli army and recovered from oblivion for the doc.) It is the detail of war, the way in which, willy-nilly, everyone, at the front or not, was sucked in that is so upsetting. Much of this was ultimately absent from *The Great War*, replaced by a war memorial sense of piety.

But one shouldn't be negative about the achievement of *The Great War*, or indeed the kind of television that it represented. Each episode was viewed by an astonishing nine million people in Britain, and it was shown around the world. I suspect that it remains one of the most watched documentaries. Representing the national culture, indeed the national mood, is the principal purpose of a public broadcaster, and the BBC has always done this admirably. But the corporation, and other public broadcasters, was less good when it came to individual voices. The idea that these voices – authors' views, but those of so-called 'ordinary people', too – should also find expression proved harder to accommodate. There have been legions of squabbles between irate producers, BBC executives – the so-called Platonic guardians at the top of the organisation – and those in government. In most instances, but not always, these ended in compromise but marked a small advance. Yet the demarcation between the claims of individual authorship and the obligations of the BBC were never laid down. How creative were you allowed to be at the BBC? Was it a forging house of national talent, or was it an organisation supplying a service within the concept of a national culture? Most documentaries shown by the BBC were conceived in a spirit of watered-down Griersonism. They presented no ideological challenge, and they were, at least relatively, free of authorship. But there were occasions when a film-maker seemed determined to cross the carefully erected boundaries. The most important of such instances concerned the fate of the genius Peter Watkins.

In addition to the political controversy stirred up by TV documentaries, audiences could easily be upset by them. When the BBC showed a version of *1984* (1954), viewers called to complain that the scenes involving rats had caused them distress. The most distressing film made by the BBC in the 1960s proved to be *The War Game* (1965), and it couldn't be shown on television for another twenty years. A young film-maker, Peter Watkins, was lured to the BBC for his sense of independence. His first project was *Culloden* (1964), a recreation of the 1746 battle that resulted in the destruction of Highland society. To tell what had happened, Watkins adopted contemporary devices: a brilliant, highly partisan script that mimicked in tone the BBC's impartiality; and news-style interviews in which Jacobite and British protagonists, privates as well as generals, addressed the camera directly. The film is all the more remarkable because Watkins appears to have anticipated how far it was possible to go in relation to a mass audience. *Culloden* may depict the last battle on British soil, and judged by the level of casualties it was a minor affair. But by the standards of *The Great War*, and indeed those of much contemporary war coverage, it goes much further. It is also candid in attributing atrocities to the British army. In the 1960s, through the work of NGOs and the media coverage of wars, citizens became far more familiar with the phenomenon of mass brutality.

After *Culloden*, it was decided that Watkins should make a film about the prospects of nuclear war. For *The War Game*, he once again ventured into the idiom of popular television, creating imagined vox pops from the public, ubiquitous experts and newsreel footage. But Watkins wanted to show something wholly beyond the grasp of contemporary news coverage, and governments, too. He believed, surely correctly, that any nuclear exchange would so destroy contemporary life that civilisation would prove unrecoverable. (The conventional wisdom of the time, reflected in the building of utterly inadequate shelters, was that enough would somehow survive.) The opening scenes show an escalating political crisis that might well have come to pass. Watkins's method comes into its own when the town of Rochester is nuked. He had chosen non-actors, and the scenes of carnage are unforgettable. They are abetted by Watkins's astute manipulation of the forms of British docs. The scenes feel like Blitz footage or the platitudinous public information films of the 1940s. The commentary has the weighty authority of the BBC, and the sober-sided 'experts' (played by actors) recall stock figures of BBC authority plunged into a reality they cannot comprehend. Not a second of exposition is redundant or, it must be said, less than totally believable. Everything we see is intolerable.

Watkins, it should be clear, represented neither the budding CND movement nor any pacifist organisation. He seems to have come to his conclusions on his own. No one had been forewarned about the inadequacy of preparations for nuclear conflict, but the film-maker is at pains to point out that any measures would have proved ineffectual. We see looters executed and policemen killing the badly burnt. There is no food, no running water, and the film ends with Christmas celebrated in a bombed-out church. Much has been written about the 'banning' of the film, and it would appear that not just the government, but those in charge of the BBC (and many of them were liberal reformers) felt it should not be broadcast and, indeed, that it should never have been made. BBC records show that only one of the participants, Oliver Whitley, disagreed. People, he suggested, 'should have a realistic idea of the effect of a bomb in their neighbourhood. The BBC allowed [Watkins] to make this film. On what basis could it be said that it was wrong even to think of making a film with this aim?' It was shown to select audiences and won an Oscar in 1966. Most commentators tended to agree with the BBC's top brass, viewing the film as propagandistic (which it was not) or too likely to cause distress. One exception was Kenneth Tynan, arts critic of the *Observer*. '*The War Game* is the most important film ever made,' he wrote, with excusable hyperbole. 'We are always being told that a film cannot change the course of history. I think this one might. It should be screened everywhere on earth.' Watkins, meanwhile, had left the BBC, never to return.* *The War Game* remains a monument to what can be achieved with talent and minimal resources.

I lost count of the number of panels at TV conferences devoted to the question of whether there was a Golden Age of television. There may have been one once, when it was possible to determine what would be best for the national culture. Where state television in Eastern Europe was propagandistic, in Western Europe it rested on a quiet, often enlightened paternalism. There weren't many channels, and the restriction of consumer choice was utilised to force commercial quasi-monopolies to sustain a tradition of public service. Within the BBC, the tradition of public education survived, too. In the 1970s, the system reached its apogee. Although there were frequent collisions between those brought up in the 1960s and their elders, who now administered the system, a great expansion of original programming occurred. The principal beneficiaries of this situation were factual-programme-makers, who could choose a variety of departments in which to work. Within this sprawling bureaucracy one might spend a portion of a lifetime working on such series as *Timewatch* (history with a popular slant), *Horizon* (hard science), *Man Alive* (tabloid human interest), *Forty Minutes* (less tabloid human interest), *Omnibus* and *Arena* (mainstream arts and quirky essays), *The South Bank Show* (more art but on ITV, and by no means always lacking in challenge) or *Panorama* (current affairs, in those days made for the elite, mostly by members of the elite).

---

* He made a number of films in Scandinavia, later working with the French–German cultural channel ARTE. *Punishment Park* (1971), a dystopia set in Vietnam War America, is a radical experiment, imagining a post-trauma situation in which the National Guard is free to hunt down demonstrators.

The most remarkable instance of subsidised highbrow television was Granada's *Disappearing World*, a series of anthropological films that ran for fifteen years, few of which could now be funded by broadcasters or anyone else. Each season of television fare contained at least one longish series on a subject of importance. It was assumed that audiences would confront such behemoths without misgivings and watch them from beginning to end. The evidence is that they did.

The most notable television documentary event wasn't the work of the BBC. It was an astonishing life-altering project experienced by many millions and now requiring its own memorialisation. Many people worked on *The World at War* (1973–4), but it remains the inspiration of one man: the charismatic journalist and TV grandee Jeremy Isaacs. By the early 1970s, commercial television in Britain was being widely criticised for its lack of ambition, and it was in this context that Isaacs secured assent from his employers, Thames Television, for what was at the time the most expensive factual television series ever made. The film-makers conceived of their series as a homage to *The Great War*, and more than forty years later, *The World at War* remains captivating. The editorial choices were bold, and remain so: it was original in the 1970s, for instance, to make so much of the German–Soviet war on the Eastern Front and to cover the conflict in the Far East, even if the Bengali famines and fire-bombings of Japan were skimped. The episode on the Holocaust, later made into a ninety-minute film, was the first attempt to describe the killings comprehensively, with a description of their roots in Nazi ideology and the 1930s. Still unequalled are the episodes describing civilian life in wartime Germany, the horrifying collapse of the Reich, culminating in the Führer's poisoned dog, and a marvellous account from a female Red Army major of the taking of the Reichstag. (The only omission, unavoidably, was the Enigma code-breaking story: when Isaacs and his colleagues embarked on their adventure, its role was still a secret kept by the British elite.)

I worked for Isaacs during the 1970s and again in the 1980s, when he ran the new and innovative Channel 4. He was mildly patrician in manner and argumentative, fond of tags from his classics degree. Sharp and sometimes less than tolerant about the stupidity of others, he believed in public culture. People, he thought, should be given the chance to find out about things. Television could make up for the failures of an inegalitarian educational system. But Isaacs, uniquely among the bosses of his day, was a pluralist and a deep, almost reckless believer in free speech who regarded it as his mission to disturb the powerful and stir up debate. Staunchly social democratic, but often unable to understand why people didn't see things his way, he thought that counterviews should always be given expression. Although a large team worked for him on *The World at War*, including many who later acquired fame as historians and media bosses, it is possible to think of such collective authorship as belonging solely to Jeremy Isaacs.

Many features of his series have never been equalled, let alone surpassed. Most noticeable, given the descent of 'history' documentaries into Photoshopped fakery, is the rigorous use of archive material: not just the avoidance of staged sequences, but the clear distinction between newsreel used as propaganda and newsreel with some degree of actuality. (Isaacs was honest in admitting that most newsreel from World War II was to some degree set up, and he convincingly defended using a fresh, studio-created soundtrack.) Just as important was the seeking out and use of hard-to-find witnesses rather than off-the-peg commentators. *The Great War* had claimed to be a 'people's history', but *The World at War* realised this ambition. Yes, you can hear and see Traudl Junge (Hitler's secretary, who later appeared in *Downfall* (2004), played by an actress), James Stewart (bomber pilot), Christabel Bielenberg (married to a German and a survivor of the war in Germany) and the now notorious Arthur 'Bomber' Harris, who devised the strategy that led to the destruction of German cities by the RAF, but there are many less-known, just as interesting interviewees. They're dead now, but the camera captures them fresh and astonished. No five-minute sequence of its twenty-six episodes lacks a revealing, impassioned interview, and these come from all over the world. In terms of documentary history, *The World at War* represents the ultimate flowering of television journalism pioneered by Granada Television (where Isaacs had previously worked). There are no gimmicks, just good research and brilliantly written scripts. Isaacs leaves all judgement of witnesses to the viewer, so we can watch Albert Speer explain that he didn't really know what was going on in the camps. Do we believe him now? Then turn to Lord Avon, formerly Sir Anthony Eden, anti-appeasement hero but nowadays reviled as the author of the Suez catastrophe and attacked for failing to bomb Auschwitz while foreign secretary under Churchill. Tan-suited, with a chic tie, still elegant behind his trademark moustache, he seems genuinely apologetic, a bit lost.

Television hasn't aged well. Everywhere there is a flight from broadcasting as a medium of significance, but no one should belittle the great, long moment of public television. Something of its flavour is preserved in Robert Hughes's autobiographical essay:

> The mid-sixties was, in my recollection, a wonderful time for intelligent and serious TV in England. In Beeb-Two I never heard the word 'ratings' mentioned. It was simply assumed that you did your best to create high-quality programming for reasonably intelligent viewers, to whom you did not condescend. The sabre-toothed technocrats who would move in on the medium were not yet born, or at least not raised. The talent in and around the organization was not yet ashamed of its aspirations or, as the Murdoch boys and girls would call them now, its 'pretensions'.

The remarkable, icon-busting and -creating Hughes, for a long time the art critic of *Time* magazine, began his career at the BBC with a report on the flooding of Florence. His series *The Shock of the New* (1980) marked the first time that modernism was taken seriously in a mass medium. 'Picasso? Who does he play for?' was a joke until a handful of Australians (including the sublime Barry Humphries, Germaine Greer and Clive James) finally took on the destruction of the genteel style of cultural criticism. These were spectacular years indeed, and amid the dross of the schedule viewers could encounter minor miracles night after night. But the efforts of public broadcasters to affect culture are now arguably at an end. The grasp they had on it has gone on hold. There are still some moments of mass education coming from the BBC and a few Scandinavian broadcasters, but they must all watch their ratings now.

I sat down with Alan Yentob, who joined the BBC in 1972. He is the last in the line of believers in a Britain of 'public culture'. I'd worked with Alan, and found him to be an astonishingly good reporter, among the quickest to figure out anything. I liked his extravagance, which I'd experienced as a form of out-there protection. In his early days, he had benefited from the existence of what he called 'space' at the BBC. 'It was possible just to go off and do things,' he said. 'Documentaries are about being curious. They are about entering people's lives without quite knowing what you will bring back. When you came back, you could simply vanish for months. It was difficult to make things then. Every magazine of film lasted only ten minutes – you had to stop and reload. Films depended on razor blades. You made a sequence of images and – let's say it didn't work – you had to pull it all to pieces, and that took ages. People in those days didn't really know how to make programmes. As an executive, you had to get into films much more often than you would now. You really had to help make them. I wasn't always great at finishing my own films. But I could finish those of others.'

Individual films shown on the BBC were noticed. 'Stanley Kubrick knew about our films,' Yentob explained. 'We didn't even know that he lived in Britain, but he knew about them.' There was no policy stating that it was time to start making intelligent films, but 'someone would just say it was a good idea'. It sounded a bit like the beginnings of *Storyville*'s life at the BBC. No one had instructed me to find film-makers all over the world; it just seemed to me like a good idea. Luckily, there were others, people deep in the BBC, who thought the time for this had come. Ultimately, Alan's non- or anti-management style, coupled with ceaseless creative fretting, did succeed in getting things done. I wondered about the place I'd just left, as Alan had. The journalist Malcolm Muggeridge once wrote an acid volume of memoirs entitled *Chronicles of Wasted Time* (1972), and I could recall hours, days, months of conspicuous wastage. My activity had not really been wasted; it was kept in the films I created. Some sort of strange lesson was to be learnt here. 'Accident is important,' Yentob mused. It was how other ideas entered the system. He told me about the inspired early-1990s use of video cameras. They weren't expensive, and they proved easy to use. With relatively little training anyone could make a documentary.

And yet it wasn't that simple. You needed time for these things to happen, as well as money. His own hanging-out-with-David-Bowie film, *Cracked Actor* (1975), came about in this way. Yentob was meant to be making something that was more of a concert film, but he ended up speeding around LA in a limousine with a stoned Bowie. It's hard to see now how Yentob's film would have been commissioned, let alone found its way onto network television. The same goes for many of the ideas he pioneered on *Arena*, which first aired in 1975. In *Arena* Yentob and those working with him, the producers Anthony Wall and Nigel Finch, began to mine popular culture. *My Way* (1977), a portrait of the effects of the song and its endless replication, and *The Private Life of the Ford Cortina* (1982) were both standout moments in the series. But the most lasting *Arena* episode remains the appropriately gargantuan portrait of Orson Welles down on his luck, *The Orson Welles Story* (1982). More than his own doc *F for Fake* (1973), as much as all the reams written about Welles's success and failure, the *Arena* profile shows him as he really was – outsize in every way, sometimes rancorous and often generous, rueful in relation to almost everything. 'This happened by accident,' Yentob says.

'Mel Brooks was in a restaurant with him, and we were talking, and he got on the line, and I asked him if he would do an interview, and he said yes. So we went to Palm Springs and filmed for a day. And after that we filmed Orson again, and it got bigger and bigger. No one at the BBC was at all bothered about how long it was going to be.'

Of course, the BBC was the greatest and best place for those who tended to be male, white and from Oxbridge. Not Yentob, who heard the call all the way from the University of Leeds. But the degree of risk-taking and pluralism was unequalled. The BBC's historian Jean Seaton tells the story of the making of David Attenborough's *Life on Earth*. Shown in 1979, at the glummest period of Britain's economic slump, the films were an updated *Voyage of the Beagle*, a restatement of benign Darwinism. They were viewed by a great proportion of the British public. Much of their success comes from the apparently effortless generosity of their presenter, David Attenborough. Sir David, now ninety-two, was once a very effective BBC executive and has come to seem like a deity watching over a vanishing animal kingdom, but in his prime he was also an unassuming reporter, covering the natural world in true BBC style. This is his commentary for his still-famous encounter with Rwandan mountain gorillas:

There is more meaning and mutual understanding in exchanging a glance with a gorilla than with any other animal I know. Their sight, their hearing, their sense of smell are so similar to ours that they see the world in much the same way as we do. We live in the same sort of social groups with largely permanent family relationships. They walk around on the ground as we do, though they are immensely more powerful than we are. So if there were ever a possibility of escaping the human condition and living imaginatively in another creature's world, it must be with the gorilla. The male is an enormously powerful creature, but he only uses his strength when he is protecting his family, and it is very rare that there is violence within the group. So it seems really very unfair that man should have chosen the gorilla to symbolise everything that is aggressive and violent, when that is the one thing that the gorilla is not – and that we are.

It may seem invidious to single out films from the multitude of offerings from public television in its prime, but I recall, along with the BBC's *George Orwell: A Life in Pictures* (2003), the last episode of Simon Schama's *A History of Britain* (2000–2), 'The Two Winstons'. In the approved style of BBC programmes, it featured a literate on-screen presenter and many carefully filmed locations, and was scripted down to the last pause. It wasn't quite a film, but nor were the many costly series featuring literate presenters. Do we really appreciate many of these efforts, such as Alistair Cooke's *America* (1972) or the granddaddy of them all, Sir Kenneth Clark's *Civilisation* (1969)? Length apart, they seem staid, and verge on tiresome omniscience. (An exception is Jacob Bronowski's *The Ascent of Man* (1973), in which the great man appears plagued with doubts, always struggling, though the shows are harder to watch for this reason.) Schama's story of Britain seems faulty in its premise now that the dissolution of the union is on the cards, but it was daring in the way it turned the history of Britain away from schoolbooks into linked essays – a style of history befitting the time. Schama rendered the lives of George Orwell and Winston Churchill side by side through the device of Orwell's use of the latter's name in *1984*. In an hour an attentive viewer could find out a lot about the more appealing side of Churchill (Schama recalled his funeral in particular, which he experienced as a teenager, at a moment when he wasn't a great admirer of the old imperialist) and something of the dogged persistence in truth of Orwell, creator, like Churchill, of great national myths. If you want to know anything about the country you inhabit, the programme suggested, it's all here. And so indeed it was.

Think of the documentary output of the BBC in any one year, from the mid-1960s through to the 1990s. Aside from the 'strands' listed above, there were series. These were crafted for the two channels, BBC1 and BBC2. Each was carefully researched and filmed with care. In departmental meetings no one discussed how a film might be made or what it should say. Instead, we talked about the limited number of institutions still to be penetrated by the BBC. The house ethos and style were ultra-Griersonian. We should seek to express the 'interdependence' of those who lived in Britain. It was acceptable to criticise incompetence in government or draw attention to unfulfilled expectations, but our tone had to remain impartial. Much attention, understandably, was paid to the avoidance of fakery. One shouldn't criticise the rote aspect of much of this output. As producer and executive Peter Dale has observed, throughout the 1970s and 1980s, and even into the 1990s, 'millions of British television viewers sat down to well-crafted, insightful and often moving documentaries about themselves and their neighbours . . . they were appointments to view for a post-war society keen to explore new ideas, faces, ways of living – a sense of what it is to live in a liberal and tolerant society'. Taken as a whole, television documentary in Britain during the 1970s and 1980s proved to be a comprehensive portrait of its time. We'll never know how it altered the perspective of viewers, but it seems safe to assume that some came to agree with the predominantly liberal views of the producers and directors who made the films.

As for contemporary British documentary series, one need look no further than the BBC's *Hospital* (2017). In fictional series, the plots feature seemingly well-paid doctors and administrators. This contrasts sharply with *Hospital*. In one episode, the hospital is in emergency mode for twenty-four hours after the terrorist attack on the Houses of Parliament. Among the victims is the killer, his body in a locked room guarded by armed police. The BBC still values our national health system, and *Hospital* shows today's NHS in its full drabness and diversity. One of the bewildered French teenagers caught up in the attack seems lost, without phone or trousers, his face scarred and bandaged. 'You have your new look,' his friend, Yann, laughs.

Can we understand the society we are a part of? Have we lost the ability to help those in need? The British are definitively non-utopic. We attempt to solve our problems, but never truly do so. There are problems at St Mary's Hospital, Paddington, mostly because of schedules. Doctors, nurses and patients wait in exasperation, hyped-up, wondering if there is a slot available. There is also a huge problem caused by the lack of empty beds inside the NHS. After I suffered a stroke, I swiftly had an operation and a bed; if you're very unwell, the emergency system helps you very quickly. *Hospital* takes you inside the exhausting daily meetings, where the staff seem bored and near crisis. The series shows a bewildered Britain through the lens of a casualty department. The drugs the medical staff use are very expensive, and some are so new that the NHS isn't sure that they even work and is loath to dish them out; increasingly, private patients pay for them, if they can. With each passing year, the oldest in society become a larger proportion of the NHS population. Trust administrators are increasingly dealing with patients who are tired, complicated and unable to understand. One of the doctors interviewed doesn't want to take on private work, but he feels frustrated and underpaid by the NHS. As it stands, there doesn't seem to be a solution. As the staff repeatedly say, any fix for the system will require a lot of work. The employees appear to be increasingly made up of young people and immigrants, and the doctors all seem to be underpaid. It's a hard series to watch: the issues are so frustrating, and the solution seems obvious – money. As with the BBC itself, it seems as though a child could solve these issues. But we are adults, so what will we do?

Public broadcasters continue to show documentaries, but with the movement of audiences to streaming platforms, they are in an increasingly severe crisis. The commitment to continue broadcasting docs has been strongest in Canada, where the legacy of Grierson endures, and throughout Scandinavia. In France and Italy, public broadcasting took on an educational aspect for many years. The American Public Broadcasting System (PBS) was created in the 1960s, after the failures of network television were acknowledged; it came into existence as part of the mid-1960s Great Society initiatives. The creation of so many local systems, promoted in the Nixon years as a means of weakening what came to be seen as a left-wing organisation, restricted its influence. But PBS showed many BBC series, which inspired it to create its own. On a small scale, and with striking success, PBS began funding documentary films. These were increasingly made by independent producers. Classics such as Ken Burns's *The Civil War* (1990) followed in the successful path of historical series. From the vantage point of the present, the PBS films about African American culture and its two series about the Vietnam War (1983 and 2017) seem to be its legacy.

The past described in such films is recent, and entering it still feels alarming. Henry Hampton's *Eyes on the Prize* (1987) covers, over fourteen hours, the civil rights movement, from its 1950s origins to the traumatic year of 1968. It's a story of hopes fulfilled, but the films don't contain a note of triumphalism. They explain the attitudes of segregationists such as George Wallace and Orval Faubus, but they are as sharp about the havering government and the splits within the civil rights movement, between Martin Luther King and his supporters and the more radical voices that had all but drowned him out by the time of his death. One should admire these remarkable films for the sheer richness of their African American voices and the many instances of heroism they display. The Vietnam War is commonly viewed as the defining moment in the empowering of television news coverage, but it's clear that the civil rights struggles were just as important in forming American views – not least those of politicians such as JFK, RFK and the doughty, still spurned LBJ. Episode six, about the march on Montgomery, is a masterpiece, but the issues the films describe have come to acquire a different sort of familiarity, because they show just how difficult it would be to change attitudes and how, ultimately, changing the law isn't enough. Progressive Americans thought it would be enough for the federal government to guarantee voter access to African Americans. 'We're willing to be beaten for democracy,' a marcher says. But it wasn't enough, and fifty years later the existence of Black Lives

Matter shows the limits of formal democracy in guaranteeing equality. Executive producer Henry Hampton's series made possible the forensic, brutally eloquent *Malcolm X* (1992) and *Citizen King* (2004), an extraordinary, sustained elegy; and also Stanley Nelson's film *The Black Panthers* (2015), which finally rescued the Panther movement from the network news clichés of gangsterism, re-establishing the movement's links with the Third World strand of the 1960s and showing how far the FBI was prepared to go, illegally and with violence, in order to extinguish a movement deemed threatening to American life. In recent years, Black Lives Matter has brought these issues to the foreground once again.

The British creation of Channel 4 in 1982 came in part as a response to the pressure of independent film-makers who wanted to secure access to television. They suggested that their programmes would bring new voices to the medium. This proved to be the case. To begin with, the new channel introduced a degree of freshness and risk into what had become a staid, duopolistic system. It attracted people who couldn't stand working at the BBC and ITV. With respect to documentaries, the new channel specialised in opinionated reporting. But it also began to show international work, without editing it. For the first time, British audiences became aware of the variety of styles in which documentaries were made all over the world. The channel evolved in the direction of greater reliability. What had once seemed like innovation became, in due course and without excessive fanfare or surprise, a marketing style. By the first years of the new century, Channel 4 was notorious not for its abrasive comedies or unusual documentaries, but for the rating- and money-gathering *Big Brother*, the most successful of the many 'reality shows' into which its original quest to describe the world differently had morphed. The long-term effect of the channel was, simply, choice. In the end, what Channel 4 came to offer was more television, good and bad. It didn't change the culture of television as much as its admirers had hoped.

Anyone seeking to understand the great change that came over British broadcasting with the decline of the public service ethos should consider the fate of the successive documentaries made about the Queen and the royal family. The first of these, *Royal Family*, 105 minutes long, was screened in 1969, and was made by the then head of documentaries at the BBC, Richard Cawston. To the astonishment of Her Majesty's subjects and the forty-odd million viewers who watched the film throughout the world, the royals were shown watching television, having breakfast and awkwardly preparing a barbecue. When they weren't bemused by the banality of royal lives, the audience appeared content. But there were those who thought that the film was a mistake, because, in the idiom of contemporary documentaries, it showed that the royals were rather like us. 'Initially, the public will love seeing the Royal Family as not essentially different from anyone else and, in the short term, letting in the cameras will enhance the Monarchy's popularity,' remarked the commentator Peregrine Worsthorne presciently. 'But in the not-so-long run, familiarity will breed, if not contempt, well, familiarity.' In *The Crown* (2016), a drama series on Netflix, some scenes remain similar in appearance to its 1960s doc counterpart. However, audiences now expect drama to include the realism of scenes with which past viewers were content.

Although *Elizabeth R*, a royal portrait from 1992, passed off without incident, Worsthorne's observations were on the mark, and the royal family rapidly became implicated, willy-nilly, in the celebritisation of British mass culture. Princess Diana used the famous *Panorama* interview (1995) not just to make public her marital problems, but to criticise the hauteur of the Windsors. *A Year with the Queen* (2007) paid due homage to this development. This wasn't an exercise in 'fly-on-the-wall' film-making. Instead, it resembled in its utter absence of intimacy the formalised picture spreads to be found each week in *Hello!* magazine. Its lack of ambition notwithstanding, the series proved troublesome for the BBC, because its producers, in making a promo tape for purchasers, made it appear as though the Queen had walked out in a huff during a photo session with the photographer Annie Leibovitz.

To many print journalists, whose own methodology left much to be desired, the failings of documentaries were a sign of the frivolity of television and the inadequacy of documentary as a journalistic form. In reality, however, the offences committed by film-makers were relatively modest, and most documentaries stayed honest. But one can look at the triumph of popular television, and what observers perceive to be the relentless decline in standards, from a slightly different angle. From the vantage point of the history of documentaries, so marred by insecurity, television seemed like more than a haven. But there were also those who insisted, year after year, that television was bad for their work and that there was a huge price to be paid when one worked for the medium. Wasn't so much material in reality a substitute for the freer, more radical things that might have happened with less control? Would it be possible to envisage genuinely free television? These people were the so-called independent film-makers. Although they worked at the margins of what still appeared to be the most marginal of forms, their views steadily became more and more important.

5 : *Toujours Vérité*

Agnès Varda's *Faces Places* (2017): the ninety-year-old Varda with
the photographer JR, capturing rural and urban France with the
cinéma vérité she created in the 1960s.

The 1960s are considered not so much a decade as a long, pot-hazed, pseudo-revolutionary moment when, surprisingly, everything freed up. Those who were the right age have never lost the sense that something happened that was special and irretrievable. Much of what was invented in the 1960s has stayed with us, pillaged or rendered as parody, to be sure, but also as a genuine cultural marker. 'You can do what you want,' was a contemporary maxim, or, in the idiom of the American counterculture, 'Just do it.' Grey hairs or mortality cannot wholly abolish such insights. Film occupied a special place in 1960s culture, and, within film, documentaries had their own distinctive niche. They weren't widely viewed, but they were, in the idiom of the time, 'independent'. They were also chic, feeding other cultural occurrences.

It didn't matter if the film was dull. Suddenly, films were 'political', illustrating the left-wing causes of the time. Like most cultural terms that enter the public discourse, the notion of independent film has come to imply a degree of wish fulfilment. Films are expensive to make, and even now require industry-wide support – distributors, publicists, cinema projectors, popcorn vendors, etc. These days, most so-called 'indy' films are part-funded by the studios from whose clutches they were supposed to have escaped. But in the 1960s, it was still possible to believe that films might be made 'outside the system'. They would be made with small budgets, financed by different sources – distributors might be prepared to invest, but there were also wealthy individuals – and shown in small cinemas. They would be different from Hollywood fare – less bland.

In reality, the new film culture was driven not by ideology or cultural happenings, but by technology. And it wasn't homogenous. True, most 1960s innovation was driven by contemporary notions of libertarianism, but there were different approaches to documentary film. Three sets of technical developments, separated by twenty years, made independently produced, coherently authored documentaries possible. The first occurred in the early 1960s, when lighter 16-millimetre cameras became available, with synchronised sound, courtesy of a lightweight sound recorder known as a Nagra. Secondly, new and faster stock made it possible to do without lights, though it was still necessary to reload the camera every ten minutes. Colour stock transformed the look of documentaries, altering the potential of news reporting wherever it was used. A film-maker could hang around his or her subjects for longer. More importantly, reality could now be stalked and captured – or, in the idiom of the 1960s, 'experienced'. 'Hanging out', stoned or otherwise, was a distinctively 1960s experience, and hanging-out films became a genre of sorts. Thirdly, a variety of cameras using tape came on the market, starting in the 1980s. Filming costs fell dramatically, with cameras becoming smaller and smaller and easier to use. Lights weren't required, and the camera was small enough not to be noticed. It was cumbersome to edit tape, but by the early 1990s random access editing was freely available. This meant that you didn't have to spin backwards and forwards while assembling a film. You could store drafts and discarded sequences. And it was possible, by using a keyboard, to construct faster-moving sequences more rapidly.

Most of these innovations were cheap and very easy to use, and they have fully democratised the process of telling stories on film. They led to an astonishing explosion in documentary film-making as, decade by decade, film-makers seized on the new technology, fashioning it to their own purposes. In due course, as the cost of editing dropped, and as it became clear that television audiences could be attracted by the everyday surfaces of 'reality', the discoveries of the 1960s came to seem banal. But they were illuminating in their time, and their power has never vanished entirely.

Post-war wealth created an appetite for journalism and a revival in the fortunes of photojournalists, whose work adorned the weekly supplements of newspapers fattened by advertising. The New Journalism, pioneered in the US by the likes of Tom Wolfe, Norman Mailer, Joan Didion and Truman Capote, sanctioned the presence of reporters in stories. It also encouraged the use of devices previously restricted to fiction – flashbacks, psychological nuance expressed through the recreation of characters' feelings and, most importantly, the creation of character as well as action – thus transforming non-fiction narrative. Similar stratagems made their way into documentary film. Now the film-maker was allowed to be an author. But authorship was somehow different in film than it was in print, where it had, of course, existed uncontroversially for many centuries. Films were ultimately about what you saw, so the film-maker author was tied more tightly to the literal depiction of reality. The relationship between reality and documentary film, far from being problematic, became crucial. Films were admired to the degree that they could be said to be truthful, but they were increasingly allowed (at least in France) to speak about the level of truth they aspired to depict. This was a founding statute of the new freedoms. In Britain, the new documentaries had been known as Free Cinema. In the US, proponents of the new documentary film-making style referred to their work as Direct Cinema. In France it was known, more catchily, as *cinéma vérité*. These films haven't lost their interest; they are as fresh now as films made yesterday.

The first recorded use of the term '*cinéma vérité*' came from the cult publication *Cahiers du cinéma*, from the ethnographer Jean Rouch. Outside a small circle of ethno-film buffs, Rouch isn't as well known as he should be. Trained as a hydrographer, he returned from Africa to France in order to fight in the Resistance. In his own films and in interviews he seems bluff, a bit forbidding, matter-of-fact, with no bullshit, in a way not frequently encountered in French cultural circles. Rouch's films were made through the anthropological Musée de l'Homme in Paris, where he was director of studies for a long time. Rouch had studied the myths and social practices of West African peoples, but his subject became modernity and the stresses it imposed on humans. Although his films begin with commentary, usually read by himself, they're made in a spirit of collusion with their subjects. Rouch was criticised for his apparent acceptance of contemporary ills such as imperialism, but his films are genuinely subversive. He understood in a way that is rare among members of the French elite that people will often tell you things you don't know.

Rouch's first masterpiece, *Moi, un noir* (1958), starts with him explaining to us how the young black youth of the Côte d'Ivoire migrate to Abidjan, the new megacity, and often can't find jobs. But the film isn't an exposé. Instead, it's a first-person diary of Oumarou Ganda, with whom Rouch made the film. At first sight, and by contrast with the many efforts of outsiders to document alien cultures, the film seems bizarrely and heedlessly light-hearted. Its subjects call themselves after Hollywood stars, living inside dreams that can't be realised. What does Rouch mean by following these dreams? These young black people – Sugar Ray Robinson, Eddie Constantine et al. – have their own lives, and it becomes clear that this is the real strength of the film. Shot in colour, *Moi, un noir* is one of the most beautiful films ever made, with scene after scene straight out of a Magnum portfolio. But it remains a great film because Rouch's own authorship is evident in his care for his subjects, filtered through the sensibility of his black protagonist, who is observing other black people. They aren't objects of concern. Like the best protagonists in documentaries – indeed, like Nanook – they are themselves.

For his best-known and most influential film, however, Rouch returned to Paris and black and white. 'Are you happy?' is the question posed to Parisians at the beginning of his *nouvelle vague* documentary *Chronicle of a Summer*, made in 1960, at the moment when François Truffaut and Jean-Luc Godard had embarked on their own experiments in film. These Parisians reply with varying degrees of glumness. Paris, as Rouch and the heretical left-wing sociologist Edgar Morin intimate, was in its prime, still bathed in the existentialist culture of the Left Bank, still in thrall to the interdictions of frivolity, unless ideologically sanctioned, offered by the inhabitants of the Café de Flore, Jean-Paul Sartre and Simone de Beauvoir. You could still explain intelligently why you weren't happy in those days, and so these Parisians do, talking about love, politics, the awful Algerian War, in which the French army employed torture on a wide scale, the brutalisation of contemporary capitalism and, in the most eloquent sequence of the film, survival and the Holocaust. In a bizarre, wholly convincing way, the film anticipates the upheavals of 1968, prematurely giving voice to the young *soixante-huitards*.

Although *Chronicle of a Summer* purportedly records the views of a cross-section of the French bourgeois and workers, the film-makers relied on their contacts, which goes some way to accounting for the intimate tone of the answers – as if Jean Renoir had been reincarnated as a sociologist. (A young Régis Debray makes an appearance, and the workers are drawn from a Trotskyist group known to Morin, who was kicked out of the Communist Party. A scene with an African student reveals how emphatically white and consciously racist France was in the 1960s.) The bumbling, rumpled Morin wonders what post-war prosperity was doing to the heads of the French. He and Rouch shared a love of film theory and a very French scepticism about the capability of film-making to record the truth. Do the subjects of documentaries ever really tell the truth? Don't they end up performing for the camera? Many have circled around these questions, but these two attack them ruthlessly, both in an entertainingly literal opening sequence, where they discuss how to approach the subject of happiness, and in a long coda, in which the two men, in the spirit of a dialogue scripted in the eighteenth century by Diderot, reflect on the responses of the film's participants, reinforcing their mutual sense of scepticism by casting doubt on their entire project, even as they praise each other for their efforts.

In a very French way, however, the film tells another, much deeper story, through the lives of its two women stars. One finds love and happiness through her existential musings. The other, Holocaust survivor Marcelline, explains how young men, ignorant of the meaning of the tattoos, used the numbers on her arm to buy lottery tickets. She's caught by the camera walking from the empty Place de la Concorde through Les Halles, talking about her murdered father and how she misses him, and the film magically reaches out of the shallows of sociology into the core of individual life. Marcelline points out that when she created these scenes, she was performing – and we're left to wonder whether performance is a kind of therapy, the only way in which reality can be endured, or whether all depictions of reality are performances. Rouch believed that every film should reveal its author's point of view. He was an early influence on Godard, and you can see how his innovations seeped into fictional film-making. So modern a tone and look wasn't just a feature of the 16 mm camera and synched-up Nagra sound, and it wasn't the stylistic tic that it later became. 'All great fiction films tend towards documentary, just as all great documentaries tend towards fiction,' Godard once remarked. Rouch and Morin's masterpiece somehow manages to be both fiction and non-fiction.

Many early adherents of *cinéma vérité* – Jean Rouch, Chris Marker, even Alain Resnais – are forgotten outside the film academy, and this is a pity, because many of their innovations still feel fresh. For some idea of their influence, one must go to Jean-Luc Godard's essayistic collages of fact and fiction. 'Cinema is truth twenty-four times a second,' Godard famously declared. A film collective founded by him was named after Dziga Vertov, in homage to the great Russian's disregard of conventional film grammar and willingness to be didactic. In *One Plus One*, filmed in London in 1968, Godard cuts from the Rolling Stones recording 'Sympathy for the Devil' to some Black Power revolutionaries to a reading of *Mein Kampf* in a pornographic bookstore, interspersing footage of his own girlfriend of the day, who plays a character called Eve Democracy. He appears in the last scene of the film, bespectacled and earnest, waving black and red flags.

I must have watched all of Godard's films when they first came out. Someday, I told myself, I would ensure that films as bold as this could be made. I was less excited by his politics, which seemed bizarre, even if you were familiar with the squabbles of the Left Bank. In *La Chinoise* (1967), it appeared that Godard really did believe that Maoism would come to France, although amid the readings from the *Little Red Book* etc. he took care to qualify these views by playing around with toy weapons in a bourgeois apartment.

Not long ago, I was present at a sparsely attended showing of *Film Socialisme* (2011), the latest offering by the then eighty-year-old Godard. Superficially, nothing had changed: granddaughters of Godard's 1960s film muses perused books, while slogans half subliminally flashed on the screen. There was a long and dismally hard to read sequence shot in luridly heightened colour amid Belgian petrol pumps. Instead of the Rolling Stones, a cruise liner on which Berlusconi might have worked as a crooner served as a backdrop. As it stopped at various ports, Godard used the overweight white European passengers to deliver his habitual message about the Decay of the West. The faithful stirred in their seats. Suddenly, however, with the end of the film in sight, something did appear to happen. The film didn't exactly come around to saying anything about socialism, or indeed anything else; instead, all the elements that Godard had seemed to toy with, rearranging them to his dissatisfaction, fused miraculously. Throughout his career he wanted to show that film might be used like a pen, to write in its own language. It needn't consist of plodding narratives. Failing in this, he nonetheless bequeathed to following generations the idea that it could be done. And here, like the faint heat from an extinct sun, was a reiteration of this promise. But the promise was illusory and hadn't been kept. All that Godard managed to do at the end of *Film Socialisme*, as in so many of his other films, was recapitulate his own consciously stalled efforts. He had ended by constructing a narrative out of his own futile efforts to escape narrative.

Could film-makers really become authors? How did they set about this task? In 1968, Louis Malle escaped from the fevered atmosphere of revolutionary Paris, travelling to India. Until then, his own films had been somewhat staid, over-calculated depictions of bourgeois life, marred by stiffness and a degree of moralism, but in India he began for the first time to film whatever he saw as he saw it. In a village where they filmed low-caste women at a well, Malle's cameraman became worried by the way in which the women looked at the camera. Malle said it didn't matter, they should look as much as they liked. 'It's what I dislike about so many documentaries, this naïve *mise en scène*, the beginning of the distortion of the truth. Very quickly I realised that these looks at the camera were both disturbing and true, and we should never pretend that we weren't intruders. So, we kept working that way.'

Malle's series *Phantom India* (1969) is full of such scenes, and they still seem surprising. In his commentary, he acknowledges that he often didn't quite know what he was filming. He had been wrong about the significance of a religious ceremony or the presence of carrion crows or vultures; he had been looking for something else. The films are stronger, certainly more interesting today, for these admissions. But this wasn't how they were seen at the time, or indeed later. In the 1990s, after Malle's early death from cancer, I became interested in these films, which had been shown in Britain, causing the BBC to be banned from filming in India for some years. The colour original of the BBC version had been destroyed, but I found in the archive what was then called a 'cutting copy' – a black-and-white working print, stained and scratched – with Malle's commentary in English. Malle had a French-posh accent (he came from a family that had got rich from growing sugar beet on the plains of northern France) and he described what he'd seen, or hadn't noticed, in exactly the right way. When a new version was shown on the BBC, I had a flurry of phone calls from the Indian high commissioner suggesting that it might be risky to be showing these films again, even after more than twenty years. But he liked them. This wasn't the case with British reviewers, some of whom criticised what they saw as Malle's very French allusions to his own less than comprehending narrative presence. But I liked the way in which Malle contrived to insert himself in his films, even when this was done very indirectly. He was a passionate cyclist, and he made a brilliant short film showing a Tour de France rider falling off his bike out of exhaustion (*Vive le Tour*, 1962). It was like the best passages in his fiction films, or indeed those of his master, Jean Renoir: half-hidden autobiography, a premonition of exhaustion and death.

There are problems, to be sure, with the obtrusive French cult of the *auteur*. Recently, I came across the work of Emmanuel Carrère, novelist, screenwriter and documentary film-maker. Carrère returns throughout his work to the *grand sujet* of what we can never know or be sure of. His most successful book, *Limonov* (2012), is a biography of the eponymous Russian punk politician and memoirist. He explains at the outset that fact and fiction exist throughout Limonov's work, but he doesn't propose to disentangle them on our behalf. There's an episode in the book that is taken from *Serbian Epics* (1992), a documentary made for the BBC by Paweł Pawlikowski, in which Limonov, hanging out with Serbian nationalists on a hill overlooking Sarajevo, asks if he can fire their machine gun over the city. In Carrère's account, the action is sickening and causes him to abandon the book for a year, because Limonov appears indifferent to the fact that he might be killing someone. In the film, it's clear that the machine gun isn't trained on anything and nobody could have been harmed. There are similar crossovers in his *My Life as a Russian Novel* (2010), a real-life account of the life and death of Carrère's émigré Russian father, executed as a collaborator in 1945, and his very posh Sovietologue mother, alongside a humiliating, all-too-believable ending of an affair, in which Carrère tries to get his partner to read a pornographic story about herself published in France's poshest newspaper, *Le Monde*, on a train journey from Paris to the Atlantic coast. As a frame for the narrative, Carrère gives us an account of how he made a documentary film (the film does exist, and it isn't very good, appearing somewhat contrived) in a small town in central Russia, and the various degrees of fakery involved in finding enough to create a story capable of holding up his own very 'personal' view of Russia.

These qualities are on display, often miraculously, in the work of Chris Marker, the austere magpie patron saint of auteurism. '*On ne sait jamais ce qu'on filme*,' he remarked. Marker was oblivious to the allure of fame or money, and he lived isolated in his Left Bank studio, surrounded by his own archive, a modern hermit. He once said that his work consisted of home movies. If he'd been rich or had rich friends, no one would have seen his films. His masterpiece, *Sans Soleil* (1982), is made from an imagined letter written about travel and the world by someone we never see or identify. The text is continuous, allusive, hypnotic in a speeded-up Proustian way. And of course, like any self-respecting French utterance, it is very reflexive. Memory, we're told more than once, consists of artefacts. If we didn't have *écriture* (and now texts within films), we wouldn't recall anything. But Marker's tone is neither excessively portentous nor in the least bit patronising. His Marker-ish observer says that he's past the moment when he feels the need to find exceptional views, sites, etc., and there are small scenes, *découpages* from other films or shot by him, in places we'd never reach: a ferry in Okinawa; a cat temple in a suburb of Tokyo, with a couple who have lost their cat; the market and beach of a town in Guinea-Bissau; a town somewhere in Iceland before and after it was covered by volcanic ash. Images are sometimes blurred and messed up; more often they are of a crystalline quality. Some will feel overwhelmed by the material forced on them minute by intense minute, but these are some of the most beautiful 'found' sequences in film: for instance, the exquisite moment when Marker focuses the camera on the faces of women in an African market, who change their expressions to acknowledgement and flirtatiousness when they realise they are being filmed.

Perhaps the best way to think of *Sans Soleil* is as a performance piece or as a written essay in the shape of a film with its own aesthetic. You can go back to it, relish it, go back again. Pet themes of Marker are here: his disillusioned radical politics; his neo-Hegelian, post-existentialist obsession with history; his poring over the loss to humans represented by the end of animism; and most touchingly, his thoroughly ambiguous feelings about film and anthropology. In Japan, where many of the most beautiful moments occur, Marker, Zen-style, becomes the bow, the arrow and the target. By the end, it's possible that merely observing is what we have to do with what is given to us in the way of consciousness: the more we observe, the greater the gifts reciprocated in our direction. This may seem to be a miracle, but the real miracle is how the film does this on our behalf with one extreme, life-enhancing illumination after another.

We also owe to Marker another remarkable, wholly political film. I was sitting in a BBC newsroom the night of 11 September 1973, when the news came through that the Moneda Palace had been attacked and the Chilean president, Salvador Allende Gossens, was dead. This seemed to me, as it did to most of my generation, to be an outrage. We were certain that there was some sort of CIA involvement, and the extinguishing of democracy in Chile, one of the longest-lasting parliamentary regimes in Latin America, was a serious blow. I spent the next three days at the BBC, getting a tearful interview with Señora Allende, exiled in Mexico. I saw Patricio Guzmán's *The Battle of Chile* (1975) some years later, in the cellar of a West Village distributor, close to tears. The film was made from material shot in Chile before the coup, on stock supplied by Chris Marker, and was later smuggled out via the Swedish embassy; it seems that he helped with the script, too. The script does give an approved, Marxist version of events, reciting the usual class categories. But the film is so important and still powerful because it remains true to what it describes – and it does include a degree of authorship, remaining clearly the work of its young film-makers. Even at this distance it seems capable of recreating the horror of watching a society apparently tolerating violence and instability until a coup was expected by all parties. The last ten minutes, when fighters strafed or bombed the palace, are to this day shocking and heartbreaking. Nowadays, years after Pinochet's death and with a flourishing democratic system in Chile, the film feels no less urgent. Can we envisage another revolutionary era? Why not? Will people really not use violence (or, in the case of the Chileans, sit-ins, demos, etc.) in order to overthrow a state in the name of equality? How would we imagine they won't? Allende was a constitutionalist, and his removal and death still have the power to shock. Guzmán and Marker cleverly keep him offstage most of the time. His speeches are oddly conciliatory in tone, even when he's going through the motions of revolution. Meanwhile, the young camera teams pick out everything: the lipstick of the upper classes, the dandyish naval officers, the conspirators (including Pinochet) hiding half off-camera in groups, behind dark glasses. I can think of few political narratives as engrossing and tear-inducing as this.

There are faint echoes, still, from the distant explosions of the 1960s. Gleaning is what you do when the harvest is done, and in Agnès Varda's film *The Gleaners and I* (2000), it becomes what people do with the refuse not just of contemporary society, but of their own lives. It's also what Varda, who was then in her seventies, chose to do with her own life. Made when lightweight cameras had just come into fashion, this is an extended, Proust-inspired essay. There are beautiful scenes of the French countryside, and less beautiful sequences of those who live off rubbish. In a gentle fashion, Varda dislikes modern waste – she doesn't throw things away. Why are deformed potatoes deemed unsuitable for consumption? Grapes are thrown away in Burgundy because the best wine has to be made within annual quotas. But there are also abandoned vineyards. Lawyers and magistrates appear in the film, standing in cabbage patches to show that in France, private property laws are subject to statutes protecting the poor, often dating from the thirteenth century. There was a rich tradition of art depicting peasants of the nineteenth century at work and gleaning. In Varda's view, we would be better off reclaiming these traditions, putting an end to waste. She finds a vegetarian ex-teacher who lives off the refuse of a market and spends his evenings teaching French to immigrants. She dwells carefully on reproductions of Rembrandt self-portraits picked up in Japan, and the beautiful (and strange to her) furrows in her own hands. Some of the filming is a bit precious, but Varda has a perfect eye for the beautiful, the unexpectedly useful and, most of all, for the sheer Frenchness of French society and the gaps in which odd and precious things and people can survive. And, *bien entendu*, this is a film gleaning not just from her own life, but from *cinéma vérité*, *nouvelle vague* and all the good things she came to express through her own films.

In *Faces Places* (2017), Varda travels throughout the French countryside with the photographer JR. This is her last *essai*, full of rich photography, with JR in his hat and ever-present glasses, and insights into the relationship between the young and the old. They shoot the cranes in the port of Le Havre, a village full of goats, a hilltop town, Bonnieux, and the resting place of Henri Cartier-Bresson in a tiny cemetery surrounded by lavender and olive trees. Varda takes you to these places and introduces you to the people she loves. She and JR agree (I think) that '*photographie*' captures the '*instantané*' that, alas, doesn't last. They paste these images on walls, crates, bell towers and more. They wonder whether they are *auteurs*, but being French and looking at the images, they are really practitioners of *cinéma direct*. This is really a story about Varda, who died in March 2019, and she tells us everything she can. She tries, and fails, to see her old friend

Jean-Luc Godard, leaving a sad message on his window overlooking a lake in Switzerland. He won't see anyone. Varda says her eyes are failing, but she sees everything.

Nowadays, these innovations are lumped together, so it may be as well to pause, to distinguish the Anglo-American 1960s school from the French one. In France, *cinéma vérité* exalted a combination of the camera's eye and the intellect of the film-maker. It was thought that the camera was more capable of depicting truth than the erratic, instantly misremembered movements of the human eye. At the same time, critics agreed that film-makers should feel free to intervene in the process of filming and editing. How they did so – how, indeed, one became an 'auteur' – should always be made explicit. The early practitioners of Direct Cinema were more literal-minded. They introduced authenticity into film-making by drawing up a kind of filmic ten commandments. One must not rehearse or interview subjects. There must be no lighting, no commentary, no making subjects walk up and down, no redoing of scenes, no lighting or staging of events, no use of dissolves while editing. Among purists at least it was agreed that there should be no use of music to enhance emotional impact or disguise dull moments. Neither set of prescriptions lasted, but they have led to two different traditions which endure to this day.

6 : The 1960s: American Ways

Little Edie, the singer–actor of the Maysles brothers' *Grey Gardens* (1975), in the wilderness of Long Island, performing *Yankee Doodle Dandy*.

It's still possible, when visiting the peeling, cluttered offices of veteran American film-makers, to find, amid fire-hazard mountains of cans of film, the cameras that were used in the 1960s. They are like relics from an extinct age. You'll be surprised how heavy they seem, their lenses battered, the black paint flaking. More often than not they come with a brace screwed onto the base, for shooting from the shoulder, and sometimes, like a souvenir from a war zone, the tape used to hold them together has been left in place. And next to them you'll often find sound equipment, still with a shoulder strap, and tapes left on display to show how it was all done. The sound recorders and cameras have long-forgotten names – Éclair, Arri, Nagra – and they evoke not just a different era in technology, but a different time in film-making, when it was difficult to disguise the presence of cameras, and when indeed the presence of film-makers was a source of interest, pride or hostility. Most film-makers of the 1960s (not all, to be sure) were male. Many of them adopted an aggressive posture, as if the act of filming itself could disturb the universe, creating social change. In a more minimal and exclusively functional sense, if you carried a camera on your shoulder, you could force your way through the ranks of other cameramen, securing the interview that you needed at their expense.

One way or another, the progressives of the 1960s believed not just in action; it seemed better to actually be there and say what happened. That was what many exponents of high culture – not least Susan Sontag, with her formulation against interpretation in art – told the new generation of students. This was a new idea in the 1960s, and it played to the strengths of documentary film. What was the point of telling people what was happening, when they could see it each night? Film-makers couldn't escape the upheaval of the time, and they didn't want to. A generation older than the students, they thronged the campuses or ventured into the no-go areas of American cities, setting out to record events.

Medium Cool is Haskell Wexler's 1969 hybrid doc-and-feature essay in illusion and reality. For Wexler and his walk-on, somewhat colourlessly macho cameraman protagonist, the lens is the ultimate protagonist. Wexler's work is embedded in his native Chicago, and even when it's not on display the camera dominates the action. He was an accomplished feature-film cameraman who had also made documentaries. Commissioned to adapt a novel about a small boy playing truant, instead he criss-crossed the chaotic America of 1968 in search of reality. The script appears to have been written as filming progressed, forming a contemporary style as it happened. We open with a series of remarks at a posh penthouse party in Chicago. Here, preserved for us, are the Great Media Questions of the 1960s. Are images ever truly real? What happens to the recipients of media attention when they are filmed? Are what were known as corporate media capable of depicting reality, or is it futile to imagine that those working in 'corporate media' are capable of giving an accurate representation of what is really going on? Wexler's film wrestles with these questions. Don't look for answers, it tells us, just try looking.

We start in Washington, where the tents of the March Against

Poverty are pitched in mud. Then we go to a mocked-up hotel kitchen in Chicago, similar to the one in which RFK died. Now we poke through a disintegrating Chicago, from hospital to rifle ranges to apartments in which black militants are holed up. There are interesting scenes in a hillbilly white ghetto, with a single mother and her bright uneducated boy as a token reference to the film Wexler was making.

But Wexler's eye is taken by the apocalypse of politics. In the style of the times, he believes in direct action. Real is real, to be sure, but how real is that? And can we ever really get enough of the real? Wexler films his own actor cameraman pretending to film a training camp of the National Guard, with fake tear gas and actors playing demonstrators. Many 1960s efforts at riffing on truth and fiction now seem over-literal, but Wexler's are intense, coming from some serious need to establish that what he is doing isn't trivial. He goes at things in the style of Saul Bellow's Augie Marsh, also from Chicago. He really is authentic – the overused adjective of approval of those days. It's hard not to be astonished by the culminating scenes filmed at the ill-fated Chicago Democratic Convention in the steamy summer of 1968. Here Wexler's single hillbilly mother, in a canary yellow dress, navigates among lines of National Guardsmen as she looks for her son. This must be the only Hollywood-funded film completed in the midst of a riot in progress, and as Wexler must have intended, it out-Godards Godard. There's enough reality here to satisfy even the most jaded, media-hostile activist, and it somehow makes up for the faux-Antonioni culmination in which Wexler, having dispatched his protagonists in a car crash, appears briefly in front of camera in a scene reminiscent of Hitchcock's cameos. He tells you it's all real.

Meanwhile, distant from Hollywood, and almost any reliable source of money, working in isolation, the best documentary film-makers appear to have been doing something different. What was the best way to make a film now that it was so much easier to capture aspects of reality? The question of what documentaries were for seemed less interesting to practitioners.

Outside film studies, this world of film-makers has tended to be ignored, and they've been treated as one among many subsets of the progressive, activist culture of the time. The film-maker Paul Almond began making films in the late 1960s, and I asked him how these films appeared at the time. 'There was all the hippy and demonstration stuff in the 1960s,' he said, 'and that became hard to ignore – young people went for that. But the documentary film culture had different roots. The film-makers were a bit older and they had done different things. Al Maysles was a trained psychologist, and Fred Wiseman instructed students in the intricacies of law. You didn't go to university in order to learn how to make a documentary film. No one really knew what a film was. So they began to experiment, turning film to their own uses.'

The *cinéma vérité* found in French movies and American Direct Cinema is now lost in the past. Robert Drew had flown bombers over Italy in World War II, surviving for months behind the lines. He was the ultimate film-maker of American straightforwardness. He wanted to know how reporting could be made more truthful, but he was most interested in the degree of truth that could be captured on film, and this took him inexorably away from the existing conventions of reportage. Why explain what was happening if the new technology allowed you not just to see it, but to experience it, too? Why paraphrase? Drew, with characteristic bluntness, studied the question of why documentaries were boring. Like most of his generation, he went to work at Henry Luce's Time Life, persuading his bosses to set up a film division, to which he brought young film-makers like Al Maysles, Rick Leacock and Donn Pennebaker. It appears to have been Drew who came up with the somewhat unappealing term 'Direct Cinema', though it never amounted to much more than the notion that you had to be closer, as proffered many years before by Robert Capa. Too much commentary, beloved by network executives, created distance between viewers and what was observed. As Drew's more radical successors later said, why impose corporate views on reality?

All this may seem obvious to us now. Depressingly, it has become known as 'fly-on-the-wall' television. In the 1960s, it was fresh, mind-altering. You really can see what is going on. Look carefully, and you can see more than what the participants, busy with their own versions of what was around them, saw. Documentary film is in this respect revolutionary. It evolved organically; it was truthful and not safe from exploitation. In a simple way (though Drew and his fellow practitioners never said this), audiences can be nudged into deciphering film, becoming authors of what they observe. Drew and his fellow liberals believed, along with the elite of the time, that democracy could be improved – people could become better citizens. This is the idealism that makes these 1960s films so hauntingly important and fresh. They really do tell us something important about democracy.

The great breakthrough of Drew and his colleagues can be seen in *Primary* (1960), which recounts the efforts of the forty-two-year-old senator John F. Kennedy to become the 1960 Democratic candidate. The film contains one of the most famous shots in the history of documentaries. We first see JFK from behind, entering a hall packed with his supporters somewhere in Wisconsin. The crowd parts as he enters, but reluctantly, and for the next two minutes he makes his way from one supporter to the next, shaking hands, chatting, doing all the things that politicians must go to some school to learn, except that he does it better than the rest of the pack – we can see that at once. Robert Drew, Al Maysles, Donn Pennebaker and Ricky Leacock all worked on *Primary*, and it flawlessly fulfils the new criteria for Direct Cinema: no set-up scenes, no messing about with musical scores, no interviews, just scene after tidily constructed scene. In Wisconsin, Kennedy ('a millionaire, Catholic and Easterner', as the tersely written and delivered commentary informs us) confronted the 'Happy Warrior' Hubert Humphrey, a stalwart of the Democratic Party, bumbling, indefatigable and, as poor Hubert touchingly concedes, just a little dull. Superman, as Norman Mailer observed in a contemporary book of essays, had come to the supermarket, and this is the story told by Drew and his mates.

But the film has a different resonance now, showing in scene after scene (often incidentally, in the corner of the screen, or when the election scenes open up onto wider vistas) what small-town white America was like. This isn't a rich place at all and people don't have good teeth, though they wouldn't think of themselves as being poor. Into this America, looking like candidates for a picture spread in *Hello!* magazine, come JFK and Jackie. Jack hasn't yet acquired his mature turns of phrase, as he speaks in a gravitas-aspiring I'm-not-Irish monotone, while her voice is surprisingly squeaky. They seem cold and removed, ill at ease, like minor European royalty given a less than pleasant assignment. They look as if they want to get home to Georgetown. Nonetheless, they are far from ordinary. We know that Humphrey will be vanquished, that he will always seem second-best, a failure in the brutal game of politics, but he fits better into this harsh America of failures than they do.

Ultimately, following a well-established pattern in documentary film-making, Drew found Time Life too restrictive and corporate a place, and he left, creating Drew Associates. Witnesses, also predictably, described conditions at the new venture as chaotic. 'It was hell, particularly if you were a woman,' one survivor explained. *Primary* had been screened for the Kennedy brothers, and it had given JFK ideas about how film might be used to further his own purposes in government. Out of a series of meetings in which Kennedy was determined to seek a suitable opportunity came Drew's second, wholly remarkable political film, *Crisis* (1963). This is the astonishing account of the stand-off between the Kennedy brothers and George Wallace, the governor of Alabama, over the admission of two black students to the University of Alabama. Drew and his colleagues were able to film the confrontation as it occurred. This was to be the first time that anyone was allowed to film the progress of a crisis from inside the Oval Office. The film was, in a real sense, a commissioned piece, made for propagandistic purposes, but it never had the air of representing any official position.

The closest anyone had come to a depiction of power had been CBS's Ed Murrow's ill-fated guided tour of the White House, in the hands of a faltering Jackie. The film starts with intercut breakfast scenes of Bobby Kennedy and Governor Wallace, in the Montgomery, Alabama, gubernatorial residence and in the Virginia suburb where Bobby lived with his outsize Catholic family. We get to see, pertinently, that Bobby's cute blond children are looked after by a black nanny. Drew is a freak for details, a small-scale, shot-by-shot addict of incremental insights. Much of the film is given to describing the build-up to the crisis in RFK's Department of Justice and around the Montgomery campus. There are interviews in which elderly segregationists get a chance to say, absurdly, that blacks will be happier not being at university with whites. These are assertions that the film is quick to contradict, but it never judges such people adversely.

The political-media process proves fascinating, as we see it unfold in one detailed scene after another. *Crisis* is the first film account, perhaps the first coherent account in any medium, of the interpenetration of media and gesture in the new politics. The Kennedys wish to crush Wallace, while giving the impression that they have been generous and broad-minded in extinguishing him and his ideas; they cannot afford to do otherwise, given the need to retain support for the Democratic Party in an increasingly hostile south. They must at least appear to be fair. To this end they dispatch an aide, the bald, charismatic, chain-smoking Nick Katzenbach, to Alabama. Governor Wallace, of course, understands that he has been beaten, but he plays for the network cameras by being defeated gracefully, in the southern style. In its depiction of politics, *Crisis* remains a film that uncovers what goes on behind the scenes, in a way evoking the fictional *The West Wing*. But it is also something more: a ringing, utterly convincing depiction of the 'values' of a liberal America that is bent on activism, and also of how people should behave. It helps that the Kennedys aren't wholly likable, and that it isn't clear whether they care much about the fate of the two black students whose future they're sponsoring. They are interested in their own reputation, but on this occasion this coincides with the way America should be seen or experienced by its citizens. At one point, rocking in one of the less than comfortable office chairs favoured by the Kennedys as relics of Cape Cod upper-crust life, RFK says how bad the crisis has been for the reputation of the US.

The American upheaval, however, could be recorded in a less earnest way. We can still experience how sudden it was, changing everything about the country irrevocably, by watching the music documentaries of the time, from *Monterey Pop* (1968) to *Woodstock* (1970). It is like watching a culture unbutton itself and then undress completely. On a more intimate scale, film-makers could begin to examine the sudden arrival of celebrity on the scene. Careful about how their properties appeared, agents and studio PR people proved happily negligent when it came to film-makers. *Meet Marlon Brando* (1966), from Drew's cameraman associate Albert Maysles, now working with his brother David, showed the star acting bored and insouciant when it came to promoting a mediocre film, flirting outrageously with a female journalist and taking the piss out of the appalling accent of a Frenchman, to a comic effect the great man never attained otherwise. But it was another of Drew's finds, Donn Pennebaker, who invented the modern documentary as a serious cultural form. Pennebaker is in his nineties now, as nice and unassuming as people say he always has been, but it's nonetheless hard to believe that he didn't know quite what he was doing when he received the assignment of accompanying the hardly known Robert Zimmerman on his 1965 tour of Britain. 'No, I really didn't know who he was, really I didn't,' he says. 'I'd left Drew because I wanted to work on my own. I wanted to be a genius, you see. I had a family and I worked two years in advertising, and this job came along.'

The action starts with Dylan holding up cards to match the lyrics of 'Subterranean Homesick Blues', while the poet Allen Ginsberg lurks further down a shabby mews. Pennebaker says that this wasn't his idea at all; it 'just seemed to occur to us all'. It would seem that Dylan wasn't really aware of performing for the camera; he, too, like the people he and Pennebaker encountered, didn't know what a documentary was. In between jump cuts and jerky pans, there are set pieces of brilliantly unadorned spot-on film-making. The troubadour trashes interviewers, talks kindly about inspiration to teenage fans in Liverpool, drives from one seedy hotel suite to another in hearse-like black monster cars and gawps at the interior of the Albert Hall. In the background, there is a constant reminder that this is the Swinging Sixties, heralded by *Time* magazine and touted as evidence of a newly hedonist, post-imperial Britain that didn't really exist outside a few postal districts in chic and entitled west London. Dylan isn't the cosiest person you've ever met, and he doesn't enjoy the presence of the pompous or ungifted. Asked by *Time* if he cares what he sings, he shoots back: 'How could I answer that if you have the nerve to ask me?' The reporter Horace Freeland Judson appears as a model for the eponymous Mr Jones in Dylan's 'Ballad of a Thin Man', and his exchange with Bob is an unsurpassable 1960s moment. 'If I'm going to find out anything, I'm not going to read *Time* magazine,' Dylan says, taking aim at America's most influential source of information, ''cause they just got too much to lose by printing the truth.'

Time: What is really the truth?
Dylan: Oh, you know, a plain picture of, let's say, a tramp
    vomiting, man, into the sewer. You know, and next door to

the picture, Mr. Rockefeller, or Mr. C. W. Jones, you know, on the subway going to work, any kind of picture. Just make some sort of collage of pictures which they don't do. They don't do . . . Because the guy that's writing the article is sitting at a desk in New York, he's not, he is not even going out of his office. He's going to get, all these fifteen, ah, you know, reporters, and they're gonna send him a quota, you know.

Time: That's not me . . .

Judson believed that the confrontation was contrived for entertainment. 'That evening', he said, 'I went to the concert. My opinion then and now was that the music was unpleasant, the lyrics inflated, and Dylan a self-indulgent, whining show-off.'

There was, it would seem, no written contract for the film, and no one interfered. Dylan came to see the completed cut, sitting through it in the dark, and said: 'That's fine.' He then left without another word. Donovan, the British Dylan, is the butt of many of Dylan's borderline cruel jokes, and somewhere around minute thirty you can witness Dylan's attempts at typing as an accompaniment to his then girlfriend Joan Baez's marvellous voice, before he gives up, awed by her and unable to complete the song he's working on. 'Bad news, bad news came to me where I sleep,' she sings. 'Turn, turn, turn again.' This is the real stuff of 1960s culture, from which our own was made. A *Guardian* reporter assures us that 'the bearded boys and the lank-haired girls, all eyeshadow and undertaker lipstick, applaud the song and miss, perhaps, the message'. The Dylan phenomenon wasn't as simple as that, even in those days; his own performance affected audiences as much as his lyrics. But he was going to change the way we looked at the world, and Pennebaker had found a film language capable of making what he had to say natural. The film still has the power to imply that everything could have been so different, while telling you just how it was in the 1960s, when it all did seem authentic.

Like others of his generation, Pennebaker continued to make films for the next forty years. He filmed concerts, such as David Bowie's *Ziggy Stardust* (1973), and, with his partner Chris Hegedus, edited several years later the remarkable footage from a rowdy and absorbing debate about feminism in New York that Pennebaker 'happened to have shot', creating *Town Bloody Hall* (1979). The film captured the state of feminism in 1971 and was left half edited in the style typical of Pennebaker, who tended to have numerous projects on the go at once. Germaine Greer and Norman Mailer aren't the stars, but they describe the New York feminist scene that Betty Friedan, Jill Johnston and Susan Sontag wrote about at the time. Pennebaker later said: 'I couldn't have done it without Chris Hegedus.' Hegedus is the architect of the films, with a vision of the features that could emerge from their recordings. She understands the stories from the inside and can picture how the final film will look. Pennebaker–Hegedus films are, like their makers, distinctively American in their optimism, without authorial intervention or, unless it was strictly necessary, interviews. *The War Room* (1993) was their most spectacular result, a flawless, non-judgemental rendering of Bill Clinton's new electoral management techniques, which led, despite setbacks caused by the candidate's liability to scandal, to his election. The only recommendation Pennebaker has given to film-makers is that they should read a lot and be watchers. 'The world isn't that depressing,' he said. 'It may seem so, but that's because you don't watch enough. I think it's important.'

As a psychology graduate, Albert Maysles made his first film, *Psychiatry in Russia* (1955), in Russian mental institutions. Unexpectedly, the film doesn't focus on the abuses perpetrated on dissidents at the time. Instead, it's a somewhat scholarly account of the Pavlovian therapies utilised by Russian doctors, and how these fitted in with the notion that in a socialist utopia no one could be mentally sick, only temporarily out of kilter with the legitimate collective aims of society expressed through labour and normality. Maysles contrasts the brutal practicality of the Russian system with the Freudian views prevalent in the US, but he shows, too, how poor the Soviet Union is, afflicted with alcoholism. There is a very Mayslesian acknowledgement that the stressed, underpaid and dedicated doctors are doing their best under difficult circumstances. In 1962, Maysles and his brother David set up their own company and began to make their own films. I met Al when he was in his late seventies, and once spent two mornings with him in Rio, in search of the right pair of trainers. Shortly before his death, I spent an evening with him in southern Israel, near the wire-strewn fortified border. Like Pennebaker, he was the ultimate optimist, the bearer of happy and uplifting illustrations regarding the applicability of his film-making practices to everyday life. 'Reality is providential,' was one Mayslesism, delivered in the style of a contemporary Benjamin Franklin. He really did believe that his art was improving mankind. 'You don't need a point of view,' was another.

Maysles believed that it was best not to approach anything with preconceptions. If one remained devoid of dogma, it was easier to find out the truth. Another Mayslesism, carefully cultivated, was that his short attention span had made it easier to become a great documentary cameraman. 'I can't focus on things long enough,' he said, when our conversation flagged. 'It really helped me, because I was always thinking and looking at what would come next.'

In 1967, the Maysles began work on what seems like the most improbable success of that decade. While their contemporaries were focused on the new culture of revolt and hedonism, they went in search of Bible salesmen. As an undergraduate, I worked for two weeks as an ad salesman in the Empire State Building. We were paid next to nothing if we didn't sell, and the successes of our colleagues – they were often old and had spent twenty years at the game – were posted on a board. Selling is what drives everything in the world, but few films describe what it is to sell. Meet the Gipper, the Rabbit, the Bull and the Badger (*Salesman*, 1969), four middle-aged men in bad suits trying to sell Bibles in New Jersey and Florida. They aren't big on the scriptures; they are lost and borderline-impoverished people, some Catholic, some not, attempting to sell fifty-dollar illustrated Bibles. The Maysles brothers paid for this masterpiece, and it seems to have cost a not wholly inconsiderable sum. They distributed it themselves, and it cannot have made much money on its first screenings. But Vincent Canby, the all-powerful film czar of the *New York Times*, liked it:

For one reason and another, I've seen *Salesman* three times, and each time I've been more impressed by what I can only describe as the decency of that point of view. The movie's lower-middle-class, Roman Catholic-oriented landscape is not particularly pretty, nor are the indistinguishable hotels (the film was shot in New Jersey, Chicago and Florida) or indeed the hard-sell tactics employed by the salesmen as they pitch their $49.95 Bibles to lonely widows, Cuban refugees, boozy housewives, and to one young couple that can't even pay its rent. 'Be sure to have it blessed,' a salesman reminds a customer to whom he's just made a sale, 'or you won't get the full benefit from it.'

Canby was shrewd in spotting the decency of *Salesman*. Everyone in the movie seems to soak up the Maysles' empathy, even the Mid-American Bible Company's pious 'theological consultant', Melbourne I. Feltman, who, at the Chicago convention of sellers from throughout the US, urges the salesmen to go about their 'Father's work', adding: 'God grant you an abundant harvest.' *Salesman* goes beyond a spirit of mockery; this is because the salesmen really are no less vulnerable than their customers. Take Paul Brennan's performance as a cocky, beady-eyed drummer who finally succumbs to 'negative thoughts' after a long period of being unable to make a sale. 'I don't want to seem negative,' he confesses to a colleague as he drives aimlessly through the fake Moorish architecture of Opa-locka, Florida, after a fruitless day, 'but all I can see here is delinquent accounts.'

While they were at college, Al and his brother had worked as salesmen – the equivalent, in American business, of the much-reviled yet also loved Japanese salaryman. Brennan knows too much about what he is doing to do it even adequately, and thus fails. What are we to make of this insight? *Salesman* has become more and more appropriate with each passing year. It doesn't matter what is sold – Bibles, trainers, political nostrums – the law of the market, which is based on the poor attention span of customers and salesmen alike, dictates that from Donald Trump downwards, they will all, finally, become obsolescent. Faithful to their principles as makers of Direct Cinema, the Maysles neither celebrate this insight nor do they bemoan it. Unlike the Bibles he sells, unsuccessfully, Paul Brennan shows us the way. But it's a way to nowhere much, which may tell you something about our world.

The Maysles' biggest and darkest success came, appropriately, by accident. They were commissioned to record the 1969 Rolling Stones tour of the US, which ended with what was supposed to be a 'West Coast Woodstock': a free concert at the Altamont Speedway, near San Francisco, attended by more than 300,000, which was held to make up for the fact that the Stones hadn't performed at Woodstock, thus abdicating their deserved place in the pantheon of the counterculture. Far from replicating the peace and love of Woodstock, however, Altamont proved to be a disaster. Four people died, one of them stabbed by the Hells Angels tasked with keeping fans away from the stage. The Maysles were present throughout the violence, and they continued to film from their ringside perspective. They would be criticised for this, but one must be thankful that they did. *Gimme Shelter* (1970) is something distinctly more interesting than even the ultimate in rock films. Later, the Maysles intercut the slippage into anarchy as the Stones perform with the bemused, borderline impassive reactions of Mick Jagger and Charlie Watts as they view the scenes on an editing machine. At the time, *Gimme Shelter* appeared to depict the end of the 1960s. No, humans liberated from society weren't ennobled, Rousseau-style; it was stupid to have even temporarily nursed such illusions. Was Jagger's style of pouting and dancing a cause of the mayhem, or were the Stones, who seem nonplussed, lost for words, as little in control as anyone else?

I first saw *Gimme Shelter* in Manhattan's West Side on a rainy afternoon, and I emerged dazed and beaten. Was this what we'd come to? Watch it now, however, and it becomes possible to strip out much of the cosmic angst of the *fin de* 1960s. These days we're jaded by screen violence, but the stabbing of Meredith Hunter hasn't lost its power. I suspect younger audiences today would be more shocked by the huge quantities of drugs consumed and the berserk, orgiastic bad sex on display. But the film offended many of those who flocked to see it. In her *New Yorker* column, the critic Pauline Kael (who had also attacked *Salesman*, alleging that it was inauthentic and heavily staged) suggested that the Maysles brothers had somehow created a vast reality show in which 'events were created to be photographed', and that the murder wouldn't have happened without their collusion. The Maysles responded to her claims with indignation. 'No actors were used in *Salesman*,' they said in a letter to the magazine that was never published. 'Miss Kael seems to be implying that we, as film-makers, are responsible for the events we film by suggesting that we set them up or helped stage them.' Surely, however, the Maysles were right in this instance, though one could also suggest that Ms Kael was prematurely on the button, anticipating by several decades what may ultimately be seen as a consequence of the 1960s film-making tradition: the widespread setting-up of events for what became known as 'reality television'. *Gimme Shelter* is a far more straightforward exercise in looking at what is in front of you. Far from being an epitaph for the 1960s, the film describes, in astonishing detail, what happened at Altamont. It depicts without second thoughts the campy insolence of Mick Jagger in his prime and remains one of the best accounts of the raw power of rock 'n' roll, even as it reminds us how poorly organised concerts can end in mayhem. At the very least, the Stones appear to have been disturbed by what they had set in motion.

Grey Gardens (1975) is the first documentary to stage an experiment in real-life performance, turning its raw material into an odd, yet wholly appealing, hybrid. This isn't a profile of its two characters, though it seems to be such in the first few minutes. The Maysles brothers appear in the film, but not as its authors. It belongs entirely to its protagonists, Big and Little Edie. Ultimately, all we know about their lives comes from them, and *Grey Gardens*, one of the greatest films of past decades, exists as their autobiography. Throughout, there are echoes of Tennessee Williams, and certain scenes appear made for the stage; this is how the two women act out their lives. For them, and ultimately for us as we watch, the performance is real – and it's superior to anything one can see in the theatre. The film charts the bizarre survival of a mother and daughter living in poverty and decrepitude as members of the American upper class. 'It's very hard to live nowadays,' says Big Edie. 'Everything is very hard.' She lives with her daughter, Little Edie, in a twenty-eight-room house in the posh resort of East Hampton, surrounded by dozens of cats, opened cans of food and yellowing copies of New York tabloids. The pretext of the film was a decision by Big Edie's niece, Jackie Onassis, to contribute $30,000 – a sizeable sum in those days – towards stopping their house from falling to pieces. The Maysles' film satisfies any level of prurient curiosity in its investigation of high-tone family members fallen on evil times. But it is also a film of a unique, starry performance and, more touchingly, an account of how, in desperation and loneliness, humans cling together. Big and Little Edie re-rehearse their pasts continuously, as if they are about to bring off a final act. But the act turns out to be their own lives; acting is what they have left, for each other, and for the neighbours (who appear in a cringe-making dinner), the handyman (whose efforts they constantly contrast with previous handymen) and, of course, the Maysles, who double up as inter-lopers and unique recorders at what often seems to be a court of sorts. You feel sorry for Little Edie, with her bizarre snoods and curtain-or-towel dresses. She reads from astrology books about the wisdom of acquiring a Libra husband, and tells us that her mother stopped her from marrying into the Obolensky fam-ily, as if we would all know who they were. One can choose to believe these things or not, but it is clear that she gave her life away by sequestering herself with her mother and the cats. She does seem to enjoy the ceaseless exchanges with her mother, and in a remarkable scene shows us that her own life skills go beyond acting out her own past – to swimming. 'I tell you, if there's any-thing worse than a staunch woman . . . S-T-A-U-N-C-H . . .' is how she describes her own father's absence of real regard for her, and her performances – most of all the terrific *Yankee Doodle Dandy* number in the main hall, happily free of cats – are ter-rific. The photos of her mother and herself as debutantes, a life before them, are heart-rending. *Grey Gardens* has been the basis of a musical (Little Edie did a wildly unsuccessful cabaret act) and an HBO movie. Innumerable camp routines have emerged from the travails of Big and Little Edie. But the two women remain sig-nificant because they are, as they no doubt wish to be, capable of describing the final years of the old American rich. They are great characters, too, as they know; in the idiom of their class, troupers.

Documentaries and feature films give a sense of the times in which they were made. They are portraits of their decade. This can mean that films have only brief windows of relevance. However, these 1960s films, although tied to their time, seem to increase in relevancy with age.

Another series that originated in the 1960s and spread through time and space to the present is the Fred Wiseman cycle. It comes as a shock to think that Wiseman's forty-plus-year experiment of chronicling American institutions through the medium of documentary film began so long ago. Wiseman has become the dominant figure in American documentary film-making, probably the individual who has most influenced the way in which documentary films are made and discussed. In the US, and probably elsewhere, you cannot think of making a film without acknowledging, if only in reaction to them, the ideas of Wiseman. But it would be wrong to think of him as a dogmatic figure. He has never told anyone how to make a film. What he has done, in his rare and usually laconic pronouncements, is give a full account of how he makes his films, and how he came to his own conclusions about film-making.

Wiseman's father came to the US from Romania in 1890, aged five, and became a lawyer, taking care of the interests of Jewish refugees from persecution in his spare time. His mother wanted to be an actress but ended up keeping house and cultivating what Wiseman describes as a great talent for mimicry, which she passed on to her son, along with the ability to listen, patiently and endlessly. Wiseman, by his own account, wasn't a good student, but what he most enjoyed was sitting in the comfortable chairs of a library reading poetry. He came to film, unusually, after teaching law at university. In his somewhat enigmatic, terse account of how his films are made, he makes it clear that he doesn't really like documentaries, rarely watching them. He was influenced by a spell in 1950s Paris, where he encountered the work of Samuel Beckett, and by what used to be called 'close reading' – the highly textual study of poetry popular in universities during the 1950s, practised by professors eager to discipline their students through exposure to literary culture. Although Wiseman claims to have disliked law, a contentious lawyer's passion for literal accuracy seems to have stuck with him, defining the rigour present in his films, as well as their remorseless adherence to detail.

Wiseman treats the sequences in his films as if they were lawyers' briefs, to be worked on again and again. His films are constructed from words, laboriously assembled. Wiseman doesn't pre-interview or 'research' his subjects. He prefers to walk straight into the place or institution that he has chosen. Filming is based on 'hunches', and he's careful to shoot a considerable amount of material. Wiseman painstakingly creates his films out of individual incidents. They follow each other in sequence, like our own life encounters, as if we were making a film while trying not to adhere to the conventions of narrative. He records sound (rare for directors) and (still rarer) edits his own films. There's no music in them, and sequences are always shown in the order in which they were shot, though some are omitted. For Wiseman, editing is how the film becomes a 'fiction'. Through the process of assembling and reassembling, the material ceases to be borderline random, acquiring whatever meaning he chooses to extract from it. The meaning is a gift of Wiseman's, who is the films' author. But it's always clear that the films retain their own autonomy, and they can be 'read' in different ways. Thus, they remain a gift offered by reality to us, though it's also clear that the gift is ultimately Wiseman's.

Describing his editing process, Wiseman can sound like a long-lost existentialist come back from the 1950s Parisian Left Bank with gold in his hands:

I have to constantly ask myself the following kinds of questions: Why are the participants saying what they are saying? What are the implications of the choice of words spoken or not spoken? What is the significance of a gesture, a tone or change of tone, a look, a walk? What inferences can be made from choice of clothes? I do not know if I am right about the inferences I make, but I have to have a theory about what is occurring in order to make the choices as to whether I want to use the sequence, how I am going to edit it, and finally, if and when I might place it in the film.

The rest of us might think of such a process as a canny rearrangement of recorded reality, making so-called 'real life' less messy, but Wiseman says he is creating a 'fiction'. He adds:

> The film has to work for me on a literal level and at its periphery as a metaphor or at least an abstract statement that is more than the literal meaning of each sequence. While there is no way of my knowing what influenced me, I like to think that the greatest influence on my editing of the films has been the attention to close reading I was taught in college and the novels and poems I have since tried to read with care.

When I read this, some small disruption of consciousness occurred to me. I, too, was once addicted to 'close reading', spending hours juggling the effects of metaphor and rational exposition in difficult texts. I set up my own experiment, resolving to 'read' Wiseman's films. For close to a week, I sat in an intense Paris heatwave, watching early Wiseman in a smallish hotel room. At times, I imagined myself in the midst of an existentialist narrative of my own creation: 'The Man Who Loved Wiseman'. From time to time I did venture out in search of steaks or Chinese food; I indulged more frequently in glasses of wine. But I was never bored by the experience for a moment; I was captivated. Wiseman's films aren't like the 'non-fiction novels' of his time. Never quite fragmentary, they do have narrative qualities. But the narratives relate to the individual lives that we see, as is normal in life. The novelty of his method consists in the way that every scene is exploratory. Many of these experiments don't quite come off, but the failures are not without significance, because they enable us to consider why or how such successes come to us. What does it mean to understand anything? If we knew that, we would certainly understand life better, and maybe participate more skilfully in our exchanges with our fellow humans. Wiseman insists that all this isn't easy. All he can do, legitimately, is show how it might be done. I finished the week wishing that I'd staged the same experiment many years earlier. If I had, my life would have been significantly different, though I am still not sure in what way.

I remain uncertain that Wiseman's work is truly fictional, because it is purposive, unlike 'real' fiction, seeking to document the way in which Americans try and often fail to coexist. Wiseman constructs his stories depending on what he has reclaimed from oblivion – once in filming, the second time in editing. His work lacks the miraculous fictional capability of somehow finding out more and more, as door after door opens up, one corridor and room after another. But I can't reproach Wiseman for this apparent failure. The meaning of film is a hard taskmistress. What you find out from observation is limited by what you cannot find out, and Wiseman is honest enough to depict this. I think that he does often manage to find an 'abstract statement' – or let's just say that he does so on good days. Interestingly, and rarely remarked upon, is the limited use of narrative in his films. The concept of 'closure' would not mean anything to him, nor indeed would the Hollywood-derived idea that film-makers must try to leave their audiences in a place that is happier than where they found them. Instead, he asks us to begin to decipher questions such as: how do we begin to comprehend what's around us? Is there anything to comprehend? Is there really anything that can give us comfort? From my overheated Paris week, I concluded that Wiseman offers illumination and frustration in equal portions.

I met Wiseman a few times. He struck me as formidably determined, not just in defence of his films, but in his non-tolerance of whatever bores him. I'm sure this is a consequence of having listened to so many thousands of hours of often inconsequential human goings-on, and then attempting to transform them. Wiseman isn't, as film-maker Errol Morris has suggested, a misanthrope. He's tolerant; I sense that he even sometimes likes his fellow humans. But his films aren't always optimistic about the prospects of humanity, though they can be funny. In the 1950s, when he was a young man, sociologists used to write about how individuals might survive in what was beginning to be referred to as 'mass society'. Wiseman isn't a sociologist or a political scientist. He has a deep aversion to elites and offers no solutions that I can discern. But he is exercised by the struggle of humans to survive, and not just as a lepidopterist might look at butterflies. In much of his work, he looks on with sheer admiration at the successes humans achieve by merely staying alive. I think this is his legacy. If we don't think of ourselves as individuals, how can we live?

His first masterpiece, *Titicut Follies* (1967), was filmed within the sombre premises of Bridgewater State Hospital, a place run mostly by the inmates and a few scattered staff. Many have described the film as a vision of hell, and its long penumbral shots in which the naked and vulnerable bodies are seen in counterpoint with the uniforms of guards recall Ken Kesey's 1962 novel *One Flew Over the Cuckoo's Nest* and the successful 1975 film that was based upon it. Many scenes look like the black-and-white raw material of Francis Bacon's paintings. I marvelled at its bleak, involving images of solitude. There's nothing to praise in *Titicut Follies*, and yet the film isn't an assault on contemporary psychiatric practices. Although the inmates are locked away in cells, they aren't wholly in isolation from their guards. The first and last scenes, in which the inmates perform their annual variety show with the guards, tell a story of crude, often patronising collaboration between society and those who are locked away. There's the notorious scene in which a guard shaves Jim, a raucous old man, while the others ask him whether he's going to soil his cell again. 'Shit isn't important,' old man Jim says; it's clear that the ritual – shitting and cleaning up – is performed each day. Joshing the old man is what the guards do, and they ask him, not unaffectionately, what he used to be. Enraged, his mouth cut by clumsy shaving, Jim screams that he was once a teacher.

Wiseman regretted the editing of another scene in which the force-feeding of a patient is intercut with the preparation of his dead body: he thought it violated his strict injunctions about never going out of chronological order, and it gave the impression that the man had died as a consequence of being given too high a dosage of meds and then being force-fed. But the scene doesn't give that impression: one can think of the images of the dead man as some sort of an ending to his torment. This is how we all end, the scene seems to say. My second viewing enforced the sense of how difficult it is to 'draw conclusions' from Wiseman's work. It really isn't clear exactly what messages he wants us to draw from his film, and maybe it shouldn't be. It would be better if places like Bridgewater didn't exist, but they do. At the very least, we should know what happens in them. There's another scene in which a young patient, Vladimir, confronts a board of experts, requesting to be let out. We never find out what's really wrong with him, and he suggests that he's getting sicker as a consequence of his time in Bridgewater. Can facilities like this make people mad? The board appear confused by his suggestions, but they aren't hostile. Like the guards, they're nonplussed by the phenomenon of madness. They fall back on rote language and routine. Vladimir is classified as a schizophrenic and not released. I feel I know what Wiseman felt.

Titicut Follies is one of the most important works of the 1960s, but it wasn't shown widely for many years. In 1967, the government of Massachusetts tried to get it banned, claiming that it violated the patients' integrity, despite the fact that Wiseman had permission from the hospital authorities. In a series of legal wrangles, Massachusetts judges first ordered the film to be destroyed, then banned its general release – the first time that a film was banned in the US for reasons other than obscenity, immorality or national security. It was shown only in 1991, after a judge finally ruled that so many years later 'privacy concerns' were less applicable. Wiseman, however, always believed that the privacy criteria invoked before the courts were misleading. Rather, politicians were embarrassed by the existence of places like Bridgewater, and the film was banned for that reason. He was right to draw this conclusion.

I set out to watch Wiseman's late-1960s films and found I could do this without wanting to venture into the overheated streets. I might feel I was tiring of the relentless application of the Wiseman method, but when I did, I began to try to calculate how many hours he must have stood silently, mike in hand, listening; and how he then had the patience first to view the same material prior to editing, and then watch it several times more as he edited the sequences, cutting as much as an hour down to five or seven minutes. Increasingly, in their examination of so-called social reality, film-makers are drawn to the extreme and the deviant; this is, in part, a concession to how familiar audiences have become with the raw material of hospitals, police stations, etc. Wiseman was lucky to be filming at a moment before television had annexed these subjects. He was also lucky, in those long-lost years when anything was allowed for film-makers, to be able to cast his own coldish eye on anything he wanted. *High School* (1968) is the first attempt on Wiseman's part to penetrate the apparent normality of American institutions. What could appear more normal than a school with three thousand pupils in a mainly white, Jewish suburb of Philadelphia? Critics tend to focus on the authoritarian aspects of the teachers and what the film reveals about the collision between authority and the youth of the late 1960s, but the film is richer and more equivocal in its message. There are cringe-making classes in deportment for the girls and grotesque, snigger-inducing lectures to the boys about respecting virginity, etc. Through the bizarre chemistry-lab effort to simulate space travel, however, it becomes clear that respect for mainstream America isn't unpopular. One Jewish teacher boldly tries to interest an indifferent class in the music of Simon and Garfunkel. 'It's nice to be individualistic,' the teacher says. 'There are certain places to be individualistic.'

How and where individuals can survive receives additional attention in Wiseman's surveys of a Harlem hospital (*Hospital*, 1970) and the Kansas City police force (*Law and Order*, 1969). It might seem difficult to ask anyone to revisit an emergency room, now that the experience is a staple of peak-time television, but Wiseman's film, the first to provide such an experience, is rawer than its successors, more probing. The film spares us neither the helplessness and embarrassment of the patients nor the uncertainty of the doctors. A fear of death irradiates all procedures at the East Harlem Metropolitan Hospital, but Wiseman's doctors battle on, day by day. Their task isn't just to forestall death, which they appear to manage admirably, but to get the best for their charges out of what was then called 'the system' – the endless bureaucracies into which the poor and the infirm were daily and brutally shoved without ceremony. What should we think of our institutions? Maybe we should begin by looking at them. As Wiseman reminds us, this is no simple task. In *Law and Order*, he visits the Kansas City police. The force is mostly white, and those they catch in the process of committing petty crime are black. But they also help black victims of crime: the best scene in the film involves a white policeman helping a dazed elderly black woman recover her handbag, from which a purse has been stolen. Wiseman's point throughout the film is that policemen are much like us. They have careers and pensions; they want to be paid more; sometimes they make mistakes. But they are doing jobs that we ask them to do, and in that sense they are like us. I'm sure this is true, but sentiments such as these are indeed the staple of thousands and thousands of hours of television. I am not sure that a being from another planet, viewing all of this, would be able to distinguish Wiseman's effort from its rivals.

I once sat next to the author Joan Didion. She admitted to having watched lots of daytime television because it was so boring and she wanted to find out how others watched it. I asked her what was the most boring book that she had ever read, and she said without hesitation that it was Edmund Spenser's *Faerie Queene*. 'I read it at Berkeley,' she said. 'The desk in my room faced the street. I had to turn the desk away not to get distracted by an empty street.' I had felt the same about Spenser, but hour after hour of Wiseman didn't have this effect at all. The argument, patiently delivered in one film after another, is that they need to be that long, as otherwise it would be impossible for him to do justice to the lives of his protagonists. I'd started off being irritated by never knowing who his characters were and never being told what happened to them later. He has shot every scene in every film in every corner of the US, and none of them have conclusions.

These objections dropped away when I watched what still seems to me his best film, *Welfare* (1975), filmed within the social support system of New York. It begins with Polaroid photos of those who enter the system – a reminder that the system, like Jeremy Bentham's Panopticon, exists to keep records of everyone that passes through its various portals. Then we see rows of people waiting, all ages, genders and races. They look tired and battered. They remind me of what Christopher Hitchens once wrote about being seriously ill: that you enter a black-and-white zone. Everything may look the same, but in reality it's different; you know just how impossible it will be to get out of this place. Without acknowledging that this is the case, the people arrayed here are serving some sort of penal sentence – for being poor or inadequate, or simply for having encountered so many troubles in their lives that they have finally gone under. This is the theme

of the exchanges we witness for the next two hours between petitioners – those who are, for one reason or another, rejected and
deemed to be unsuitable – and case workers, guards and those
who, with palpable misgivings, administer the system.

It would be comforting to be able to dismiss the bureaucratic
system with the consoling notion that it's arbitrary or, as is often
suggested, 'Kafkaesque'. Wiseman wants us to see that it is in fact
rational, because there are, in most societies, many poor people,
and they have to be looked after somehow. Not enough money is
made available to treat them well, and this is how we want it to be.
We also want these people dealt with so that we don't encounter
them, because their travails are embarrassing to them, and we'd
rather entertain the fiction that they somehow deserve their fate.
Anywhere you care to look in the so-called developed world, it
is assumed by the fortunate that the poor cheat, abusing the generosity of others. The New York writer A. J. Liebling once wrote
an article entitled 'The Undeserving Poor', in which he tracked
down the story of a poor woman criticised for wearing mink as
she sought assistance. It turned out that the coat was far from
grand. I spent two years of my life making films about poverty
that were to be shown globally, and I made two discoveries. The
first was that poor people have lives that are far more busy and
eventful than everyone else's. Their lives are taken up by activity
– this is evident in the ceaseless, desperate, one-stop-from-the-
end activity on display in Wiseman's film. The second thing is
that people are fascinated by the lives of those who are less eco-
nomically advantaged than themselves. To get them to watch,
one must avoid abstractions, as Wiseman does. It all comes down
very simply to seeing people for what they are and, more importantly, observing how they shape up.

A Chinese film entitled *Petition* (2009) tells the story of a court set up in imperial times, where one might challenge the injustices of officials by posting a petition through a letter box. Petitioners waited, often for years, for a verdict on their case. The Beijing court had been relocated to what looked like a suburban post office, but waiting times were no shorter under communism, so petitioners lived in a slum surrounding the court, often remaining there for as much as seven years awaiting a verdict. Wiseman's petitioners face a similar problem. They don't wait as long, but it seems just as long to them. *Welfare* didn't show the American way to be as casual as the Chinese one, but both assumed that people could wait indefinitely. The American system is never explained to us, but it never appears to lack rationality. Somewhere at the outset of Wiseman's film there's a long conversation about a dog:

> Agent: We're not, we're not giving assistance for your dog.
> Client: I know, I know . . .
> Agent: We're concerned about you, right?
> Client: Between the dog, me and my friend, we work it out. We work it out between me and the dog.
> Agent: In other words, the dog can stay with your friend.
> Client: It's my dog, but I don't know. I don't know if he wants the dog to stay. I'm not sure. That I would have to work out with him. Like I said, I might be able to work out a furniture situation with, or and, the dog, I don't know. But the fact that I came down here was that I was told that I would have a place to go, which is an apartment, and that, and that is where I could take my dog and live, and, and, and work for a living.

Sometimes, out of sheer frustration listening to the plight of others, the state employees crash into these exchanges. It's easy to spot when the agents run out of any pretence of civility. They're exhausted. Some of the addicts, including a beautiful young woman called Valerie, are clearly beyond help, but the case workers do their best, even when they are being shouted at. There is one memorable scene lasting fifteen minutes in which petitioners humiliate a young case worker. A man who describes himself as a veteran insults one of the black guards, and the latter explains, patiently, that he was a veteran, too, in Vietnam, 'in a war that had nothing to do with me'. 'Why are they talking?' another worker asks off-camera. 'Because I have nothing better to do,' the guard explains in fury. And so it goes on; for hours it really does go on. You can be shocked, but never resigned. Nothing Wiseman has done suggests that nothing can be done. He gives the last word to a man who has been ill, whose life is wrecked, and who has been stealing bars of chocolate since his cheque for $147.35 went missing:

I'll wait. I've been waiting for the last hundred and twenty-four days since I got out of hospital, waiting for something. Godot. But you know what happens, you know what happens in the story of Godot. He never came. And that's what I'm waiting for under this great society of ours where everybody is equal under the law, you know. Lincoln said that, didn't he? All men are created equal? Lincoln never took an army physical, you know. He should have known better. What's equality? Equality's when somebody has and somebody hasn't and the one that hasn't tries to rip off the one that has, and the one that has tries to keep what he's got, and there's nothing in the middle any more. It's either you have it or you don't have it.

Forty years later, nothing about *Welfare* has dated, least of all the references to Wiseman's favourite dramatist, Samuel Beckett, the author of *Waiting for Godot*. Among the many lessons of Wiseman's work is that one should never confuse cynicism with the legitimate desire or obligation to shatter illusions. He is the ultimate non- or anti-utopian; like Dylan, he offers the prospect of what can be 'gathered from coincidence'. That may be all that we can legitimately expect, as Wiseman certainly believes. His vision emerged from the 1960s, but it's no less valid in our time.

7 : Ultra-Reportage

Nick Broomfield's *The Leader, His Driver and the Driver's Wife* (1991): the anti-hero, white supremacist Eugène Terre'Blanche, kisses a recalcitrant baby. 'You must be spivvy among spivs, gormless among the ignorant,' says Broomfield.

At one point in my career there was an attempt to make me into a screen presence. I'd never thought of myself in that way; indeed, I'd felt myself disbarred from this activity through lack of hair, a post-Eton mid-Atlantic accent and, worse, a disposition to look at the complicated side of things. But I found myself on the Eurostar, on the way to meet unfamiliar groups of people who were part of what was termed the Far Right. European coverage had veered between ignoring them or, what seemed worse, treating them like members of political groups. But they were growing in influence, though at that time it would have been hard to anticipate the inroads they would subsequently make. How did one approach members of the Far Right? Did one upbraid them? I wasn't sure. In a spirit of desperation, I tried out a variety of approaches, settling for something short of brute confrontation. I recalled a film I'd once made with my friend Christopher Hitchens. He'd provoked most of the bigots we encountered into open antagonism. This was, to be sure, good television, but it seemed to say more about Hitch's rudeness and ability to get under the skins of others than it did about our subjects' views. But I had more luck than I could have hoped for. Many of the racists I encountered were unschooled in media, dropping their guard.

The more skilled, such as Jean-Marie Le Pen, a man who believed in torture and the expulsion of Muslims from France, were happy to engage in what appeared to be a game of chicken with me. I'd pretend to ask Le Pen questions, and he'd pretend to answer them. After some minutes, he'd throw me a bone, as one might an annoying and persistent pet. What he gave me was good enough to use but short of outright offensiveness, and thus within the permitted area enjoined by France's strict laws on hate speech. In this spirit of half disclosure, we rang the bells on Le Pen's favourite subjects: the Holocaust was 'a detail of history' (disputing the details led to denial of the atrocities), the non-integration of Muslims was 'fundamental' and the corruption of the French political class 'absolute'. Then I was dismissed. Heavy-gutted, shambling, Le Pen remained surprisingly fit and, within his own self-imposed limits, mentally agile. He had one eye made of glass, and my memory of him is of a singular blank stare that one could interpret either as contempt for liberal journalism or as acknowledgement of a job well done. We didn't like each other but, bizarrely, we appeared to get on.

Much of what I did was down to two colleagues: a much-loved, mild-mannered Turkish friend, Celal, who'd persuaded me to undertake this bizarre task; and Christian Poveda, a remarkable director-cameraman who came from a family of exiles from Spain with an anarchist past. Poveda was shot in the back of the neck and killed some years later, when he went back for one last interview while making a film about teenage gangs in Salvador. Bulky, profane and genial, he appeared to be the caricature of a news cameraman, a ridiculously brave and stubborn man who used his lens as a projectile, sticking it into the faces of our surprised subjects. But he was also an acclaimed war photographer and, I began to understand, someone who felt personally affronted by the bad state of much of the world. He hated those who misused their power, evading interrogation about their views or motives. We were nearly beaten up many times. I was assigned the task of finding as many ways as possible to ask the same question, until our prey responded either with a snarl or by walking away. I looked at my efforts again recently and was surprised not to be wholly disappointed. What I'd done sometimes seemed to be a caricature of news reporting, but the rawness had achieved something; the dressed-down, show-them-what-you-do-as-you-go style is popular now in places such as Vice News, which is watched online by young people throughout the world. *Journey to the Far Right* (1999) was used for a long time in European journalism schools. I'm not sure whether it put many supporters off bigotry, but it did approach the question of how often the people who would become known as 'populists' would resort to coded utterances when addressing their followers. Shortly after the film was shown throughout Europe, I was in a Paris taxi on the *Périphérique* with a talkative driver who described himself as a communist. He'd asked me where my accent came from, and when I said I was British but with a French mother, he embarked on a long monologue about how he didn't like the coldness of the Brits, their obsession with class and money. But he had seen a British reporter giving a bad time to '*les fachos*' on television. Upon the realisation that it was me, he insisted on stopping and buying me a bottle of champagne. I called Poveda to tell him what had happened, and he laughed.

To the media-minded, everything is a journalistic opportunity. In the space of a few years, reporting has gone from being a tolerated, fitfully admired activity to something deemed worth only of reprobation. The shift in attitude is in part due to the rise of social media, bringing with it the notion that everyone can be their own reporter, via varieties of 'citizen journalism'.

But the sinking of journalistic prestige is also to do with the failing economics of the newsroom. There's not enough money to carry out good print reporting, and in what are quaintly termed 'electronic newsrooms' there's too much space to fill. Even in the most favourable accounts of news reporting today, a note of disappointment creeps in. A visitor to the shiny Newseum, just off Pennsylvania Avenue in Washington DC, might be forgiven for thinking they had gone back in time, when phrases like 'the lying press' (*Lügenpresse* in German) weren't current, and a successful US presidential candidate hadn't built a campaign around the notion that reporters should never be believed. Just as important in the flight from news is the notion that somehow what we see or are told about shouldn't be so dark. Here is the philosopher and populariser Alain de Botton talking about the failings of news:

> Before we despair at the calamities that apparently surround us on all sides, we should remember that the news is ultimately only one set of stories out there, no more and no less.
>
> Our nation isn't just a severed hand, a mutilated grandmother, three dead girls in a basement, embarrassment for a minister, trillions of debt, a double suicide at the railway station and a fatal five-car crash by the coast.
>
> It is also the cloud floating right now unattended over the church spire, the gentle thought in the doctor's mind as he approaches the patient's arm with a needle, the field mice by the hedgerow . . .

I'm never sure how to respond to such sunny assertions. Yes, the world is dark, and reporters shouldn't always go for darkness. But the problem, surely, is that so much news reporting doesn't go beyond the bulletin board; for a variety of reasons, reporters find that they cannot. I never embraced Martin Bell's formulation of a 'journalism of attachment', because we'd rather reporters just looked at things for us. But done properly, looking implies other activities, and I admire reporters who do just that, slipping out of judging and back again. No coherent boundaries exist between reporting on television, making films or indeed calling yourself a film-maker. 'I'd rather be called a paedophile,' a BBC executive once said, in exasperation at the pretentiousness of film-making culture. 'I'm just a hack,' the film-maker Adam Curtis says. What he really means is that he's happy to report. We should value real reporters more than we do. Poveda would become disappointed whenever I failed to nag or insult one of the racists we were pursuing. '*Il faut les frapper, les cons!*' he'd say. When I had struck at them, he was happy.

Jon Snow, of *Channel 4 News*, told me that reporters increasingly come from the rich, professional classes, but that those running the newsrooms need to understand both privatisation and poverty. He doesn't abide by the 'journalism of attachment', and nor does Harold Evans, the world-renowned former editor of *The Times* and *Sunday Times*.

Are reporters supposed to have views? Self-evidently, however you answer this question, they do exist. They are suppressed, partially allowed, encouraged or applauded, depending on the whim of a publication. It must be evident that 'objectivity', however it is defined, is a code of sorts within journalism. Readers or viewers expect publications not to adopt positions too overtly, except when these coincide with their own. Reciprocally, reporters, whose job it is to find out things, feel protected by the mask of not taking sides. There's nothing wrong with a poker face. But there's another, less easily defined area in which the views of someone looking at something are foregrounded and journalists should be able to attest to what they've said. The legendary head of the BBC during its prime in the 1960s, Hugh Greene, said that there were some subjects, notably racism, where no degree of impartiality was required. In Edward R. Murrow's day, the frontiers between having views and not having them weren't yet defined or patrolled, and in this sense the early years of broadcasting resemble our own post-broadcast era.

Each day, on my way to my new offices at the BBC, an eighth-floor space constructed around the biggest newsroom in the world, I'd pass a small blue plaque on a nondescript 1930s block of flats. The plaque told me that Edward R. Murrow had lived there during the war. These days, Murrow is perhaps over-memorialised as the enduring conscience and patron saint of broadcast news. No television series dealing with the ethics of journalism is complete without quotes from him. But Murrow was a more complicated figure in his own lifetime. His father was a poor farmer from North Carolina who sold up and moved to Washington state, working in a sawmill and then on a railroad. Murrow was educated at Washington State College, where he was tutored in speech and drama by an admiring teacher who spotted his exceptional gifts. Graduating in the 1930s, he organised students' tours to a stricken Europe and became involved in finding asylum for exiled graduate students and professors. Murrow did have his own views, certainly. He was hired by CBS in 1935 as an organiser of 'cultural stuff', and he happened to be in Europe, signing up opera performances, when Hitler invaded Austria. Too late on the scene, or perhaps too conscious of his lack of Harvard, Yale or Columbia expertise, he didn't, unlike his near-contemporary John F. Kennedy, blame democratic politicians for their supineness in the face of their enemies. But he knew on what side he (and CBS and America) stood. At the same time, his reports appear irradiated with a form of anxiety.

Wearing the best shirts from Jermyn Street, Murrow offered a point of view that was subversive, one that saw him partly banned from CBS by William Paley, the smart entrepreneur who understood the economics of national radio and television. However, his reporting made him the star of Blitz-era London. Murrow may have been reckless, but he didn't want his coverage of cities in wartime to be a farce; he was tough. Tuning into his show *London After Dark* was said to be like being transported to the fires in London, where he broadcasted from the roof of the BBC. He went where no reporters had gone quite yet, visiting twenty-five bombings in Europe. Murrow was a pioneer venturing on unmarked paths. This is almost understood in the long, half-ironic *New Yorker* profile of him in 1953, in which the reporter described how long Murrow took to write his radio editorials, how he sweated before delivering each one of them, and how much neat whisky and London broil he required to wind down. Murrow's after-dinner seriousness bordered on self-parody:

Talk sometimes dies when it's seen that Murrow is no longer taking part, or even listening, but is leaning forward and staring at the rug, his elbows on his knees and his fists slowly beating each other, an unattended cigarette in his mouth, glowing and subsiding with his breathing, and the smoke from his nostrils enveloping his face in a dense, infernal cloud. The cigarette may burn to his lips before he plucks it out, crushes it in an ashtray, and picks up the conversation where it was dropped several minutes earlier. This portentous condition of mind persists to some extent when Murrow is at the microphone. On the air, his manner of speaking often conveys the impression that he knows the worst but will try not to mention it . . .

Within CBS, Murrow was described as 'the voice of doom'. You can view samples of his work in the garish circumstances of the Newseum in Washington DC, but the best way to comprehend his achievement is to take it neat, via YouTube. Blink through a cheesy, over-memorialising PBS doc, and you will have some idea of what it must have felt like to be sitting in a small town in still neutral, America First territory and knowing, through Murrow's words, that planes were busy setting fire to London from the air. Go to the most striking moment of Murrow's television career, in 1954, when he set out to destroy the repu-tation of 'Tail Gunner' Joseph McCarthy, persecutor of those he deemed to be crypto-communists, purveyor of large, mainly imaginary lists of the disloyal and, in the view not just of lib-erals but many conservatives of the day, the greatest threat to the republic. Murrow, it is said, didn't tell the management of CBS that he was about to attack McCarthy. He had hesitated for many months, though it appears that he was encouraged by the response to a story he and his team had done about the son of presumed leftists who was threatened with the loss of his job in the army. It seemed to Murrow that the time was right. You can see him sweating through the crude kinescope record-ing and faltering as he reads from a script between the clips of McCarthy baiting his victims. This isn't a performance so much as a record of someone trying to perform, conscious not just that he may fail, but that the penalties for failure are great. Murrow's closing quote from *Julius Caesar*, about looking into ourselves, is apposite and non-rhetorical. We may be sure that he thought that many people who could have opposed McCarthy and didn't, including himself, were to blame for his ascent. And we can be sure that Murrow wished that any expedient should be employed to end the career of the senator from Wisconsin.

Murrow's coup has been the subject of many analyses, and it is described with surprising accuracy in George Clooney's film *Good Night, and Good Luck* (2005). Would McCarthy have fallen a few months later without the intervention of Murrow? Did Murrow, given air during the newly created peak time of the networks, not find himself exercising disproportionate power, even if he'd chosen a fitting enemy? The downfall of McCarthy is described in Emile de Antonio's *Point of Order* (1964), in which you can see him destroyed by his peers. But it is hard to imagine that these senators weren't affected by Murrow; his broadcast was covered extensively by the press. It was the first multimedia event, heralding the 'echo chamber' effect observable in the tweeting and retweeting of today. Many more people knew about his assault than watched it, but this increased its power. It's clear that the management of CBS, including William Paley, had misgivings about Murrow's onslaught. This was in part because they were legally obliged to allow McCarthy a right to reply in the following weeks, but that cannot have been the only reason. Murrow worried over the sheer extent of his own power. Was it appropriate to use this new medium, and the power of near-monopoly, to destroy a politician? Later, he said that he regretted that such power hadn't been available in the 1930s, when it could have been put to good use; but he also said that in a democracy, such efforts were appropriate only very rarely. Murrow was at heart a radical New Dealer who believed that the American promise was best fulfilled by giving everyone a fair chance. *Harvest of Shame* (1960), a film he made about the lives of migrant workers, is an extraordinary, unfiltered expression of personal outrage. Murrow believed that broadcasting must be a 'world classroom'. Broadcasters such as himself must use the medium to draw attention to the blights of privilege and poverty. Although *See It Now* (1951–8), the series he made with Fred Friendly, paraded its journalistic neutrality, there was no doubt about what he meant to say. He was a poor executive, and he hated his time behind a desk attempting to run the US Information Agency (USIA) for JFK's Camelot of internationalism. He was worse than burnt out by the time he died of lung cancer in 1965, ten years after he had first reported on the possible connection between smoking and cancer, sucking on a cigarette as he spoke over images of the disease that destroyed him.

I met Fred Friendly many years ago, in his office filled with agitprop artworks from the 1930s by the likes of Ben Shahn. Genial, open with advice and bearing a surprising resemblance to the version of himself later played by George Clooney, Friendly told the usual stories about Murrow. But it was the degree to which he insisted that Murrow was one of a kind that impressed me. Murrow didn't have to go after big corporations, he didn't have to attack television in the way he did a few years later, referring to it as 'a box full of lights'. His criticism of his former friend and boss Bill Paley was imprudent, perhaps ill-judged. Although he and Friendly had argued endlessly over the shape and purpose of broadcast journalism, Friendly told me that Murrow never liked television. 'It was not what he thought his career was about,' Friendly said. 'He belonged to radio, in his view.' I asked Friendly whether it wasn't the corporate attitudes that had got to Murrow. 'Well, it was that,' he replied. 'But it was also the system that he had helped to put in place.'

Later, I encountered another view of Murrow when a friend sent me to lunch with Don Hewitt. Like Friendly and Murrow, Hewitt had enjoyed a long career at CBS. He was polished in speech, beautifully dressed, silky in manner, with the demotic style, half drawl, half steely, of successful male television executives. But his own views on broadcasting were very different. He had perfected CBS's political convention, with the stings and graphics beloved of generations of television producers, and invented *60 Minutes*, turning it into the most lucrative CBS property. Hewitt referred to his own journalists – polished reporters such as Morley Safer and amiable brutes like Mike Wallace – as his 'tigers'. When I asked him about Murrow and CBS, he didn't reply immediately. Instead, he told me about his 'wet bar theory'. According to Hewitt, a viewer should be able to get up from the couch, go across the living room and mix a martini, then return to the couch and sit down, without having his concentration interrupted. That was the principle he'd employed on *60 Minutes*, and it was clear that he thought that Murrow didn't measure up to it. Hewitt evolved television journalism for millions, but he also appeased the channel's desire for a family and arts network. He didn't mind if journalism was to be a minor part of CBS.

Television has become an unregulated free-for-all, most of all in the US. The questions posed by the experiences of Hewitt and Murrow remain. They feed into any serious consideration of documentaries, too. Hewitt was responsible for the most

immediately engaging factual journalism in the history of broadcasting, but he also contributed to the ascent of celebrity. The
real subjects of *60 Minutes* were Hewitt's tigers and their successors. I'm sure this wasn't what Hewitt and his ilk meant to happen, but the consequences were to be seen everywhere. Can one
say what one wants within the medium, without interference? If
one does say what one wants, who will listen? Does one have to
go outside television in order to say what one wants? Some sort
of decay in television has occurred, and it certainly never reached
the promise evoked by Murrow. But documentaries depend for
financing upon some major source of money. Although private
sources have increased, the roots of documentary, most of all in
Europe, are in television. So the arguments about what television
is supposed to do persist, colouring documentaries.

The most vigorous battles in Britain occurred in and around
the space occupied by *World in Action*, Granada's long-running
experiment in documentary journalism, launched in 1963 and a
near-weekly fixture of the ITV network until 1998. You can watch
World in Action now on DVD and enjoy its antiquated boldness,
but its full radicalism requires some explanation. Often the films
are full of jump cuts and rapidly processed film. This seems to
have been a conscious anti-aesthetic decision based on the perception that urgency came from a negative attitude to style. Films
were made by pairs of producers and directors. *World in Action*
was a very male, somewhat chauvinist place; its producers wore
leather jackets and were familiar with the writings of Gramsci.
Classlessness was de rigueur: there were few people at Granada
who would admit to having received a private education or sending their children through one. One could forgive such minor
hypocrisies because the reporting was so good. Many *World in*

Action directors, such as Michael Apted and Paul Greengrass, went on to make highly successful Hollywood films, but the work they did for the series was pure investigation or, more rarely, observation with a strongly slanted view. The roots of the programme lay in the vigorous, investigative, leftish tradition of tabloid newspapers such as the *Daily Mirror*, and to begin with it hit out at anything its creators found to be corrupt or inept in British society.

The success of *World in Action* was made possible by leftish management, headed by the redoubtable entrepreneur and cinema operator Sidney Bernstein. After a rocky start, it was cushioned by the monopoly profits of commercial television. But the programme's progress was characterised by ceaseless battles with the regulatory authorities, which Granada appeared to relish even when money was wasted in the pursuit of controversy. 'Part of its success was owed to the fact that the Granada team . . . refused to succumb to the moral blackmail through which the British establishment seeks to smother any story that could cause them embarrassment,' Denis Forman recalled. 'Time and time again we would be told that a forthcoming programme would be against the national interest, would damage irrevocably our foreign trade, or would cause a loss of confidence in the police force, the army or the navy; we became accustomed to listening to heavy breathing from top civil servants, from ministers, sometimes from lawyers.' To their credit, Bernstein and his colleagues stood behind their creation. But it was the status of Granada as a protected monopoly, on which public service obligations had been imposed by law, that allowed them to do so.

World in Action reached its peak in the 1960s, when its style of grainy immediacy came to define the decade, in the same way that news magazines and photojournalism described the 1940s. In the 1970s, it excelled once again: film-makers were able to confront the decline of Britain with a series of investigative pieces that made most contemporary television appear half-hearted and evasive. Through *World in Action*, Granada developed the idea of the documentary drama, in which actors were used when it was impossible to film an event. Docudrama is widespread now, and the term often seems no more than a claim for a degree of authenticity for a film that is, in its essentials, fictional. The first Granada docudramas were stark affairs, telling the story of the meetings between Czech politicians and the Soviet Politburo in 1968, or the mistreatment of Russian dissidents. 'They were made with next to nothing,' says director Leslie Woodhead. 'This was an experiment we were engaged in. How did we tell what happened when no film existed? We went to an abandoned warehouse with some actors. There was a script truly based on real documents. And we did our best.'

It is interesting to compare the Granada style with the BBC's efforts. The BBC laboured under the burdens of the obligation to be impartial; 1960s and 1970s editions of *Panorama* appear gratuitously starchy and over-keen to appear authoritative. Good reporting was to be found on the magazine show *24 Hours*, which reflected the upheavals of the 1960s. Genuine flair and freshness, however, came from the individual voices of talented reporters, among them the remarkably stubborn Charles Wheeler and James Mossman, a homosexual ex-spy with a le Carré-ish end-of-empire view of the world who combined great writing skills with a film-maker's sensibility. In Nicholas Wright's play *The Reporter* (2007), the character based on Mossman tells how it was in the glory days of the BBC:

In those days of innocence, I used to record my voiceovers in hotel lavatories with blankets over the window to deaden the traffic noise. Then I'd pack up the film, the tapes, the cutting order and send it to London like a Christmas parcel. Days later a telex might arrive, laconic, brief: 'Your story transmitted, twelve minutes.' Very occasionally, 'Well done.' The only time I saw the film myself was when I returned to London. Then I'd watch on a monitor in Lime Grove Studios, a leaking hell-hole at the back of Shepherd's Bush Green, tenaciously clung to over the years on the grounds that outward luxury would be superfluous to a department so superior to any other as BBC current affairs.

Mossman's films now appear a curious blend of sophisticated, often wayward scripts with remarkable images, wildly unevenly edited. But his own voice is what lingers long afterwards. He was permitted to have views, and the images he sent back weren't excessively repackaged. Charles Wheeler's style is less literary than Mossman's. He is remembered within the BBC as the ultimate reporter and the embodiment of the BBC's house style of precision and impartiality. Wheeler was slight, soft-voiced and amiable in a carefully guarded way. He batted away compliments with practised assurance. Ultimately, he wrote nothing about reporting, or his own life, but the archive of his reports from a burning Detroit or cold war-era Berlin gives some notion of the source of the Wheeler mystique. He was a reporter, not in the sense that one might feel called to be a lyric poet, but in the way one becomes a lens grinder or a microbiologist. In a Wheeler report, there are few adjectives; no style is perceptible. Instead, you are with him, you feel what it's like to be standing where he is and seeing what he sees. He doesn't paraphrase or relay the voices of others. He is his own voice, and nothing else. One of his greatest coups came after he secured the script for a Republican political convention, reading it out deadpan, peering over his spectacles. He seemed to hate and despise any degree of delusion. In that rarest sense, and with his appalling candour, the modestly persuasive Wheeler is the perfect successor and counterpart of Murrow. Both stand somewhere on the boundary between television and documentary; both retain the power to trouble, with their awkward presence as well as with the hard truths they convey.

In the long-running series *One Pair of Eyes* (1967–84), the BBC continued with the tradition of the reporter-observer. Nowadays, such overtly small-audience, elitist experiments are hard to find; polemics have replaced the more leisurely observational style. But investigative journalism, despite many efforts, was never the BBC's forte. As late as 1981, recently released documents reveal, the director-general, Sir Ian Trethowan, felt obliged to send a *Panorama* episode dealing with the British secret services to MI5's legal officer for advice. He passed the many suggested cuts on to the programme's editor. During the 2003 Hutton Inquiry, which dealt with the BBC's coverage of the Labour government's famous memo stating that Iraq was in possession of lethal weapons, there were many (including the judge) who appeared to think that the corporation had no business looking into such things; as a national public broadcaster, it should restrict itself to news that was already public, acting as a recorder of the national debate rather than breaking stories. The BBC didn't heed such views, and its news reporters supply remarkable stories each day – many now coming from women, who were significant by their absence in its earlier days. But it's hard not to think that the kind of reporting once in evidence on television is becoming harder to find each year, as the cuts bite deeper and the ultimate patrons of television – politicians, regulatory bureaucrats and even audiences – turn away from what is difficult or controversial. At the same time, reporting has flourished in a different way thanks to documentaries, either outside television or on its margins.

It may be that audiences know that there are generations of hard-nosed, über-stylish investigators already out there. Nick Broomfield, known for his obstructive boom mike, is one of the most well known. 'Elephant traps are such fun,' he says of *The Leader, His Driver and the Driver's Wife* (1991). 'They are all to do with your knowledge of people, which becomes so intimate that you know exactly how they are going to react when you do something.' Superficially, Broomfield's film is about things that don't happen: his repeated failures to get an interview with the South African white supremacist Eugène Terre'Blanche are played for comic effect. These culminate in a marvellous rag-losing rant from the Leader when Broomfield shows up fifteen minutes late. You sense just how much Terre'Blanche hates Broomfield, not just because the latter is a journalist and an interloper, but because he's British and the Leader is an Afrikaner with a background of 'heavy drinking, heavy meat-eating and heavy womanising'. Nearly thirty years later, however, you view the film differently. It tells the story of hopelessly disorganised Afrikaners on the edge of conceding power to those over whom they had brutally ruled, and no one has ever done this better than Broomfield, in the scenes with JP, the Leader's driver, who is decent and lost and gets on well with black Africans. But it also reveals much about the psychology of those who were called fascists then, but whom we've now come to call 'populists'. Broomfield's father came from Czechoslovakia during the 1930s, and the film displays a sixth sense when dealing with the levels of collusion that go into supporting bullies such as the Leader. When he made this film, Broomfield hadn't appeared on camera much, and one can see him edge into the role of reporter, shamelessly utilising his own gifts of diffidence and impertinence and playing off his own style against a ruthlessly flat, 'objective' commentary delivered in the best BBC style. In the end, the film is so successful because of what Broomfield calls 'luck': the capacity to be in the right place at the right time, when nothing in particular is happening and then something finally does, such as the moment when the fat-arsed horse carrying the equally fat-arsed leader nearly throws him off.

Broomfield lives in Malibu, when he isn't to be found at his old mill in Sussex. Among executives and some film-makers, he has a reputation for raffish arrogance; part of this may come from the way that he has broken so many of the rules of his generation. Although he often wears T-shirts, they are well cut, and a faint aura of dandyism surrounds him. I once went to see a BBC bigwig with him, and later I received a call in which the BBC man expressed some surprise at finding Nick to be 'less spivvy than he looks'. I was astonished by this remark. What I should have replied is that if you make the kind of documentaries he does, it helps to have protective coloration. It's good to appear innocent even when you aren't. 'You must be spivvy among spivs, gormless among the ignorant,' Broomfield has said. But the good looks and superficial fun of many of his films fail to hide an essential seriousness of purpose. His father was a skilled industrial photographer ('from the working class'). He is able to hang out with people, while always seeming separate. After up-and-down private schooling, which he detested, he fetched up at the newish National Film School, run by the redoubtable Colin Young. Here he discovered that his early interest in social comment needed narrative. But it wasn't until his South African jaunt that he learnt how to use himself on camera, styling himself as a reporter amid the chaos.

Some of his films do display signs of tricks overlearnt. Mostly, his pursuits stylishly go nowhere and end by saying what we already knew about their quarry – Mrs Thatcher and the egregious Sarah Palin, for instance. Sometimes the leftism of the 1970s creeps up on Broomfield, but he is a remarkable reporter. There must be a reason why so many, such as Louis Theroux, Michael Moore, Morgan Spurlock or the impressive Danish director Mads Brügger, have borrowed from his mix of derision, gaucheness and suavity. When I worked with him on *Kurt & Courtney* (1998), a lengthy, ultimately frustrating account of the Nirvana frontman's suicide, I was astonished by the lengths to which he went in order to secure interviews and the degree to which his chosen subjects enveloped him. He never seemed cynical, even if he did frequently display some signs of exhaustion at the sheer awfulness of much of what he observed.

In the US, Broomfield didn't seek out the conspicuously weird or brash. He was never really a photojournalist like Weegee or a tabloid hunter, though he was drawn to murders and deviance. Instead, he looked at people on the borderline, those who, like the Hollywood madam Heidi Fleiss, the dominatrix artistes of New York and, yes, Kurt and Courtney themselves, remained somehow on the periphery, unable or unwilling to cross the American threshold dividing those who were accepted from those who weren't. Often his films seemed to conclude that there was perhaps less dishonour in remaining outside.

'Nick is at heart a very serious person,' Kim Longinotto told me. 'He really does get shocked. And he has become more shocked as time goes by.' This is demonstrated by his long-standing interest in the fate of the murderer Aileen Wuornos. *Aileen: The Life and Death of a Serial Killer* (2003) is Broomfield's best, as well as his darkest, venture deep into America. In order to fully understand the boldness of Broomfield and Joan Churchill's doc, it helps if you have watched his 1992 film that delves into the commercialisation of her trial (*Aileen Wuornos: The Selling of a Serial Killer*). Aileen was a prostitute who killed seven of her clients. Some of these might have been acts of self-defence, but it's evident that neither her lawyer nor the police care much about this; the latter are too busy painting her as evil in order to sell movie versions of her life. There's a terrible account of her lesbian partner, who turned her in to the police, and a series of equally awful scenes with a horse ranch-owning patron who takes Aileen under her wing and wants her to plead no contest so that she can be executed, joining Christ. One can imagine some level of prurient collusion in a film about the selling of Aileen, but Broomfield, when he finally meets her, sympathises with her plight because she seems more honest than most of the people who are determining her fate.

Broomfield has always grasped the heedlessness that goes with the American sense of ultimate promise. In this respect, unpretentiously and in small scale, his films now seem prophetic. We're entering a part of the world in which no protestations of fact or virtue seem to mean much, and most things, including justice, seem to be for sale. This is the theme picked up in the second film, which tells the story of Aileen's last days, ten years later. Broomfield is present at her final appeal hearing because his first film was entered in evidence by Aileen's lawyer. But Aileen, once again, has changed her mind. She now maintains that she killed the johns in cold blood, but ultimately she tells Broomfield (unaware that her words are being recorded) that this isn't the case. Aileen wants to be finished, she wants her life to be over. Nobody really cares about her. This is the unsettling revelation of both films. Aileen is crazed, and perhaps she always was, but that doesn't make her someone you don't want to understand or with whom you can have no sympathy. (In an aside, remarking on the fact that Aileen was declared sane enough by a psychiatrist to be executed, Broomfield wonders what one would have to do to be spared by reason of insanity.) Broomfield is an opponent of the death penalty, but really this is a film about how no one can be bothered with Aileen. There's a terrific last interview with her in which Broomfield, having attempted to get Aileen to forgive her mother and failing, is witness to an explosion of her rage. She still thinks the police are out to benefit from her life. All Broomfield can do is say he is sorry when she ends the interview, and it's clear that he means it. 'It opened me up as a person,' he said later. 'It was very painful. I think it's a sensitive film about someone it would have been very easy not to have been sensitive about.'

By far the most well-known documentary film-maker from the US is Michael Moore. His open style riles traditionalists and draws in swathes of audiences unlikely to be seen at any other factual screenings. He is the most outsize, successful presence in documentary film. Moore teases audiences of fastidious film-makers by asking them how many truly popular films they have watched recently, mocking them when they can't recall any titles. He grew up in Flint, Michigan, where eighty thousand workers toiled on the crucial component of the American Dream known as the automotive industry. Early in life, Moore became aware of the fraying of the social fabric, even as he continued to love what was going on. As he explains in his autobiography, he didn't like documentaries:

> Documentaries felt like medicine, like castor oil – something
> I was supposed to watch because they were good for me.
> But most were boring and predictable, even when I agreed
> with the politics. If I wanted to listen to a political speech,
> why would I go to a movie? I'd attend a rally, or a candidate's
> debate. If I wanted to hear a sermon, I'd go to church. When I
> went to the movies, I wanted to be surprised, lifted, crushed, I
> wanted to laugh my ass off and have a good cry . . . I wanted to
> glide out onto the street as if I were walking on air. I wanted to
> feel exhilarated. I wanted all my assumptions challenged . . .

Moore ran a local paper for ten years. He then moved to San Francisco to work for the radical magazine *Mother Jones*, returning home when he was fired. His return coincided with the announcement by General Motors that thirty thousand workers would be fired when the factories were moved to Mexico. Moore explains that he didn't know how to make a film, but, working with the New Yorker Kevin Rafferty, he began to make *Roger & Me* (1989). Made for $160,000, some of it obtained by remortgaging his house, the film records Moore's fumbling attempts to make a film, even as he tracks the scale of the disaster enveloping his own past. In scene after scene, we are introduced to the bemused inhabitants of Flint: a bailiff, young laid-off workers about to leave, a rabbit breeder living off social security payments, superannuated celebrity visitors such as Pat Boone and

Anita Bryant. A GM lobbyist, sacked shortly afterwards, tries to explain that all is for the best in free market capitalism, and even if it isn't, there's nothing that can be done. The ravaged heart of Flint is rebuilt, with a museum commemorating its own ransacked car plants, but this, too, goes bust.

Moore tries to interview Roger Smith at the GM headquarters in Michigan, at a country club and at the annual general meeting, where he gets the following non-response:

Moore: Mr Smith, we just came down from Flint, where we filmed a family being evicted from their home the day before Christmas Eve. A family that used to work in the factory. Would you be willing to come up with us to see what the situation is like in Flint, so that people . . .?

Smith: I've been to Flint, and I'm sorry for those people, but I don't know anything about it, but you'd have to . . .

Moore: Families being evicted from their homes on Christmas Eve.

Smith: Well, I'm . . . listen, I'm sure General Motors didn't evict them. You'd have to go talk to their landlords.

Moore: They used to work for General Motors, and now they don't work there any more.

Smith: Well, I'm sorry about that.

Moore: Could you come up to Flint with us?

Smith: I cannot come to Flint, I'm sorry.

Watch Moore's films now and they seem familiar. His devices have been used so many times by others. He assails exponents of free market capitalism with a series of gags or entraps them with shrewd interviews. His films have an air of improvised journalism, though the effects are extremely calculated, with well-devised, highly rehearsed pranks. They often omit details, sometimes in their haste to convey the Moore message, often because he cannot be bothered with too much baggage. But no one should complain about his adoption of a political stance, which is overtly expressed. Moore is polemical, leftish, anti-authoritarian; his on-screen truculence enables him to avoid the self-righteousness of left-wing commentary. His commentaries eschew even-handedness as much as those of his adversaries on Fox News do. But there's a largeness of heart in what Moore does, represented by his presence and shambling gait. Even when irate, he seems capable of generosity, unlike his foes. His films are true depictions of what it is to be an American.

In Moore's next film, *Bowling for Columbine* (2002), he conducts an inquiry into gun control, taking as his starting point the murder of high-school students in Columbine, Colorado. The 'bowling' of the title comes from the allegation, later shown to be false, that the teenage killers went bowling before the mass murder. Moore isn't interested in more gun laws; he tells us that he's a member of the NRA, sympathising with the many Americans who carry guns. He goes to Canada, noting with approval that seven million guns are in private hands, but that Canadians don't kill each other on the scale that Americans do. His real theme is American fear, and how this is instilled in Americans by the mass media. The violent history of the US is real enough, but other cultures are just as violent. What irks Moore is the American failure to look at anything very clearly. Americans remain immured in their own mythology of success, even in the face of the abject failure of much of their world. They never really want to change anything. It isn't clear whether they could, even if they wanted to.

And yet in his films we do encounter those who, unexpectedly, can see what is wrong. Usually, these aren't rich or powerful people. A powerful nostalgia for a vanished, ordinary America pervades all of his films, but there is no sense that Moore or America can fix what is broken. The film closes with him interviewing an ailing, pre-Alzheimer's Charlton Heston, a figure deeply identified with the gun lobby, who won't apologise for showing up at pro-gun rallies held just after killings. Heston is vague about the reasons for American violence; it's not clear whether he has lost the energy to debate or simply doesn't care. Moore leaves behind a photograph of a child who was killed by a six-year-old handling a gun at school.

Moore was much criticised for this interview, and there are many who dislike his films. To the *New Yorker*'s film critic, Pauline Kael, *Roger & Me* was 'shallow and facetious, a piece of gonzo demagoguery that made me feel cheap for laughing'. Moore did get to interview Roger Smith, as a film by two Canadian film-makers revealed. He has said that it wasn't a real interview, and that it took place before he started *Roger & Me*. If he had interviewed Smith, Moore suggests, General Motors, seeking to discredit his film, would have gone after him.

Fahrenheit 9/11 (2004) was Moore's most successful, and most criticised, film. 'The film is so flat out phony that fact-checking is beside the point,' Christopher Hitchens wrote in *Slate*:

> If I write an article and I quote somebody and for space reasons put in an ellipsis like this (. . .), I swear on my children that I am not leaving out anything that, if quoted in full, would alter the original meaning or its significance. Those who violate this pact with readers or viewers are to

be despised. At no point does Michael Moore make the smallest effort to be objective. At no moment does he pass up the chance of a cheap sneer or a jeer. He pitilessly focuses his camera, for minutes after he should have turned it off, on a distraught and bereaved mother whose grief we have already shared. (But then, this is the guy who thought it so clever and amusing to catch Charlton Heston, in *Bowling for Columbine*, at the onset of his senile dementia.) Such courage.

Fahrenheit 9/11 cost $5 million and took an astonishing $160 million at the box office.* For many, it became the only credible account of the 11 September 2001 terrorist attacks, standing in for the official lies. Much of the film recounts conspiracies involving the Bush administration and the Saudis, implying, probably correctly, that the government wished to get the Bin Laden family out of the US. It never seems that Moore wholly grasped the viciousness of Saddam Hussein's regime, and his depiction of happy Iraqis at a moment when the country was subjected to international sanctions is ridiculous. But he was among the first to identify and depict the heedless arrogance of Bush and his entourage. What, truly, did the US mean to do in Iraq? How did it hope to introduce democracy or improve the lives of Iraqis? Moore's simple questions receive no answers. They have never been answered. The sequences where he attempts to ask congressmen why they don't send their sons and daughters to

---

* The film was to be distributed by Disney, who withdrew their funding and support, to be replaced by the Weinstein Company. Moore later sued the Weinstein Company on the grounds that the distribution costs had been inflated. The lawsuit was finally settled in 2014.

Iraq are telling. So is his overall view of a society so glutted with the exercise of power and so habituated to violence that it can no longer fully comprehend the consequences of its actions.

It would, nonetheless, be wrong to make too much of Moore's numerous elisions and partial truths. His job, as he has often stated, is to entertain. Long before Trump and his supporters picked up the refrain, Moore was saying that the version of events supplied by 'mainstream media' was misleading. He tells his audiences they mustn't believe in anything they are told by politicians or corporations. He made possible the clever satire in Jon Stewart's *Daily Show*; it seems likely that he contributed to the widespread distaste not just for politicians, but for reporters, too. I'm not sure what Moore really thinks about this, but his autobiography reveals how unpopular his views became. In the post-9/11 hysteria, his driveway was filled with excrement, and he was the recipient of numerous threats. After he was attacked in the street, he was obliged to hire twenty-four-hour guards, some of them ex-Navy Seals. For two years he contemplated abandoning documentary film, on the grounds that it was too dangerous. In a different way, therefore, Moore has proved to be almost as influential as the output of Fox News. And, whatever you think of his film-making style, that is a signal achievement.

In 2016, Moore was among the first to acknowledge that Trump would win the election. In *Michael Moore in Trumpland*, in a speech delivered to an audience in Ohio, he's at his best as he addresses 'every beaten-down stiff and forgotten worker'. He tells them they've been given, in the shape of Trump, 'the fucking human Molotov cocktail they've been waiting for'. He is completely at ease with the audience, anticipating what they must feel about minority-rights politics ('gays next . . . transgenders

... a fucking hamster in the White House?'). He doesn't like the Clintons and never voted for them, but he conjures out of disappointment and rancour his own vision of how Americans might nonetheless fit together if they decided that they should, willing a state of greater equality and solidarity into existence. This isn't a film, but it's among the best things Moore has done. Many of the snootier reviewers disliked his 2018 film *Fahrenheit 11/9*, in which he charts Trump's career and the discomfort of working-class Democrats. Moore truly understands poor Americans, describing in every film their fury and discontent.

Super-reportage has flourished as mistrust of the stale conventions of news reporting and 'fake news' causes audiences to reject what is routinely, from left and right, described as 'mainstream media'. In Britain, a post-Broomfield school of social observation now exists, featuring (usually male and borderline scruffy) talents such as Louis Theroux and Sean McAllister. Previously, such reporters would have appeared as ordinary television presenters, but their presence can now be experienced differently, as diarists and authors, as well as reporters. The same transformation occurs in Morgan Spurlock's best film, *Super Size Me* (2004), filmed over thirty days during which he eats only McDonald's food, gorging himself three times a day with the company's prime offerings. By consuming 5,000 kcal (the equivalent of 9.26 Big Macs) per day, Spurlock gained 24.5 lbs, a 13 per cent body mass increase, leading to a cholesterol level of 230 mg/dl. It took him fourteen months to lose the weight gained from this experiment.

The most daring and funniest of the new tribe is Mads Brügger, a bespectacled, bald, genial, pinkish Dane. Derision is his forte, as it is Moore's, but Brügger expresses a gleeful, borderline manic variant of distaste. None of his films go after individuals; the implication of a Brügger film is that this would be absurd given the state of the world, which verges on insanity. But his comic explorations are grounded in factual accuracy. His parents were journalists and he runs his own talk show on a Danish radio station. In person he is shy, curious and polite, with an elaborately mannered command of Danglish. He can no more shed his sense of the absurd than he could transform himself overnight into the sort of robot-speak news presenter impersonated by the comedian Chris Morris. In *The Red Chapel* (2009), Brügger travels to North Korea with two disabled Korean-born comedians. With the assistance of Mrs Pak, they devise a performance for members of the Korean elite; they end by taking part in a commemorative procession as it sweeps through the streets of Pyongyang. But their show, as they point out to Brügger, is a pretext for his determination to expose the cruel absurdity of North Korea. He does this by reading aloud from a treatise published (if not written) by Kim Jong-il. His exchanges with Mrs Pak, while elaborately polite, reveal her own fitful grasp on reality. He gets her to admit that the disabled are often packed away in camps, where they are neglected and starve to death. But Mrs Pak is either game or wholly immune to any comprehension of Brügger's strategy; she tells him how much she loves the disabled duo and the awful act they devise. Whenever I've seen the film with an audience, I've sensed an embarrassment evident in the rustling or coughing. But that is what Brügger wants. Some things are so terrible that they can be credibly depicted only by recourse to savage satire. Maybe you do need to lie in order to depict the truth, but you must never lie about what you do or what is around you in plain sight, which is what North Koreans are forced to do, daily and as a matter of survival.

For his most daring exploit, *The Ambassador* (2011), Brügger buys the right to a Liberian ambassadorship in the Democratic Republic of Congo. He dresses up as a colonist in pith helmet and breeches as he takes up residency. Befriending two pygmies, he listens to whale music with them and has himself paddled up and down a lake. He also gets them drunk. I was on a jury with an African film-maker who refused to discuss Brügger's clowning, so offensive did it seem to him. But Brügger insisted that he wanted to expose the *Tintin*-style racism that had dominated European views of Africa. The fact that no one objected to his mission was surely significant. He was able to purchase a match factory, setting himself up as a businessman. It wouldn't have been possible to document this level of corruption without adopting a disguise. Other people of colour I met agreed with Brügger and enjoyed the film. One could argue that a more straightforward approach to corruption, executed in the by now familiar style of television journalism, would have had less impact; or one could conclude, with some regrets, that Brügger was lucky to come from a culture in which clowning in the name of journalistic endeavour was still a protected activity.

Most people attempting to understand the world nowadays make no distinction between news and other forms of factual description, in much the same way that print reporting and images are now more or less indistinguishable. Is there a future for documentaries as reportage? I found clues in the sheer porousness of the new media world. In 2014, the BBC, as part of an economy drive, began to send fewer and fewer London reporters to trouble spots. Overnight, a transformation occurred, with fewer and fewer safari suits on display. The old BBC standards of reporting were still in place, but the voices had changed. Nelson

Mandela's funeral was different when it was recounted by a young Johannesburg-born black woman. A longer film I commissioned, *Nelson Mandela: The Myth and Me* (2013), by Khalo Matabane, gave expression to the deep ambivalence surrounding 'Madiba''s mixed legacy. It said what the host of white-inspired commemorations hadn't really wanted to say: that the personal heroism of South Africa's first black leader hadn't compensated for the incompetence and corruption that followed the partial dismantling of apartheid. Surely reportage would benefit from different voices; it should, in many instances, be personal. I recalled the resistance I'd first encountered during the 1990s, when I tried to formulate such modest recommendations. 'You mean you want to send Salman Rushdie to report on a local fire?' a critic asked. Well, no, though this would have been an interesting assignment. Who knows, maybe the great man would have developed an interesting argument about arson. Many years later, I was able to get Japanese female director Kyoko Miyake to make *Brakeless* (2014), a film about a suburban train crash outside Osaka in which 106 people died and 562 were injured. It turned out that the train was going too fast because the very young and inexperienced driver was terrified of losing his job due to the near-barbaric work practices of the railway company. These were a consequence of the brutalist Japanese obsession with punctuality, which, the film argued, permeated every corner of national life.

But media politics change slowly, and there were many who waited more than half a lifetime for opportunities that should have been made available to them. I first encountered the redoubtable Sue Lloyd-Roberts as part of a collective tasked with depicting 'minorities', among whom were women, on film for the new Channel 4, back in 1980s Britain. A debutante turned socialist and feminist, with a marvellously distinct classy accent, she didn't fit in easily with the anti-nuke, egalitarian campaigning style of contra-Thatcherism. But she worked with different broadcasters, always able to hold her own. Finally, she was installed at the BBC, becoming what colleagues, in admiration as well as envy, described as the Hopeless Cause Correspondent. Her own style of journalism, which involved taking ridiculous risks to go to places where women like herself were not welcome, was a consequence of the arrival of the Sony Hi8 video camera. Video jockey became her vocation, enabling her to make risky, provocative films, one after another. 'I remember thinking at a very early stage that if you were interested in what I was doing – campaigning journalism and human rights – three burly men with a large camera and a big fluffy phallic microphone is not the tactful way to interview a rape victim in a war situation,' she once said. And yet her output retained a surprising level of humour. She told an imam who was a proponent of female genital mutilation, on the grounds that it prevented clitoral itching, that she had never experienced the symptom in sixty years. In Saudi Arabia, she made an entertaining film by attempting to buy undergarments from an embarrassed male shop worker, thus illustrating the absurdity of a religious regime that didn't allow women to drive or unveil in public and stopped them serving each other in shops. And yet she was modest about her own ground-breaking style: she seemed to baulk when I suggested making a documentary out of her own archive. We were still talking about the project when she went into hospital for a stem-cell transplant, and she died shortly afterwards.

Another pointer towards the future came from the early death of Tim Hetherington during the 2010 Libyan conflict. He went from covering homeless shelters and boxing gyms to becoming a successful war photographer, and from there he moved into documentaries, in West Africa and then Afghanistan, where he made *Restrepo* (2010), an account dripping with hazard, filmed with the writer Sebastian Junger, of an American platoon marooned on a hilltop base. But Hetherington also worked as an investigator for the UN in Liberia and made installations of his own work. 'I want to record world events, big History told in the form of a small history, the personal perspective that gives my life meaning and significance. My work is all about building bridges between myself and the audience,' is how he aptly described his short career. Hetherington saved every scrap from his voyages and left behind a formidable archive of his own work, testifying to the notion that these days one doesn't have to choose between professions. What the vastly talented Hetherington did choose, however, was danger, and that, of course, is how he came to die, at the top of his game but taking risks one wouldn't wish on any friend or colleague.

Among gatherings of the tired, the impoverished and the exhausted, it's customary now to deplore the decline in standards and budgets. Would you want to start out as a freelance journalist or reporter these days? Would you risk your life with the limited security now afforded by impoverished broadcasters or up-and-coming outfits like Vice? It's easy to identify with the moaning, but understanding has a way of appearing where it's needed. The economics of broadcasting thirty or forty years ago favoured reportage, but the circumstances of the cold war, in which people did feel they needed to know about the world, were a factor, too. It would be bizarre not to realise that the current state of the world requires just as much attention. Those who have made money out of the enormous shift from print and broadcast media to online have begun to see what the demise of journalism – not just in print, but on film – implies. Just as important is the fact that people still want to become reporters. Not long ago I went to Gaza, and when I returned I hunted down recent filmed reports. One of them, made by two young Hungarians, looked at the circumstances in which ill-trained ambulance crews with no resources dealt with the aftermath of bomb attacks. It was the sort of purist reporting favoured by *World in Action*: immediate, visceral in its power and, with its images of the picking up of stray body parts, both hard to watch and impossible not to stay with. Then I found some reports by a young Brit who'd dropped out of college, living for some time under bombardment in Gaza. He sounded more like Charles Wheeler than Ed Murrow, but there, so many years on, one could witness the same tight-lipped outrage. The world, as the poet Robert Lowell remarked, 'out-Herods Herod', but one must believe there will be people prepared to risk their lives on our behalf to record what happened and why.

8 : Screamers

Claude Lanzmann's nine-and-a-half-hour epic *Shoah* (1985): Szymon Srebrnik
survived Chelmno by disposing of the ashes of fellow Jews and singing songs to
please Nazi guards and bureaucrats. 'Statistics don't bleed,' says Arthur Koestler;
'it is the detail that counts.'

The first image is of a woman wearing a scarf, crying at the spot where she buried her son. Four years after the fall of Srebrenica and the massacre that ensued, she's finally able to visit his grave. But it's apparent that this isn't the only family member Saliha Osmanović has lost. Her husband and her other son Ramo were among the 7,414 Muslim men and boys murdered by soldiers of the Bosnian Serb army between 11 and 14 July. Now we see her husband forced at gunpoint to cry out for his son. 'Tell him to come down to the Serbs,' a soldier says, and he does, with fear in his eyes. In another sequence a Serb asks a beaten, dehydrated Muslim marching with his hands on his head whether he is afraid. 'Of course I am,' the man says, with the same blank look.

I can recall finding these images amid a pile of old cassettes in the rundown premises of a local television station in Tuzla, an eastern Bosnian town. I'd stayed in Sarajevo, in a house with plastic sheeting for windows, just after the siege was lifted, but nothing quite prepared me for the desolation of Srebrenica. Just outside the town was the shell of the Dutch base in Potočari, from which the town's Muslim men were taken to be murdered. In the old centre, there was no life outside a solitary café blaring the new MTV channel. It was cold as well as dank, and I felt, not for the first time, the presence of ghosts. 'I was too late,' the protagonist of Albert Camus' *The Fall* tells us silkily, after failing to rescue a young woman who jumps off a bridge in central Paris when he is on his way home from a good dinner. 'We are always too late.' I contemplated the low-quality, grainy VHS footage of a man screaming for his son to come, when he knows that he will be killed anyhow, and that if his son comes they will both die. This, to be sure, was our film's start and end. But I also dreaded what it might do to my colleagues, and a few months later the director was to be seen sitting in a London club, tears streaming down his face, as he read a book recounting what happened at Srebrenica.

People of my generation have seen the same images year after year. One is the visit to the perpetrator, usually now living in comfort in an obscure modern suburb. The others are pits at the edge of a village somewhere in Europe where victims were disposed of. People came to believe that reminding people of the atrocities was itself a valuable activity, but it had its own sharply defined limits. We wondered how much difference it would make. Politicians like to say atrocities 'should never happen again', but they would, and not just film-makers, but judges, journalists and therapists could do nothing to repair the damage. While on trips to and from courtrooms, or to pits in the countryside, I thought a lot about the purpose of informing others. I remembered that one should never refrain from something just because its consequences weren't assured.

By now, numerous trials later, and as a result of the accumulation of more than a million pages of court transcripts, lists of the dead and investigative accounts, the massacre of Srebrenica must be among the most researched atrocities in human history. Leslie Woodhead's film *A Cry from the Grave* (1999) hasn't dated in the least. It follows the individuals involved as they struggle to make sure that the plight of Saliha and the women of Srebrenica won't be forgotten, and that some of the perpetrators can be brought to justice. The enormity of so many dead emerges from these small-scale individual stories. 'We had roses in the garden,' is how a widow evokes the life she and her husband had in Srebrenica while Yugoslav communism still existed and neighbours didn't collude in mutually inflicted atrocities. Srebrenica was at one time a good place to live. We meet the ex-cop from Marseille turned investigator Jean-René Ruez, as he picks his way among exhumed bodies poking out of white bags. We hear from some of the four hundred and fifty hapless Dutch soldiers serving in the UN force, underequipped and ill-prepared to handle the flight of twenty-five thousand locals. We meet survivors who made their way out of the columns of the doomed. Most heart-rendingly, we're told the story of Hasan Nuhanović, a young man who worked as an interpreter for the Dutch, translating from Serbo-Croat into English. Hasan brought his family to the 'Dutchbat' base. Abruptly, in a rare instance of decisiveness shown by the UN troops, he was told that he could stay on the base, but the rest of his family must go with the Serbs. They were killed. Hasan says he will never get over the moment when he let them go. He might have thought of taking a pistol from a Dutch officer, but he didn't. 'At that moment, you have no brains left,' he explains. 'You're obedient because you feel you have to obey. And they, too, obeyed, they just walked to the gate.'

Leslie Woodhead made anthropological films for many years. He has a feel for the Balkans, a degree of admiration for these hardy, old-fashioned lives. The film is filled with images of the dark, mountainous backdrop to the massacre. He doesn't judge the perpetrators; he doesn't need to. Instead, he calmly marshals the evidence as he recounts what happened hour by hour, day by

day. There is an interview with the local Muslim warlord Naser
Orić. (Unlike the Serbs, Orić does admit to killings, but he says
they were committed in self-defence. He was later tried in The
Hague and acquitted.) As Woodhead points out, Srebrenica
was 'a catastrophe witnessed by camcorder'. The Western media
were present to record the rash promises made by the French
commander General Bernard Janvier, who committed to making Srebrenica a UN-supported 'safe haven', without having any
means to protect it. It is the Serbian footage, however, that is most
remarkable, not just the material from the edge of the execution
pits, with men assembled ready for their death, but the bragga-
docio of General Ratko Mladić, the conqueror of Srebrenica.
Mladić is to be seen strutting around the town and sitting down
with the Dutch troops and a representative of the townspeople.
This might seem rash, but it's clear that neither he nor his soldiers had any idea that they might be brought to justice. Footage
from the film was used at the war crimes tribunal in The Hague
during Mladić's trial, and I was present a few years later when
the film was shown to an audience of Serbs in Belgrade. It was
at a heavy-rock venue, and within the large audience one could
sense the unusual horror at the stark images. 'This happened in
Europe at the end of the century,' Woodhead tells us in his own
commentary.

I am not sure how another *Cry from the Grave* would be
greeted now in places such as Syria or Yemen. I have no wish to
criticise Woodhead's film, and I feel that it remains one of the
best things I did in my career. True, it was viewed by many millions, but what does that mean? (I'm pleased to find that another
film about Srebrenica, *A Town Betrayed* (2010), was made in part
to counter our own film, and that it was rightly dismissed as Serb

propaganda.) I ensured that the BBC showed more films not just about the Balkans, but about human rights. I also began to learn about international human rights law and sat through parts of Slobodan Milošević's and Radovan Karadžić's trials. I sought out Geoffrey Nice, the man who had spent much of his career prosecuting Milošević, only to see the former Serb president die in captivity before judgement could be passed. The Hague was only in appearance at a remove from the spookiness of Srebrenica. The ghosts were here, too, in the courtroom and the ultra-clean, dull bars where lawyers drank more than they should have before wobbling off on their bicycles. What was it like to spend so much of your life in proximity to atrocity, unable to ensure it didn't happen again? Weren't we all in this position? I went with Woodhead to the annual reburial of the remains of those murdered, witnessing the transfer of numerous small, green-covered coffins to the huge plot adjacent to the Potočari base. I was disappointed by the degree to which grief had become politicised, while realising that this was inevitable. But my real feelings were deeper and harder to acknowledge. What did we think we were doing when we made films about atrocity? Why and how should we cover it?

As a student, I hitch-hiked to Dachau, Mauthausen and the places in southern Austria where in 1945 the British army handed over the Cossacks to the Red Army, knowing that they would be killed. Two decades later, when making films about Eastern Europe, I found I wanted to visit places like Chelmno, Auschwitz-Birkenau, Treblinka, Bełżec, Sobibór and Majdanek. I went to every death camp site I could find in Poland. I'd nag my colleagues and get them to swap the rusting steelworks and decrepit Stalinist new towns for the privilege of standing in the rain and snow looking at featureless mounds or forests, or broken remnants of crematoria. Strangely, I was never depressed by the experience, because I was finding something out, even if I didn't know what.

I once got myself locked in a death camp at closing time and had to bang on the door in the style of those trying to attract the attention of Macbeth's porter. Another time, I got an Oxford don drunk in the intense Polish January cold on the ramp at Auschwitz, with what in those days was known as 'kiosk vodka'. 'They never made anything here,' he said, gesticulating in the direction of the adjoining labour camp, Monowitz. 'They never really made a single gym shoe.' I have no belief in transcendence, but I feel it's legitimate to want to know what happened in these places. It may be, too, that one can learn something from whatever haunts the woods, fields, crumbing ramps or railway lines around which so many were killed. I felt the same in Tuol Sleng, the *lycée* of Phnom Penh to which the victims of the Khmer Rouge were brought; one can see photographs of the enemies of the people brought there for execution and the beds on which they were tortured. I also felt the same around a marsh near Lviv, in Ukraine, to which the inhabitants of a nearby town were taken and shot. And of course, over the years, the fire-blackened villages of Bosnia have had the same effect on me.

But simply listing the deaths isn't enough. You really do need the literary genius of someone like Primo Levi to evoke the enormity of what happened. Film is slightly different. Film, so much more than the exhibits crowding Holocaust sites – reconstituted railway cars, facsimiles of orders from the bureaucracy, endless heartbreaking photographs of the vanished – just might make it possible to think how it all happened. No footage that we know of exists of the real business of the camps. If it did, it would have been taken by members of the bureaucracy, which means that it would have been brought into existence for a purpose. Indeed, an account of the Kraków ghetto exists. Many scenes were removed, and it was later described as Nazi propaganda. The power comes from watching what you're meant to see, and then realising what you cannot.

In 1943, the Polish underground activist Jan Karski, posing as an Estonian, witnessed the killing of Jews at Bełżec. Smuggled out of Poland, he was introduced to the writer and émigré Arthur Koestler, who wrote a pamphlet based on Karski's discoveries, turning it into a script for the BBC. 'My name is Karski,' the script began. But the meeting had a profound effect on Koestler, who was appalled by the sheer difficulty he encountered in convincing people that killings were going on. In 'On Disbelieving Atrocities', written for the *New York Times* in 1944, he describes himself and those like him as 'Screamers'. Such people, he says, do succeed in getting through to others, but only for the odd ten minutes of half-distracted attention, before the human desire not to know reclaims the listener and oblivion prevails. 'A dog run over by a car upsets our digestion; three million Jews killed in Poland cause but a moderate uneasiness,' Koestler tells us. 'Statistics don't bleed; it is the detail that counts. We are unable to embrace the total process with our awareness; we can only focus on little lumps of reality.' He recounted a recurring dream in which he was being strangled to death by the side of a road in a wood while people walked by. 'I scream for help,' he said, 'and no-one hears me.'

But once events reach a certain scale, as they did in 1945, they become impossible to ignore; once the news networks relented, the facts were unavoidable. The 'lumps of reality' were judged to be too large and indigestible, and a similar fate awaited attempts to record on film the reality of the German death camps. In 1945, Sidney Bernstein was working both for the British Ministry of Information (MOI) and the Supreme Headquarters Allied Expeditionary Force (SHAEF). Among his tasks was the creation of films as countries were liberated, and to that end he enlisted the help of his friend Alfred Hitchcock, who came to London from Hollywood. At the end of April, British troops entered first Buchenwald and then Belsen. Bernstein gained access to Belsen, staying there a whole day. That night, he and the Australian journalist Alan Moorehead drank a bottle of Scotch, with no apparent effect. The next day, Bernstein made plans for a film entitled 'German Special Film', which would be shown to German audiences, but with an English version for world distribution. In his memo to SHAEF, Bernstein, with memorable curtness, defined the function of the film:

(1) By showing the German people specific crimes committed by the Nazis in their name, to arouse them against the National Socialist Party and to cause them to oppose its attempts to organize terrorist or guerrilla activity under Allied occupation.

(2) By reminding the German people of their past acquiescence in the perpetration of such crimes, to make them aware that they cannot escape sharing the responsibility for them and thus to promote German acceptance of the justice of Allied occupation measures.

In his quest to record what had happened, Bernstein sent sound crews to enhance the efforts of military cameramen. He seems to have worried about the credibility of the film, demanding that they must photograph 'any material that will show the connection between German industry and the concentration camps – e.g. name plates on incinerators, gas chambers or other equipment . . . in particular attempts should be made to establish the firm which built the camp . . . the makers of the tattooing and/or branding machines used for numbering prisoners'.

Without knowing it, Bernstein was creating the grammar of modern documentary film. *German Concentration Camps Factual Survey* (1945), as it was called, with the understatement for which bureaucrats are famed, is one of the most brutally testing films ever made. It's a monument not just to the painstaking aesthetic and empirical sensibilities of all those who made it (or finally completed it over seventy years later), but to the power of factual film. I've watched it many times, and each time I see it, I feel it's possible to understand more: about the atrocities it describes, of course, but also how one can observe human endurance and steadfastness in the face of horror. The title seems to me both to mask the film's importance and to proclaim the merits of a non-poetic style of description. It's best just to know, the film says. Don't decide you don't want to. As soon as the footage arrived in London, however, there were misgivings. At the MOI, no one disputed the veracity of the footage, but they thought that people might not believe it was real. 'It might have a boomerang effect since people might query its authenticity,' one memo suggested.

It's not entirely clear what role Hitchcock played, but it seems that the very long takes were his idea. It was he who thought of getting Eisenhower and Churchill to read out a message at the end of the film and got the young, leftish philosophy scholar Richard

Crossman to write the script. The film begins in a near-leisurely, almost reflective style, far from the stridency of newsreel. 'In the spring of 1945,' says the narrator, over bucolic springtime shots of the German countryside, 'the Allies advancing into the heart of Germany came to Bergen-Belsen. Neat and tidy orchards, well-stocked farms lined the wayside, and the British soldier did not fail to admire the place and its inhabitants. At least, until he began to feel a smell . . .' Then we see, slowly, in long takes, what the British soldiers encountered. But the film also describes, painstakingly, the enlistment of SS guards to shift cadavers, the survivors crowding around their torturers, and the local German townspeople, most of them holding handkerchiefs to their noses. Crossman's script, written while viewing the footage, is a small miracle. He relies on the accumulation of detail, to devastating effect, minute by minute. Some sound was recorded in the camp, and there are extraordinary extemporised addresses – from a choked-up private, a padre and an officer whose words are trans-lated into German for the cowed local dignitaries. A scene in which survivors can shower in hot water for the first time – one must assume in many months – is revelatory, among the mir-acles of documentary. After its definitive, gruesome catalogue of wickedness and apathy, the film ends with Crossman's warning, which is still more than relevant today: 'Unless the world learns the lesson these pictures teach,' he concludes, 'night will fall. But by God's grace we who live will learn.'

Bernstein viewed portions of the film that had been edited, before leaving for Hollywood and his business ventures with Hitchcock. The film wasn't completed until 2015, when archiv-ists at London's Imperial War Museum finally finished assem-bling the material, creating the film as Bernstein and Hitchcock had envisioned. It has been suggested that it was abandoned because the British Foreign Office didn't want to evoke sympathy towards Jews. (This remains the view of André Singer, who produced *Night Will Fall* (2014), a documentary based on the Hitchcock–Bernstein material and containing additional material from those who survived Belsen or came as liberators.) This seems improbable, not least because the film doesn't stress the fact that most of the victims were Jews, instead (in line with contemporary anti-fascist views about why the war was fought) choosing to depict how many different nationalities comprised the death toll. It seems more likely that the ever-pragmatic British came rapidly to feel that the post-war devastation extended to the millions of Germans now in their charge, and that efforts to allocate mass blame were likely to be ineffective – an attitude which, to judge by the great numbers of Germans who continued to believe either that the Holocaust never occurred or that it wasn't their responsibility, was short-sighted. But the images and words remain for all of us, and they are extraordinary in a way that is hard to describe, redemptive. They do insist that we will somehow be wiser or better if there is nothing that we don't know.

Now that there are monuments marking killing fields across Europe, it has become hard to recreate the level of ignorance that prevailed. As late as the 1970s, films declared that such images should not be shown, as evidenced in Daniel Anker's *Imaginary Witness: Hollywood and the Holocaust* (2004). It is well known that gas-company sponsors didn't want survivors to mention how Jews had been killed. Some Germans only found out about the Holocaust as late as 1978, through the fictional Weiss family, who featured in a television drama series entitled *Holocaust*, which was watched by a staggering 50 per cent of the West German population. *Holocaust* was too cleaned-up, and the fact that its protagonists were German Jews rather than Poles or Romanians or Greeks, or members of the other Jewish communities shipped to the east, made it parochial.

It is in this context of part-willed unknowingness that one must now think of the bravery of *Night and Fog*, Alain Resnais' 1955 documentary. If you come across this film randomly, on late-night television or on an obscure website, you might think you have seen it already, so familiar are the images and so influential has Resnais' elegiac style become. Resnais didn't want to make a film about the camps, but he was persuaded to pursue the idea by the scriptwriter and Auschwitz survivor Jean Cayrol. It was not a happy experience, and Resnais was overcome by nausea when editing it. He was attacked for his pains. He was criticised in Israel for not saying that most of the victims had been Jewish, while the German government scandalously tried to get his film removed from the Cannes Film Festival. A separate, more ideologically correct version was made for East Germans. It was shown on television in France in 1956, becoming a classic, and was repeated on all the public channels in 1986, following the desecration of a Jewish cemetery. Resnais was a central figure of the French avant-garde and he constructs his vision of annihilation out of a series of static, memorial-like tableaux – scenes of railway tracks, camp museums, hair, spectacles, etc. I know many who regard the film as a defining influence on their career. Scriptwriter Cayrol's closing message hasn't lost its power in the least. 'Who is going to warn us of the arrival of fresh executioners?' he asks. 'We pretend it all happened in one place and one time, and turn a blind eye to what surrounds us, not hearing the ceaseless cry of humanity.'

In the 1990s, I criss-crossed northern Germany with a young German, in search of neo-Nazis. As we waited for these punk-ish teenagers with nose rings and tattoos, often wearing fake Wehrmacht uniforms, we talked about what it meant to be German. She told me that I could never imagine what it was like – to have always in the background a past that you could neither escape nor deny, and to experience a vestige of reproach for actions that you couldn't have committed. The Holocaust had become boring as a consequence of rote teaching, she told me. I said that I could understand this, though I might also have said that there were worse burdens. What I didn't say to her, not having read Koestler's essay, was that it wasn't so bad to be a Screamer. Maybe she should think about the astonishing Claude Lanzmann, who had defied Koestler's predictions by focusing on atrocity for most of his life and had successfully altered the way the world thought.

In *Shoah*, his imperishable masterpiece, Lanzmann seems to angle himself forwards towards his interviewees, often with the air of a bantamweight pugilist. He would be overbearing if he were taller; as it is, it looks like he's seeking a resolution to some conflict hidden inside himself. As a teenager, he fought in the Resistance. Simone de Beauvoir, who was his lover for ten years, tells us that he would wake up each night, screaming, 'You are all Kapos, all of you!' For his part, Lanzmann says that he 'loved the veil that Simone cast over her voice, her blue eyes, the purity of her face and, still more, of her nostrils'. By this stage, Jean-Paul Sartre had no physical relationship with Simone, but she would read her letters to Lanzmann to him. They travelled as a three-some, Lanzmann becoming both a son to them and, for Simone, it would seem, something of an exotic. His autobiography,

The Patagonian Hare, is a bizarrely revelatory masterpiece and strangely off-putting, because Lanzmann seems so anxious, paragraph by paragraph, to prevent the reader from thinking that he is in the least bit charming, all the while insisting immodestly on his own genius. I first met Lanzmann in his book-crowded Left Bank apartment. The meeting wasn't a success. I recall mostly that he referred to 'my Shoah', as if the event, as well as the film, were his own property. When I told him I had interviewed Jean-Marie Le Pen, the grotesque anti-Semite who was the leader of the French far right National Front, Lanzmann got to his feet. 'I must ask you to leave,' he said. 'I cannot be in the presence of anyone engaged in such activities.' I could have asked him how my own pursuit differed from all the interviews he'd secured with ex-Nazis in their retirement homes, but I decided it would be better to go. The next time I met him, he again spoke for forty minutes, without stopping, about his own masterpiece. All I can recall was that at one moment he said that he didn't like Englishmen, but he had a soft spot for Spitfire pilots, having seen them fly over occupied France. A few years ago, I had lunch with him, when I was persuading him to allow a friend to make a film about how his *Shoah* had come into existence. By then he was eighty-seven years old, and he was totally charming and generous. He got his twenty-something mathematician son to join us. He wanted to leave twentieth-century horror behind and learn about physics.

There have been many television accounts of the Holocaust. Indeed, television became the way in which generations of Europeans, from the late 1960s onwards, learnt about the destruction of European Jews. No narrative, however, is as striking and overpoweringly affecting as Lanzmann's nine-and-a-half-hour *Shoah*. It was the Israeli Ministry of Culture that gave him the idea of making it. Other backers agreed to finance the film for what was intended to be its year-and-a-half-long production, but they wanted it to be no longer than an hour and a half. In the end, Lanzmann spent ten years on the film; he needed the time in order to realise how the film should be made. It seems as if he was bailed out finally by the president of France, François Mitterrand, who believed in the project and ensured that money would be available. To begin with, Lanzmann didn't want to go to Poland, out of an aversion to Polish anti-Semitism, and because he thought that all his interviewees would be best handled elsewhere. When he finally went in 1978, he saw the importance of the empty countryside. To film former Nazis, Lanzmann created a fake foundation, assuming the name of the Institute of Contemporary History, based on the premises of the magazine he edited, *Les Temps modernes*. He called himself Claude-Marie Sorel, after the French anarchist theoretician. To film the ex-Nazis without their knowing, he kitted out a VW van. It was necessary to 'cheat the cheaters', and to this end he created a miniature camera, a *paluche* – a 30 cm camera capable of transmitting blurred images to the minivan outside – which he concealed in a bag, while sound was captured via a small microphone attached to his lapel. He interviewed several Nazis in this way, including the ineffable Franz Suchomel, who was in charge of transports and processing stolen goods at Treblinka. Lanzmann was caught out while interviewing another Nazi, put to flight by the man's four burly sons and obliged to jettison his camera. For months, it seemed that he might be prosecuted by the authorities, but the charges were finally dropped.

'It's a remarkable film,' Lanzmann's rival Marcel Ophüls said recently. 'But I'm not sure it's a great film.' There are no archival images in *Shoah*, no reassuring commentary, and nothing seems to happen in the right order. You're frequently irritated as you watch it. Shouldn't Lanzmann bother to tell us that not all Poles were anti-Semites? Wouldn't it be better if he gave at least a few facts and figures? But these prove to be irrelevant considerations. Lanzmann doesn't want us to approach the murder of millions in this way. He wants us to see if it's possible to remember anything at all. If we can look at the places where the murders took place, if we can hear what those who ordered them, assisted the perpetrators or somehow escaped death have to say, we may understand a small portion of what happened. And if we don't, after so many hours, that won't be his fault, or indeed ours. But, of course, it is the great economy of means of *Shoah*, as well as its length, that makes the film so impressive. Nothing, of course, can be re-experienced in real time, which is how, as Proust realised, everything is indeed lost, irreparably, no matter how hard we try. But there are slivers – memories, shadows – that can come back, and in *Shoah* they do. When Lanzmann attempted to raise money from the American Jewish community, he was asked what the message of the film was. He replied that it did not have one. Later, of course, when the film was acclaimed as a masterpiece, Lanzmann became part of the mythology surrounding it. Some have complained of his absorption in the Israeli cause, and it is certainly the case that in his autobiography and other films, such as *Tsahal* (1994) – a tedious account of the Israeli Defence Force, filled with images of tanks – he gave little attention to the plight of Palestinian Arabs. But *Shoah* remains his own life's work. Nothing else that he did is really important, and the significance of the film shouldn't be diminished by reference to the rest of Lanzmann's career or life. In a film made two years ago about the making of *Shoah* (*Claude Lanzmann: Spectres of the Shoah*, 2015), Lanzmann tells how the film, having been his entire life for the ten years it took to make, thereafter became his life in a literal sense. He went swimming in Tel Aviv shortly after the film was finished and experienced a sudden attack of exhaustion or depression, feeling that he was sinking. Fortunately, someone arrived in time to pull him out of his death-bound reverie. Lanzmann has made three films out of the material he didn't use in *Shoah*. In the Washington Holocaust museum, 1,222 hours of unused material are preserved, consisting mostly of his interviews. *Shoah* was first aired in Israel during the summer of 1986, in front of an audience composed of the Israeli elite. According to the writer Jonathan Freedland, it had an instant effect. The film 'told that Israeli audience watching in Jerusalem that the Shoah was alive in their country, too. They could not escape it. Too many people, and too many of their children, had been shaped by it.'

In one respect, *Shoah* is the ultimate crime story, filled with perpetrators and hangers-on, as well as victims. The real shock of the film, however, comes from the level of Lanzmann's own absorption in the subject matter. He recounts how long it took him to track down survivors of the Jewish Sonderkommando. It is hard not to agree with him when he said that he was right not to use the inadequate archive sources for the film. 'I was faced with the greatest challenge,' he said. 'I had to find a replacement for the non-existent images of death in gas chambers.' Documentaries are often trapped within the obligation to convey detail. At best, this can make them seem workmanlike. Lanzmann's film shows that if you look at something long enough and hard enough, the act of description comes to be the film's own wholly indispensable subject. *Shoah* is among the masterpieces of the late twentieth century, drawing on the traditions of French existentialism and *cinéma vérité*. One should think of it not just as a massive reclamation from oblivion, a reframing of the Holocaust, but a signal effort to show what can be done with the medium of film in the purpose of memory.

At the end of its harrowing, always eloquent, never distracting nine-plus hours, one of the last survivors of the ill-fated Warsaw ghetto uprising of 1944 tells us that as he walked amid the ruins, after the fires had gone out, he felt he was 'the last Jew'. No gloss is supplied here, but the film's author wishes us to think of the extinction of humanity. There are no annexations of suffering in *Shoah*, and no effort is made to proclaim any degree of Jewish exceptionalism regarding it. Somehow, Jews always did survive, the film says, but at Hitler's hands they didn't, and never could have done. They were left alone. That the Allies were asked to save them and didn't, Lanzmann tells us, is a great scandal; whether saving Jews was possible or not is something he finds, correctly, to be irrelevant. When it comes to killing, and being killed, the film tells us brutally that anyone will do; Rwandans, Cambodians, Armenians, Chinese have experienced the same fate as Jews. We should feel the same about any genocidal act, and indeed all killings. Mass killing is remarkable only because many people die, and *Shoah* is so remarkable because of the way in which it tells how people die. If it didn't so persistently take the side of the victims whose ends are depicted, it might seem like an illustrated manual. The film insists, painstakingly, on the killings: the wagons; the creaking, puffing trains; the poorly constructed crematoria; the use of so many Jews in Sonderkommando units. Utilitarian calculations about how many people could be killed, and how rapidly, were as horrendous then as they seem now; as is the fact that those recruited to clear up the mess would then be killed. The killing went on and on. It was supposed to end only when the last Jew was killed. The landscape of *Shoah* is dark. There is no redemption. Instead, we experience the interweaving of desolate landscapes and voices. The camera appears to hesitate before it enters the gravel pits, ponds and rotting brickwork, which are all that endure from so many of the killing sites. The film wants us to enter such landscapes, even as it says that real entry is impossible. The aesthetic strategy of *Shoah* is, therefore, a one-off, unrepeatable: it tells how its intentions cannot be fulfilled, even while adamantly insisting that nonetheless it must be done.

Lanzmann once said that if any images of gassing were discovered, he would refuse to use them, because they would have been recorded as the property of the oppressors. I'm not sure that this is a good argument, but by now it is clear that no images will ever be found. No other film like *Shoah* exists, and one must hope, admittedly without excessive grounds for hope, that none will be necessary. Of course, it was necessary to trick the Germans interviewed into depicting the system they administered. Of course, too, it was necessary to prompt and cajole survivors, and to insist that they had an obligation to relate what they had witnessed. It is not a film excessively concerned with Polish resistance to Nazi rule, and the participation of Poles in helping Jews isn't evident here. However, the interview with Jan Karski, the sole Gentile witness outside the ring of perpetrators, is remarkable in its vividness. He shows how empathy isn't a feature of co-religionism and ethnic solidarity. He is truly a just Pole. (Lanzmann has also made a shorter film out of the testimony of Karski, in which the latter recounts, memorably rising from his chair to recreate the dynamics of the encounter, his meeting with Felix Frankfurter,

Supreme Court judge and intimate of FDR. 'I don't believe this,' Frankfurter said to him. 'I know you are not a liar, but I don't believe this.') Ten years ago, the role of Catholic Polish peasants, who were, as Lanzmann depicts, at best indifferent to the plight of Jews, might have seemed to have been depicted in *Shoah* vindictively, and it is certainly the case that Lanzmann's barbed questions display his own contempt and dislike of the Catholic peasantry on show. But the Polish peasants do in turn display a historic, shameless anti-Semitism. It is clear how much they detested their richer, better educated neighbours, and that they were happy to steal the goods and properties of vanished Jews. Poles are still arguing about the question of the massacres committed by their fellow countrymen between 1939 and 1942, when Jews were rounded up and sent to ghettos. A law was passed in 2018 by the right-wing Catholic Polish government criminalising the term 'Polish death camps'; it would seem that anti-Semitism in Poland, far from being over, lingers on as a national original sin. Those still in doubt regarding this question should read about the critical, anti-Semitic treatment meted out to Jan Gross, the historian who wrote about the 1941 Polish massacre of Jews in the village of Jedwabne, and indeed the endless efforts of nationalist Poles to pretend to this day that the massacre either didn't happen or wasn't the work of their Jew-hating countrymen.

It is irrelevant to complain that Lanzmann 'set up' his interviews with survivors, forcing them into saying what he wanted. The scenes with the boy who sings, Simon Srebnik, are unbearable, but this is because this grown-up, broken man can somehow revisit the hell of his childhood, 'where everything was death', bringing it back to us and to himself. We can assume that this is what he wanted to do, and what Lanzmann allows him to do. In any case, most of the interviewees are eager to talk because they wish to convey what it was like. Their testimony is carefully organised, deliberate. No therapeutic dimension governs what still seems to be the centrepiece of the film: the revelation of Avraham Bomba, while cutting hair in a Tel Aviv barber's shop, that he had to cut the hair of town acquaintances who wanted to know what would happen to them. One fellow Sonderkommando recruit had to cut the hair of his wife and her sister before their death. How or why should we begrudge the film for telling us this? Bomba doesn't want to tell us what happened, but he does want us to know, and for that reason there is no spirit of coercion:

> Bomba: I can't. It's too horrible. Please.
> Lanzmann: We have to do it. You know it.
> Bomba: I won't be able to do it.
> Lanzmann: You have to do it. I know it's very hard, and I
>   apologise.
> Bomba: Don't make me go on, please.
> Lanzmann: We must go on.

Bomba talks about the hair shipped to Germany. Then he enters what for Lanzmann is the core of the film:

> They try to talk to him and the husband of his sister. They
> could not tell him this was the last time because behind them
> were the German Nazis, SS men, and they knew that if they
> said a word, not only the wife and the woman, who were dead
> already, but also they would share the same thing with them.
> In a way, they tried to do their best for them, with a second

longer, a minute longer just to hug them and kiss them, because they knew they would never see them again.

Lanzmann describes his encounter with Bomba in his own inimitable, somewhat bombastic style:

> The camera kept turning, Avraham's tears were as precious to me as blood, they were the hallmark of truth, its incarnation. Some have discerned in this high-risk scene a degree of some kind of sadism in myself, whereas I regard it as an ultimate expression of piety, which implies not tiptoeing backwards when you are confronted with something painful, but instead obeying the categorical imperative of finding out the truth and conveying it to others.

In the end, *Shoah* is best judged not by what it tells us, but by the degree of pain and the sense of utter irreparable loss it can elicit in the telling. By the standards of empathy it sets – because no other film has ever attained, or even attempted, this ambition – it remains a masterpiece.

After the 1970s, when the human rights movement attained a certain maturity and it became plausible to imagine that the actions of liberals might somehow restrain governments, a parallel culture of human rights journalism grew up. Film festivals or events commemorated this development. It would be churlish to criticise such occasions and the films shown there, and I went to them if not happily, at least with a sense of obligations discharged. They would begin with Chardonnay and a speech from a celebrated actor who recounted a familiar narrative. Yes, the liberal audience was told, the world was in desperate shape. Offenders included a roster of governments, some of whom (the less powerful, or the ones that could do least damage to the organisation in whose name we were assembled) were named. Usually, the film we would then watch was built around the same narrative. Afterwards, I'd slip into similar conversations with colleagues. We wouldn't want to say that we hadn't enjoyed the occasion or indeed the film, but it was clear that we hadn't. This, I suspect, was because what we had just experienced smacked of official culture. We could say that we were present only because somehow this was our cause, but there was nonetheless something not wholly satisfying about what we'd just seen and experienced. But one could say, too, that the existence of such events implied some degree of continuous interest in the parameters of atrocity. Sparrows could fall, providence notwithstanding, but mass killings, though they might take decades to punish, couldn't go unnoticed.

A few years ago, I found myself at the edge of it once more, this time in western Ukraine. *What Our Fathers Did: A Nazi Legacy* was an investigation by the human rights lawyer Philippe Sands into the circumstances in which many of his family had perished during a 1942 massacre. But the narrative was richer and more complicated, including the fact that the founding members of international law had been educated at the nearby university of Lemberg, or Lviv, as it was now called. I became familiar with the rival theories of Raphael Lemkin, who devised the legal opinions surrounding the concept of genocide, which he had defined, and Hersch Lauterpacht, whose work stressed individual responsibility, and who wrote much of the prosecution opinion defining crimes against humanity. Sands had legal textbooks with him, and he appeared limitlessly interested in the potential of his subject and irrepressibly optimistic about the potential of human rights law. In one location after another, I ticked off massacres that the world wouldn't have known about, or at the least would have found a way of diminishing. We knew about the Cambodian genocide. We knew far more about catastrophes such as China's persecution of peasants and businessmen in the early 1950s and Mao's disastrous Great Leap Forward, followed by the insanity of the Cultural Revolution. Joshua Oppenheimer's films had helped uncover the Indonesian massacres of the 1960s. The notion that no genocide had taken place in Armenia in 1915 was still proffered by the Turkish government, but few believed it. Of course, the Putin government was busy partially rehabilitating Stalin, restoring him as a nationalist Russian icon, but the revelations of the post-communist era about the Gulag wouldn't go away.

In the end, therefore, the light had been let in. The world had somehow shifted in its attitudes. Naturally, media people talked about atrocity fatigue, but they might not have meant what they said. I was sceptical about the idea of humans not responding to revelations of atrocity. I thought that Arthur Koestler was wrong. Humans may not like to accept bad things about themselves, but with persistence some sort of knowledge can be lodged in the world's brain so that it never quite goes away. Of course, its impact has to be ensured by reminders, but that's to be expected. It depends on the talent and the persistence of those making the reminders, not just on the presence of Screamers.

I was sure that no such fatigue-induced oblivion existed when I went to a New York cinema and sat through the Oscar-winning *Son of Saul* (2015). This astonishing film, by young first-time Hungarian director László Nemes, doesn't really follow a plot. He wanted to 'immerse the viewer in an experience . . . not illustrate'. Contrary to the approach of Lanzmann, who left the interpretation of events to the mind of the viewer, *Son of Saul* leaves nothing. For most of the nearly two-hour film, the camera remains on the face of its protagonist, Saul Ausländer. What we find out about the killing sites comes through blurred backgrounds and the haunting mix of languages from the camp's guards and their Sonderkommando helpers. 'We are all dead here,' Ausländer says, and his own frenzied moves – removing the dead, searching for a package in an adjoining camp factory, avoiding blows, feeding himself – are as close to a non-life as one can have without being dead. There's Ausländer trying to bury a boy who may or may not be his son, a breakout of desperate Sonderkommando squads, a final killing after guards are told where the escapees are by a local boy. For most of the film, the question of what it was like is posed. So, what was it like? What *is* it like? What is it like *now*? Killings are something we can see and know about, without ever comprehending them fully, because some things are beyond comprehension. In its modesty and utter commitment to depicting truth, this is what the film tells us, minute by minute. Of course, *Son of Saul* could not have been envisioned without Lanzmann's grand effort and all the other films that preceded or followed it. *Son of Saul* is an individual act that rests on a deeply collective effort. Such films have changed the way things like this are thought about. Lanzmann admired the film, and it is thanks to him and *Shoah*'s survivors (and all the other survivors of atrocity) that those who died can linger like a ghostly presence in each frame.

9 : Docquake

Leon Gast's *When We Were Kings* (1996): the epic life of Muhammad Ali shows both the glamour and the sordid underside of pugilism, alongside the brutal spectacle of a notorious African dictator.

Truth is hard to find. Nowadays, lies fill the pages of newspapers and magazines. As the minutes and seconds pass, it seems that truth is disappearing. I cannot think of a sector of news media that currently describes our past, present or future accurately. I've wondered if you can ever have the 'truth' in fiction, but I agree with Mark Twain that the truth is stranger and more interesting. What does he mean by 'possibilities'? How much of fiction is 'true'? The lines between the two are blurring at a rapid pace. In this post-truth landscape, how do we differentiate between them? Docs seem to be the last bastion. There is a version of truth in every documentary; the most important ones, I think, have at some time had a single truth in their story. In documentary production, an editing suite is full of files showing different constructed realities. If one of the realities works, it becomes the truth in the film. As the concept of truth becomes more elusive and confusing, through the narrative of documentaries we can at least find moments – in a face, a walk, a conversation – that offer a glimpse of it.

Sitting in nondescript BBC offices, riffling through the piles of plastic video cassettes, it took me a while to realise how lucky I was to be working in my particular field. I watched Barbet Schroeder's 1974 autobiographical farce, *General Idi Amin Dada: A Self Portrait*, a film whose narrative is controlled by the domineering general. Among the scenes is a swimming race against ministers, entirely rigged in his favour. I wanted to find new films with different voices; I hadn't considered the voice could be that of a dictator-cum-joker.

After I came across Schroeder's film, I returned again to *Paris Is Burning* (1990), Jennie Livingston's magnificent, game-changing exploration into the gay and transgender, AIDS-shadowed 'Drag Balls' of 1980s Harlem. 'Voguing' was a dance adapted from the pages of the fashion magazine, later taken up by Madonna. Most of the very young poor kids (gay or trans, pre-, post- or non-gender-altered) in the film would flock to 'balls' in shabby community halls, where Livingston filmed them. The scene was part of a larger project of self-identification by this community. You could become part of a 'house' if you performed, and the performance consisted of doing whatever pleased you. On the surface Livingston (and the others who made the film – a roster of up-and-coming New York film-makers) is fascinated by the varieties of camp. One can read the film as an application of Susan Sontag's *Against Interpretation*, a canonical work that influenced generations of New York writers and film-makers, or as something that might have come from a more empathetic Andy Warhol. But the vision is deeper here, more steadfast and more loving. It consists in seeing how true liberty allows anyone to be what they want to be. A more subversive insight is that true beauty is inextricably connected not with transgression, as is commonly supposed, but with the circumstances of personal freedom. Watch this film for the brief, wondrous life and death of Venus, a teenage transwoman and precocious expert in the economics of sexual favours, and the sage parting words of the middle-aged Dorian Corey, as she paints around her sad eyes before donning a mega-tutu. 'I don't think you have to make a mark on the world. You make a mark on the world if you just get through it.' Watch it, if only for the truth of her statement, as you only need to watch it to understand its truth.

When We Were Kings (1996) is certainly the best film about Muhammad Ali, and it vies with Martin Scorsese's *Raging Bull* (1980) for the title of best pugilism epic. It may also be the best film ever made about the glamour and sordid underside of the sporting life. It's a wonderful insight into 1970s Afro-chic and the long-lost Runyonesque culture of sports promoters and writers, as well as a traveller's-eye insight into the brutal spectacle created by that most notoriously cruel African dictator, Mobutu Sese Seko, 'Africa's Stalin', with his cane and his leopard-skin hat. *When We Were Kings* deservedly won an Oscar, yet the film was made by accident and took twenty years to complete. Leon Gast had been hired to film a James Brown concert accompanying the Ali versus George Foreman fight. The music is magnificent and sexy, the African colour hokey and seductive. The fight itself is described blow-by-blow by two stalwart, highbrow boxing buffs, Norman Mailer and George Plimpton. Prime world championship boxing was once that good and that heroic, and there was a time when Africa promised an identity shift for people of colour in America. Forget the dark side of boxing promoter Don King, and the even darker memorialisation of 1974 Zaire, and recall Ali in his late prime. He's a hero out of Shakespeare, alternately cruel in his putdowns of the hapless giant Foreman and endlessly, touchingly generous with the Zairean children massing around him wherever he goes. 'Ali, *bomaye*,' is the chant – 'Ali, kill him.' Minute by minute, you can see Ali transfigured, turned into a great leader, an inspiration, 'the hero of his time', as Spike Lee says. Ali wasn't the favourite, but he overcame Foreman by using the ropes – 'like a man leaning backwards out of the window' – and knocked his massive adversary down in the eighth round, seemingly by a form of boxing ju-jitsu, using Foreman's muscled bulk against him. After the fight, Ali was asked by Plimpton to compose his own poem, and this message, worthy of inclusion in any book of quotations, comes at the end of Gast's great film: 'Me / We.'

Now to *Southern Comfort* (2001). Bob Eads lives in the woods, and he begins by telling us how well he gets on with the 'good ol' boys'. Swiftly, though, Kate Davis, in her beautiful retelling of the last year of his life, uncovers the sheer singularity of this narrative. He grew up as a girl called Barbara ('my cross-dressing days . . . a poor little boy stuffed in drag'), and was married and had two sons. He hung out in the gay community because he was accepted there; it was this association that most upset his mother and father. (His father won't appear in the film, but off-screen he states he can still see Barbara in Bob and is disappointed that the person he regarded as his daughter didn't grow up to be president.) The doctors told Bob that since he was past the menopause, he didn't need a hysterectomy. Now, he's dying of uterine cancer. His story might come over as mawkish, but Bob is wise and devoid of self-pity. He lives with his partner Lola (a transwoman), his adopted son Brad (a transman) and friends, in a droll, black-edged, barbecue-smoke-filled forest. His grown-up son comes to visit and calls him Mom. Near to extinction, Bob is serene in a Zen-like way, helped by morphine. Life has consisted of being kind, and when that was not possible, being ruthless while hurting others as little as possible. He has no time for religion, or indeed any other form of consolation. 'Younger guys', Bob explains, 'feel that if you don't have that piece of flesh swinging between their legs, they're not a man. Being a woman or a man has nothing to do with your genitalia, it's what in your heart or your head.' Davis's film came out before same-sex marriage or LGBTQIA became mainstream, and it harks back to the real sacrifices made in the name of self-definition. And Bob, as far as human beings go, isn't short of miraculous. 'What a curious thing it is to be so uptight!' reflects Lola, after his death. 'Nature delights in diversity – why not humans?'

The Natural History of the Chicken (2000), a bizarre but brilliant film, does more than ponder the age-old 'which came first?' question. Not even the least-addicted TV-watcher can avoid the copious doses of wildlife programmes pumped our way nightly. Rarer are shows that investigate how humans do or don't get on with animals, what we think of or do to them. The Australian director Mark Lewis has made a career out of investigating the anomalous interactions of humans and animals. Many of us eat chickens, and for the most part chickens have lives that are nasty, brutish and short. Some, however, are cherished by their human protectors or kept for special purposes. Miracle Mike, a headless chicken, is alleged to have made a lot of money for his owners, and he's the star of this wackily absorbing narrative. (Mike allegedly expired because his owners mislaid the syringe used to give him water and liquid nourishment.) But there are many other appealing fowls on display, not least the fighting cocks bred in small houses who woke their suburban neighbours daily, until they were silenced by a court order. Lewis doesn't tell us that chickens are especially intelligent or likeable, but he does show how badly we treat them and how they could be allowed to have better lives. The film is shot in a lurid range of bright colours, giving its American suburban locations a wholly appropriate air of *The Wizard of Oz*. You may still be eating chicken salad after you've watched it, but you may also feel it has allowed a chink of light into the darkness surrounding what humans still call the animal kingdom.

Truth of the kind that is on display in these films can be so strange, so unexpected in its reach. I'd spent a large part of my early career around the media scene wondering why I was never quite doing what I wanted. Why wasn't I making really good films? Was it the system? I still look back at endless moments in the 1990s in a spirit of dazed astonishment. There wasn't any perceptible event that made me aware that something special was happening to docs. I can't claim prescience, but I can say how it seemed. First, the nondescript offices where I worked filled up with cumbersome VHS cassettes, then with DVDs that never really worked. Next I became aware of how far outside the normal boundaries of television those who contacted me tended to be. They weren't always British, or white; they didn't always know anything about journalism or indeed film-making. They would just tell me they had things to say. Many of these new films appeared to come from the US, but I realised that there was no national distinction applicable to these newcomers. They merely arrived, like the babies distributed by storks in Disney animations, and would be there, awaiting a life. 'Do something with me,' they would plead.

It took me a while to comprehend that these offerings, though they might have been made in the hope of earning money, were in fact gifts. Anything about them could be used, reused, discarded, appropriated and reappropriated. They would exist for different groups of people in wholly different contexts. For me, they were inseparable from the new media of the day, which was spreading globally. There were people who thought it was yet another plot of what remained of the privileged white world to take over everything. But from where I sat, in a remote, under-surveyed, neglected part of the BBC, in what had once seemed to be a closed citadel of the patriarchy, doomed to Anglo-localism, it became apparent this change was the best opportunity of my life. I could open up this fortress to fresh voices. I could distribute wealth and, perhaps more importantly, contacts and advice. I wouldn't exactly be creating a system to find films throughout the world of the kind I'd dreamt of, but I'd be helping it along.

What was so special about these new films that I encountered weekly? They were made in their own way, seeking not just a form within which what concerned them could be expressed, but a space, too. They couldn't easily be squeezed into the schedules beloved by television and its schedulers. More important was the fact that they seemed to embody a degree of authorship never seen previously. Back in the 1960s, there had been something elitist about the idea of an author, even when the pronouncements came from the very democratic Fred Wiseman. These films told me that observation was in itself good. They relied on voices. In the simplest sense, many of them offered voices to those whom they depicted. But the films also had an authorship that was identifiable. Their makers had wanted to say something. Using film, using (at times misusing) their subjects, they contrived to do more than record or depict. They really did describe.

These docs are easily classified: as films about art, as observation, as profiles of people, as hanging-out films, crisp essays, etc. Bewilderingly, Terry Zwigoff's astonishing portrait of the cartoonist Robert Crumb (*Crumb*, 1994) is all of these. It has a lot to say about America, its mainstream and its outsiders, contemporary art, caricature and pornography. It's a family story and an altogether unflattering look at its protagonist. Framed by Crumb's abandonment of the US for a life in Provence, it goes back to his origins in late-1960s Haight-Ashbury. Crumb hates to be called a counterculture guru. The roots of his angry, often abusive art lie in the 1950s blandness of the US and his brutal father. He has two brothers: one keeps to his bed (and kills himself just after the film is finished); the other lies on a bed of nails, literally. Crumb is most eloquent in relation to his Mr Natural series (an old man with a beard), which includes a woman with a plug instead of a head being given to an acne-covered teenager. Some of his drawings are caricaturally racist. In a brilliant interview, the art critic Robert Hughes says that Crumb is 'the Brueghel of the late twentieth century – and there wasn't a Brueghel of the first half'. Zwigoff's film explains that we need artists like Crumb. We're told he masturbates three times a day. He's angry towards women, yet it's clear that although he says – correctly, because he is indeed honest – that he's never loved anyone but his daughter, they do find ways of loving him. He abandons humans, yet Zwigoff doesn't press this, choosing not to indulge in clichés about the cost of art. Do we like Crumb's art because it's rooted in the failings of humans and what they call 'culture'? Or is he just a wayward humourist from the now distant underside of the 1960s? *Crumb* lets us decide. Political correctness makes it hard to imagine such a film being made nowadays.

Another feature of these films was the notion that they must end up in cinemas. Would documentaries ever make any money if they were released theatrically? Was there such a thing as a 'theatrical documentary'? It is still routine to find writers in the *New York Times* or elsewhere bemoaning the poor performance of documentaries and casting doubt on their prospects of survival in the dog-eat-dog market. In reality, there is still a small market for them in the US. They perform no worse than independent films; a fortunate few per year gross $5 million or more, and some do very well indeed. In the latter category are the films that win an Oscar or are nominated each year: one can cite *An Inconvenient Truth* (2006), Al Gore's lecture about the evils of global warming, which took $24 million, and Michael Moore's *Fahrenheit 9/11* ($220 million), *Sicko* ($24 million) and *Bowling for Columbine* ($21 million). But it is necessary to set these figures alongside DVD sales (though these are now falling precipitously) and, of course, income from television.

Documentaries shown in cinemas aren't necessarily the best films of the year. They are successful because they have been well marketed, or because their subject matter chimes with the tastes of the multiplex public. Frequently, they are on display because the people who have bought them wish them to qualify for Oscars. (The rules governing the submission of films for the Academy Awards change bewilderingly, but one constant is the requirement that financiers find cinemas in New York or Los Angeles, so that the films can at least be seen in a movie theatre before the DVDs are shipped to the Academy members.) But the annual Oscar nominations mean that within the film world, docs are taken seriously, albeit as a niche form. Documentary film-makers are noticed, they are important, and their films' merits are proclaimed on billboards in Hollywood each January. These films enter the cultural bloodstream in a way that they would not if they were merely shown on television or on university campuses, and this means that the ambitions of documentaries are significantly raised. At the very least, they are something more than an offshoot of the vast television industry. With documentaries being increasingly shown now on streaming platforms such as Netflix and Amazon, films that previously had a limited theatrical run are reaching new audiences. Famously, Netflix doesn't release its viewing figures, but we can be sure there are huge numbers of new documentary fans.

In a less tangible fashion, this also means that documentaries have found their way into the surrounding film culture. They have become part of how we see the world. In this respect, their relatively poor performance at the box office is less important. It is possible to see documentaries influencing other film-makers, as well as writers and activists. They are linked now to campaigns, through the books, blogs and online articles written about them or the subjects they depict.

The first film I saw that gave me a sense of something new was eight years in the making and nearly three hours long. Steve James's 1994 Chicago epic *Hoop Dreams* follows the basketball careers of two sixteen-year olds, William Gates and Arthur Agee, from the Cabrini projects in Chicago. I'd been sent a low-quality cassette by a friend, and idly watched the first few minutes. He called me to ask whether I'd watched it. 'Get past the first sixteen minutes,' he said. 'You'll find they get a new camera then.' He was right, and I was grateful to have persevered. 'This is one of the best films about American life I have ever seen,' the critic Roger Ebert remarked, when the film was first screened, and more than twenty years later it is hard not to agree with him. William is the steadier of the two boys; he seems destined to follow in the tracks of his idol, NBA star Isaiah Thomas. He manages to keep his scholarship place at the suburban (and Catholic) private high school, St Joe's. The pressures on Arthur, meanwhile, pile up, as his mother loses her job and his drug-dealer father leaves the family. This isn't a sports film really. It tells you how sport is a business, and an education, too. It demolishes, with precision, minute by minute, so many of the cherished lies implicit in the cult of the American Dream. But it does so without a whiff of polemical oversimplification: its characters never appear as victims and are allowed to give their own accounts. It does so with love, too, and I think of this as being down to its origins in Chicago and its authors' aversion to identity politics and dedication to what appear to be the simplest aspects of truthfulness.

I met Steve James, one of the film's three begetters, and showed another of his films on the BBC: *Stevie* (2002), about a poor white boy whom he mentored unsuccessfully while at university. James, very tall, always dressed casually, now slightly grizzled and with the patient air of a social worker or an idealistic headmaster, could be a less patrician Jimmy Stewart in a remake of *It's a Wonderful Life*. This is not a coincidence. In *The Interrupters* (2011), he follows in the wake of a community emergency group on Chicago's South Side, set up to intervene in gang violence. Most recently, in *Abacus: Small Enough to Jail* (2016), he describes an idealistic Chinese family with a small bank who are hounded by Manhattan's legal authorities. When *Hoop Dreams* was shown at the New York Film Festival, I took along a British-born novelist, and I was annoyed that she thought it was a 'white boys' film'. I cannot think of any other film that tells more clearly what it means to be poor and on the edge of giving up. About an hour into the action, Arthur's mother Sheila, who is trying to keep her family together on welfare payments of $268 a month, turns to the camera and asks us: 'Do you all wonder how I am living? How my children survive, and how they're living?' Survive they do, however, not just as a consequence of basketball, but as the result of a series of small miracles. Sheila qualifies as a nurse, and there is a beautiful scene in an abandoned church hall in which she celebrates her triumph, dressed in white. Hopeless in class, appalling at homework, Arthur is funnier and a more elegant player. William, who gets a knee injury, is probably realistic in his earlier abandonment of his NBA dreams. He becomes a Methodist pastor, ultimately, relocating to Texas in order to take his family away from crime. Arthur used some of the shared profits from the film, which made over $15 million, to set up a charity for ghettoised teenagers.

Hoop Dreams never received the Oscar it merited, but it stands now as a defining document of the conditions imposed on African Americans. It has all the qualities of a good novel – suspense, unexpected plot turns, a full and rich comprehension of humanity and, most of all, characters that you feel you can know. Another quality *Hoop Dreams* possesses is its ability to arouse indignation. Since the film was completed, both Arthur's wayward father and William's defeated brother were murdered. *Hoop Dreams* tells you what non-fiction films can do, but it offers no false hopes. It concludes that there is no immediate remedy for generations of discrimination beyond the desire and the capability, in each individual life, for survival.

At the time, I tended to associate *Hoop Dreams* with American traditions of non-fiction. In its procedure and its effects, too, it seemed to have sprung from the tradition of writing laid down in the 1960s by Truman Capote, Norman Mailer, Tom Wolfe and Joan Didion. More than Fred Wiseman's films, it had recognisable scenes and characters. In Dreiseresque fashion, it followed the existence of its characters. Steve James and his co-directors were not afraid of judgements. Working from life, the film offered the multiple perspectives of *The Executioner's Song*, Norman Mailer's one-thousand-plus-page account of the determination of Gary Gilmour to be executed by firing squad in Utah. The instinct to document exhaustively is rooted deep in American pragmatism and, as James was quick to tell me, others 'had been doing the same thing'.

Taking the advice of another friend, I recently watched *Harlan County, USA* (1976). Barbara Kopple's film begins by showing what happens in a mine, and how astonishingly hard the work is. Then we get ravishing archive footage from the 1920s and 1930s, retracing the labour struggles of America's white working class. On its surface, the film describes a year-long strike in Kentucky, depicting a distant era in American life, before fracking and the hollowing-out of the economy, when there was a large coal industry and when battles over the right to unionise could go in favour of the workers. Kopple takes the side of the workers, but she's good at depicting the often baffled mine owners – the mining company is owned by southerners – in the isolation of the Appalachians. Lingering around miners' homes and social clubs, the film builds up a picture of the mining community from the inside. But Kopple also goes to shareholders' meetings and demonstrations on Wall Street. No one had made a film about a strike at this length, no one had listened to working-class America in this way. The mix of anger and modesty in the voices is distinctive; so, too, are the battles between goons and miners, which seem closer to what Dashiell Hammett wrote about in the 1930s than the present. In 2016, Appalachia voted for Donald Trump. Many of the mines have gone, and this part of America is stuck in the past. Kopple's film has become an epitaph of sorts, but it also testifies to what you can find out if you simply stay with people long enough, and in this sense it seems utterly of our times.

A discovery I made around the turn of the new millennium was that it was okay to like stories. The argument, most eloquently laid out by John Birt and Peter Jay in *The Times*, was that the prevalence of on-screen images was somehow vulgar or inappropriate, a legacy of the roots of television news in tabloid journalism or its offshoot, documentaries. There was 'a bias against understanding' in television, which threatened the rest of the media like a contagion. Nowadays, television is anchored within the idiom of storytelling. Documentaries have contributed to this tendency. They have also enthroned narrative, for better or worse, within a wider culture. Unlike print stories or non-fiction books, or indeed novels, documentaries supply the frisson of the real. But this wasn't the case in the 1990s; it was beginning, but it wasn't yet acknowledged. I'd emerge from viewing these new films to be greeted by looks of blank incomprehension. On one occasion, I recall telling a well-known BBC figure about a show I'd just seen about the tribulations of a Finnish vacuum-cleaner salesman. 'It's a great story,' I told him. I meant that all good stories somehow jumped out of their immediate context, becoming available to all of us. But he wasn't having any of this.

I watched *The War Room* (1993) just before the Trump–Clinton debates of 2016, and was perplexed by its depiction of the beginnings of the Clinton family's rise in politics. Superficially, the film resembles so many of the Hollywood versions of American politics to which it gave rise. Get further in, and you realise that it's something bigger: a primer for contemporary democratic politics, and the best account of how, from minute to minute, politics takes place. And then you grasp that along with the sunniness, it shows the darker side of sin-based politics. You have a promising candidate, Bill Clinton, better-looking than his rivals, but with what his opponents coyly call 'character flaws'. So what do you do? James Carville and George Stephanopoulos are the perfect foils: the 'raging Cajun', with his inspirational speeches rallying party workers; and the ultra-smooth, deeply emollient speechwriter and counsellor. In an early scene, the camera is on the candidate's face when he is told that Gennifer Flowers, his shoulder-padded, blow-dried ex-mistress, is about to reveal details of many years of Arkansas assignations.

But Donn Pennebaker and Chris Hegedus's film is better than the spin it depicts. We know that Clinton will be elected and go on to display the same traits that nearly caused his downfall, but no one appearing in the film does, and the film-makers artfully recreate the uncertainty. Watch these scenes repeatedly and admire the detail: the pizza-carton-strewn offices in Arkansas from which the film only rarely ventures; the assistants on the edge of tears at crucial moments; the candidate with his perfectly coiffed wife and teenage daughter who never really wants to be on display. Despite his exuberance, Carville is the greatest exponent of the need to be serious in the intermittent pursuit of what matters. 'It's the economy, stupid', was indeed his invention. But he is never boring, not for a moment. Nor is his hilarious wife-to-be Mary Matalin, who is as smart as he is, and whom we see representing the Republican incumbent, George Bush Sr. The makers of *The West Wing* took from *The War Room* the perception that politics is addictive and those who participate really believe that they will change the world. Of course, surveying Clinton's presidency, we now know better. But that doesn't mean that someone won't come along with a different set of promises. Where would we be, the film asks, if we completely lost hope? Viewing Hillary pitted against the bouffant Trump, I knew exactly where we would be.

It has become commonplace to state that terrorism is the greatest threat to democracy, not because of the numbers killed, but because it breeds dread and insecurity. Fear is surely the ultimate enemy of democracy, which subsists on a degree of trust. I became interested in finding one such episode and seeing in what detail it could be reproduced; in creating not a laboratory for terrorism, but some sort of Petri dish in which its consequences could be experienced. Films about terrorism don't usually win Oscars, but Kevin Macdonald's film *One Day in September* (1999), about the 1972 Olympics, in which eleven Israeli athletes were killed after a badly botched rescue attempt, did. The film focused ruthlessly on a single event, recreating it as intensely as possible, without adding excessive context. It was criticised by the Palestinian intellectual Edward Said, who declared it to be 'bad politics, bad film-making' and said that it contained nothing new. Said rebuked the film-makers for having interviewed only one Palestinian, in shadow. He must have wanted the film to tell the entire story of Palestinian oppression, but I felt at the time that his observations were misplaced, and after watching the film again the day after the 13 November 2015 terrorist atrocities in Paris, I still do. *One Day in September* does give voice to the distress of the wife of the murdered Israeli fencing coach Andre Spitzer, and who would now suggest that that was a bad idea?

It would appear, from archives that have recently become available to the public, that the bodies of the athletes killed in the village were mutilated, though it's not clear whether this occurred before or after they were murdered. How should we cover terrorism? How explicit should films like this be? And how much do we risk upsetting the relatives of survivors by truthfully revealing what happened? Such questions are not resolved even now, but *One Day in September* shows, with some originality, how they were first posed. The German authorities, who had wished to make the Olympics a showcase for a new, cleaned-up Germany, were woefully unprepared. They were let down by their own violence-free vision of a New Germany; more culpably, they were just hopeless. The archive footage is so beautiful that you can understand why the athletes wanted to forget about the atrocity, but the alacrity with which the games resumed is as shocking as the speed with which the pink-and-yellow-jacketed sports presenters returned to their default mood of TV cheeriness. There is still something appalling about the way in which the German government arranged for the hijacking of a jet so that they could swap its passengers for the Palestinian killers. In a long interview filmed in exile in Africa, the surviving terrorist Jamal Al-Gashey states his case. 'I'm proud of what I did,' he tells us, pointing out that in 1972 the Palestinian cause had received very little attention. 'On that day, the word "Palestinian" was repeated throughout the world.' Al-Gashey and his fellow terrorists had wished to swap the Israeli athletes for two hundred Palestinians imprisoned by the Israelis. They weren't engaged in a project of mass murder, and I wonder what he would have made of the indiscriminate attack on Parisians. *One Day in September* remains important because it was among the first films to reach back to the beginnings of the Age of Terror.

I was as shocked as anyone by the early events of the new century. The news seemed more deficient than ever as the world careened into a spiral of propagandist statements. I found the documentaries being made inadequate. A way in, however, came from Christopher Hitchens. He'd been exercised for a long time by what he saw as the crimes of Henry Kissinger. He didn't feel that Kissinger was a figure from the past; instead, the lessons of his career were woefully pertinent. The idea of making a film about Dr K had lingered for a while. I was able to resuscitate it and got Hitch to work with two youngish American film-makers, Alex Gibney and Eugene Jarecki. As I'd hoped, *The Trials of Henry Kissinger* (2002) was raw and detailed. It had been completed quickly, but made a merit of its haste. I felt it was effective because it never became more than a work in progress. Many of Hitch's friends felt that it didn't adequately showcase his talents. I told them it was an accurate representation not just of Dr K, but of his pursuer. Hitch smoked and drank during the film. Why not be raucous? Why not try to be excessive when 'balance' has so often let us down? The film suggested that Dr K was a war criminal, and it was advertised as such on billboards in Times Square. Dr K later cornered the then head of the BBC at a corporate retreat in Bali to complain about the 'two-bit' film-makers who had besmirched his reputation. He didn't think it was the function of the BBC to bring down a reputation such as his.

Out of this experiment Gibney and Jarecki carved their own separate routes into contemporary chaos. At one time Enron was valued at $70 billion and was the sixth-largest company in the US; in 2004, it took the Texas-based energy company twenty-four days to collapse into bankruptcy. Twenty thousand employees lost their jobs, and another twenty-nine thousand followed with the collapse of the accountancy firm Arthur Andersen, which had colluded in the barely believable Enron frauds. At the time, this could be viewed as a grandiose aberration, but *Enron: The*

Smartest Guys in the Room (2005), Gibney's shrewd, numerate, blackly comic and wonderfully disabused investigation, can be viewed as prophecy. In the old days, capitalism rested on tangible assets. Enron (and firms like it) put an end to this tradition, creating a wholly new style of valuing wealth, even if the claims of the company to represent a new style of capitalism were always bogus. Rather than owning energy assets, Enron traded them. It forced up the price of electricity by withholding supplies. Clever accounting ensured that its debt mountains, which came from unsuccessful trades, were hidden in subsidiaries. These actions anticipated the sharp practices that produced the Wall Street crash of 2008.

The company was motivated by greed; it was indeed 'the dark side of the American Dream'. In a press conference, a journalist asked whether those running the company were on crack. 'It would explain a lot,' he said. Enron's chairman, Kenneth Lay, and CEO Jeffrey Skilling were Reaganesque avatars. They believed that the pursuit of 'market glory' made the Enron practices legitimate. But Skilling, prudently, unloaded much of his Enron holdings prior to the company's crash. There's a powerful aspect to Gibney's film, in the sense that it describes clearly what millennial capitalism has become, evoking the cynicism of Enron through the tapes made of traders discussing how to manipulate the regulatory statutes in California to make money. It would be naive to think that what Enron represented has been stamped out. Structured finance, as Enron called it, is still with us. Crooks still see their opportunities and take them. The real message of the film is that all business, as Adam Smith told us, implies the likelihood of conspiracy; there is nothing magic, or even special, about markets.

Jarecki's next film, *Why We Fight* (2005), was made in the wake of the 9/11 attacks, but it arose from a conversation in my own living room. Having been to Ground Zero in the weeks after the attack, watching the clearing up of dust and broken concrete, experiencing the unforgettable acrid smell, I'd become frustrated by the endless recycling of images of the buildings coming down. What we saw was impersonal and mechanical. It explained nothing. I wondered how I would feel if I had lost someone in the disaster. Wouldn't I come to hate the impersonal exploitation of grief? As Jarecki and I started talking about the causes of the conflict that was now under way, we got around to analysing a speech made by Dwight Eisenhower shortly before he left the presidency, in which the former head of America's armed forces bemoaned the existence of a 'military–industrial complex' composed of arms manufacturers and a Congress increasingly beholden to them.

Jarecki's family came from Germany in the 1930s, and he has somehow retained a European way of looking at things, even while immersing himself in the large patterns of America's recent past. He was ebullient, enthusiastic even about going straight into darkness. He wasn't afraid of tackling ideas; he knew how to offend only the right people. He made a film that linked the grief of a New York policeman with the experience of pilots sent out to drop the first bombs on Baghdad. You could watch the film and appreciate the spirit of the end of the American century, without dismissing the idea that the world in which the US was now extending its power had become dangerous in less than predictable ways. *Why We Fight* was shown in many places, including West Point Military Academy, where it became compulsory viewing for those about to become members of the US military elite.

With limited resources, I felt I could add new voices to the melee of news-cycle coverage of what appeared to be an enveloping crisis that was affecting our democracies. Alex Gibney's later efforts remain his most effective, such as his impassioned, Oscar-winning *Taxi to the Dark Side* (2007). Gibney remains professional, the most successful documentary-maker of his generation, but he has never lost the ability to be shocked by abuses of power, all the while retaining the notion that people might behave better. He is the ultimate citizen reporter. *Taxi to the Dark Side* turns the death of an Afghan driver, mistakenly arrested, taken to Bagram prison and tortured to death, into an indictment not just of brutal guards, but of the lawyers in the White House who had modified the definition of what was permissible interrogation and made it seem to Americans that they could somehow bypass the Geneva Convention, killing suspects while affirming their own status as defenders of civilisation. Gibney's narratives are never oversimplified. Unlike his subjects, he inspires trust. His work would have been confined to print media only ten years previously, but now it could be seen in cinemas. Younger people were watching these films, which I came to see as part of a new type of film journalism. Now you could simply want to tell a story that was truthful and important.

Laura Poitras's *Citizenfour* (2014), depicting the arrival of Edward Snowden in a hotel room in Hong Kong, came from this discovery. Poitras described her film as 'an escape story with a hero', but her Oscar showed how far docs had come into the previously fenced-off world of reportage. You could now debut a story on film and think afterwards about its print equivalents. Another successful piece of documentary muck-raking is Charles Ferguson's assault on Wall Street, *Inside Job* (2010). By its author's own admission, this was an attempt to indict a style of financial capitalism. Structured like an essay and narrated by Matt Damon, the film moves from one abuse to another. With a structure of chapters and the air of a formal indictment, *Inside Job* is an impressive piece of public film-making, claiming to speak for the entire American people, on whom, Ferguson is certain, a giant swindle was perpetrated. But the best parts of the film occur when he deals with side stories: the Wall Street coke epidemic, the hookers or the willingness of eminent academic economists to sell themselves to the prevailing orthodoxy. Perhaps the near extinction of world capitalism was too huge a subject to be shoehorned into one film. It is possible, too, to remain sceptical of the film's prosecutorial tone; it takes a while for one to appreciate just how one-sided and unyielding Ferguson's analysis is. He was helped along in his efforts, however, by the refusal of major players to collaborate. Are these bosses as guilty as Ferguson implies? Certainly, the many millions who saw this Oscar-winning film must have concluded that yes, they were. And with Ferguson's film, documentary attained a political importance never seen before.

It was now easy to access a multitude of new ideas. What did people think of these new film-makers? Did everyone want to make their own film? But the technology was not as simple as it seemed, and not everyone was able to take on authorship. Film-makers had discussed how and whether authorship was possible for many decades, but the new combination of editing and shooting technologies suddenly made it seem like it was. Cameras were lightweight and stock cost nothing. You could be taught merely to switch on a camera, and – *voilà!* – you were a film-maker.

In 1990, the BBC launched a series of video diaries. Shot with the latest lightweight cameras (they would seem bulky now), the films were tightly supervised. Many depicted the personal quests of the film-makers; these were expressed in the common contemporary idiom of self-realisation drawn from therapy. Victimhood was a common theme. However, *The Man Who Loves Gary Lineker* (1993) was altogether different. This was a day-by-day account by an Albanian doctor who tended his patients as best he could in circumstances of communist-era poverty. For leisure, all he could find were the soccer matches beamed faintly into Albania by Italian television broadcasters. He learnt English listening to BBC World Service on the radio, and described a fuddled private life that took him from one partner to another.

Meanwhile, the urge to disclose oneself was imminent on the other side of the Atlantic. I saw this in *Sherman's March: A Meditation on the Possibility of Romantic Love in the South During an Era of Nuclear Weapons Proliferation* (1986). The director, the southerner turned northerner Ross McElwee, starts by telling us that he has received a grant to follow in the steps of William Tecumseh Sherman, the Yankee general who torched his way across the southern states in order to destroy the Confederacy. On his way from Boston, where he is now living, McElwee discovers that his girlfriend has dumped him, and his film changes tack, becoming an effort to pick up southern belles (unsuccessfully), exorcise the demons of nuclear annihilation (half achieved, if it ever can be) and, in between these activities, describe the New South. McElwee is sometimes tart about himself and always good with his own failures. Unlike the oddly sympathetic Sherman, he never gets to destroy anything, and ultimately he proves to be no conqueror. McElwee's camera is an entrée, but it keeps him at a distance from whatever or whomever he wants to love. Nothing is natural about the act of filming, but that can be said about our efforts to live and love, too. He's interested in how the act of observation alters its subjects. You wonder what became of his subjects, such as Pat, the drop-dead beautiful would-be actress, or the naturist linguistics PhD student who lives on an island off Georgia, or indeed Ross's sister.

As one might expect, in the US documentary authorship rapidly drew from the native therapeutic process. Alan Berliner's *Nobody's Business* (1996) is a candid memoir of a grumpy Jewish father who is unable to communicate with his son and afflicted by deafness. The material is the shipwreck of old age, an ageing man at odds with his family and isolated, with little or nothing to hope for, but the film plays the part of a dutiful son. Berliner is able to hide or mitigate a certain degree of self-absorption by recourse to an impersonal, highly organised editing style, and the viewer is able to forget that his true subject is himself.

Jennifer Fox is another diarist, whose *Flying: Confessions of a Free Woman* (2007) is a six-hour experiment in feminist autobiography. Fox jets around the world, from New York to Johannesburg to rural Pakistan and India. She investigates the condition of women in remote places, while back in Manhattan she attempts to have a child and look after sick friends. Fox is a gifted and compassionate observer, and the film comes into its own as a family history, with the touchingly described death of her much-loved grandmother. Such scenes sit uneasily with the quizzing of Indian peasants about masturbation, though the contrast may tell us more than Fox imagines about the difference between rich and poor lives in the contemporary world.

Another first-person film is *My Architect* (2003), in which the film-maker Nathaniel Kahn goes in search of his father, Louis, one of the least conventional architects of the twentieth century. After his sudden death, in transit in a washroom of New York's Penn Station, his son unearths three separate families, each claiming something of Kahn Sr's life. In the end, the sheer eccentricity of Kahn Sr combines with his architectural genius to make his odd domestic arrangements seem quite natural – a conclusion reached by his tolerant and loving son. *My Architect* is a touching quest for a permanently absent father, but it's also a meditation on the nature of genius. Kahn Sr came from a very poor Estonian Jewish family. He scarred himself by putting burning coals on his face when he was three and 'captivated by light'. Brought up in lower-middle-class Philadelphia, he created his first building when he was fifty. His inspiration didn't come from modernism, which he didn't like. Instead, his masterpieces were a consequence of exposure to ruins in Egypt and the Middle East. After that, Kahn Sr worked round the clock. He took ill-paying commissions because he wanted to do good work. Among his masterpieces are the Salk Institute in California and the Yale Center for British Art in New Haven. Nathaniel, however, prefers the 'symphony boat' that Kahn built for a patron, upon which musicians can perform while at anchor, and the astounding clay-and-brick parliamentary complex in Dhaka, Bangladesh. He talks about his father with I. M. Pei, Philip Johnson and Frank Gehry, and quizzes his reluctant mother on why she loved his father so much. Slowly, the idea that Kahn Sr was indeed a genius becomes believable. He wasn't a believer and didn't talk about being Jewish, but some element of Jewish mysticism clung to him. Meanwhile, he revelled in process, as indeed his son's film does. Bricks, for him, were to be valued for their brickness. 'Nothingness mattered to him, silence mattered to him,' an Indian collaborator says. 'He cannot be an ordinary person. We call him a guru, a yogi.' The beautiful clay-brown Dhaka buildings gave the spirit, as well as the institutions, of democracy to Bangladesh. Kahn Sr sacrificed his life and his families in order to create them, but by the end of the film his son has concluded that the sacrifice was worthwhile. Who will argue with that?

I assumed there was huge effort put into these personal films, but these authors sometimes struggled to be as good as writers. Autobiographical films were a new way of memorialising ourselves, of recording memories. I got to like films that crossed over, from less personal to more. It's hard to write in a style that shifts frequently in tone and approach, and much harder to film. Luke Holland's work is reticent, indirect in an English way. He made a revealing film about the death of his own brother from cancer. He now suffers from the same incurable disease, and his short films documenting the illness are small miracles. In *A Very English Village* (2005), Holland, an urbane-seeming intellectual who discovered only late in life that he was Jewish, is living in Ditchling, a picture-postcard village in Sussex, and his account of its inhabitants doubles as an exploration of his own borderline rapturous, ironical discovery of English semi-rural eccentricity. Filmed at the beginning of this century, his films hark back to the many attempts made by Orwell and his contemporaries in the 1930s to discover what it means to be truly English. But they're edged with darkness. One episode lays uncomfortably bare the incestuous life of the resident genius of Ditchling, sculptor and designer Eric Gill, who, it is now clear, abused his daughters.

I came to associate the irruption of these highly personal films with the greater opportunities given to women directors. No

niche for female film-making existed, and places like the BBC
had offered a platform only to the likes of Molly Dineen. But now
that it was possible to make really personal films, it was clear to me
that women did this best. How do people disappear, leaving their
lives behind? Carol Morley's first ambitious film, *The Alcohol
Years* (2000), chronicles her own disappearance into alcoholic
haze via the not-very-caring milieu of the Hacienda nightclub,
at the heart of Manchester's music scene. She tells her story by
leaving herself out, bar the odd off-camera question, thus giving a
curious degree of detachment to what must have been an ordeal.
The woozy lostness of Morley's autobiography also colours her
second essay in solitude. *Dreams of a Life* (2011) tells the story of
the life and death of Joyce Vincent, found in her north London
bedsit three years after she died. After spotting the tabloid head-
lines, Morley placed classified ads in London papers. 'Did You
Know Joyce Vincent?' she asked. Slowly, people came forward
– co-workers, lovers, Joyce's sisters. They had known Joyce, but
as it turned out, they hadn't. Joyce, who had an Indian mother
and a father from the Caribbean, had been very beautiful, very
much a presence for those around her. Men clustered around her,
but she made a habit of pushing everyone away – maybe, as some
baffled interviewees suggest, because she was abused as a child,
or because her mother died when she was young and her father
never had time for her. She had made something of her life, but
for reasons that no one could quite fathom, she had contrived
to lose everything, spending time in a hostel for abused women
in order to escape a tormentor and ultimately cutting herself off
from her family. In other hands, Joyce's ordeal might have become
a pretext for homilies about the modern world, but what interests
Morley is the fragility of individual lives. These films have a way

of mixing in the personality of the film-makers and they tell you how the directors see the world. Such masterpieces rarely occur.

If you are in luck at Sundance, you'll catch a glimpse of Werner Herzog walking up Main Street. Against the half-swept snow, his beautiful Siberian wife on his arm, he looks like a visitor from a more civilised Grand Hotel world. But this is an illusion. His life has been spent describing danger, on the periphery of catastrophe. Herzog was born in 1942. His father served in the army, while his mother was a biology teacher, and he recalled the arrival of American troops. The family moved back to post-war Munich, where Herzog organised his own education, while acquiring a permanent admiration for America that distinguishes him from his generation of Germans. Wim Wenders is the same. Much of the fragile and harried boy survivor in J. G. Ballard's *Empire of the Sun* survives in Herzog's book of interviews:

> *Do you ever get bored?*
> The word is not in my vocabulary. I astonish my wife by being capable of standing and staring through the window for days at a time. I may look catatonic, but not so inside. Wittgenstein talked about looking through the closed window of a house and seeing a man standing and flailing about strangely. You can't see or hear the violent storms raging outside and don't realise it's taking great effort for this man even to stand on his own two feet. There are hidden storms within us all.

'Always take the initiative,' Herzog told young film-makers. 'There is nothing wrong with spending a night in a jail cell if it means getting the shot you need. Send out all your dogs and one might return with prey. Beware of the cliché. Never wallow in your troubles; despair must be kept private and brief.' In 1999, after a long transatlantic flight that left him sleepless, and after watching an ineptly made nature film on TV and some porn, Herzog came up with the bizarrely devised Minnesota Declaration:

> *Cinéma vérité* is fact-oriented and primitive. It is the accountant's truth, merely skirting the surface of what constitutes a deeper form of truth in cinema, reaching only the most banal level of understanding. If facts had any value, if they truly illuminated us, if they unquestionably stood for truth, the Manhattan phone directory would be the book of books … Too many documentary film-makers have failed to divorce themselves clearly enough from the world of journalism. I hope to be one of those who bury *cinéma vérité* for good.

In his quest for truth, Herzog admitted to 'playing with facts', thus struggling against the bureaucrats who ran television. He suggested that young film-makers should do the same. He'd become a proponent of what he called 'ecstatic truth', as if all truth were somehow rapturously anchored in ecstasy, or at least all important truths, while the less important aspects of existence somehow shouldn't matter too much, at least to film-makers. Meanwhile, he'd set up his own film academy, in which one might learn 'The art of lock picking. Travelling on foot. The exhilaration of being shot at unsuccessfully. The athletic side of film-making. The creation of your own shooting permits. The neutralisation of bureaucracy. Guerrilla tactics. Self-reliance.' He explained: 'I prefer people who have worked as bouncers in a sex club or have been wardens in the lunatic asylum. You must live life in its very elementary forms. The Mexicans have a very nice word for it: *pura vida*. It doesn't mean just purity of life, but the raw, stark-naked quality of life. And that's what makes young people more into a film-maker than academia.'

Herzog was right to rail at what had become the mechanical orthodoxy of documentary film-making, in which subjects were routinely processed for captive TV audiences. He took film-making from its rich-kid doldrums. His own fiction films contained a powerful dose of non-fiction, often seeming to veer into a highly sophisticated equivalent of reality television, in which the actors suffer in Herzog's search of ultimate authenticity. *Burden of Dreams* (1982), a documentary by Les Blank, is an indispensable complement to Herzog's *Fitzcarraldo*, which described the effort involved in dragging a steamer over an Amazonian mountain.

I wasn't sure what to make of these assertions. I could see the value of factual enquiry, but there was something wholly wonderful about Herzog's battles against factual tyranny. So much of German post-war history, East or West, was utterly grey. German cultural life had consisted of warnings against taking the wrong turns, and it took courage to buck this. The lies implicit in this cult of reasonableness had been frequent and horrible; having worked both in the defunct GDR and in the Federal Republic, I could vouch for this. Something important in Herzog's sensibility comes from the German Romantics, with their insistence on the obligation to be authentic. Running around the world, from volcanoes and smoking oil wells to the wastes of Antarctica, he seemed wonderfully authentic, like the ageing versions of eternally young men whom Britain let loose on the world in quest of adventure during the age of empire. He seemed to love, or at least respect, the oddballs he met in his quests. I liked the way he was always able to disguise his own excessive normality by associating himself with madmen – wholly dysfunctional characters like his 'best fiend' Klaus Kinski or mildly eccentric scientists. I could applaud, too, his insistence that some images were special and that humanity was now marooned in an endless tide of banality and impersonally distributed dreck. Herzog's best films reclaimed the act of seeing for us. At the same time, he successfully persuaded many generations of film-school graduates that seeing was somehow autonomous. If you took his *obiter dicta* seriously, you wouldn't really have to know anything. You could just go and make films, and they would supply your own store of knowledge.

My own intermittent dealings with Herzog, conducted through pliant intermediaries and emails, were hilariously at cross purposes. We collaborated on one of his less successful efforts, a sci-fi fantasy based on ice-tank footage from NASA (*The Wild Blue Yonder*, 2005), in which he imagined a planet come astray in the distant future. Some of the film was shot around abandoned supermarkets in California. I wrote to him saying I felt like the copy-editor of an H. G. Wells novel on speed; tactfully, he didn't reply. Frequently, he claimed the right to use material in the way he thought fit. In many respects, not least the voice, he resembled Orson Welles, utterly certain in his endless pursuit of contingency. 'Death did not want him,' Herzog's basso commentary tells us with regard to the ultimate rescue of Dieter Dengler, in his masterpiece, *Little Dieter Needs to Fly* (1997). Dengler is another Herzog doppelgänger, but one closer to him than the others: born in the same chaos of beaten-up Germany, in quest of something, washed up in the US, hoarding food in his isolated northern California house, still fearful.

Dieter, like Herzog, wanted to fly, because he recalled the sight of American pilots rocketing past his German village in 1945, cockpit open and goggles on their forehead. He loved the glamour of flight, and this, in the vein of Saint-Exupéry or Korean War veteran James Salter's *Burning the Days*, is the true subject of Herzog's film. Dieter emigrated to the US in order to escape Germany. He went to university, and found himself flying for the US Navy over Laos. Shot down, he was maltreated by the Pathet Lao and escaped through the jungle. He was finally rescued, seemingly by chance. Herzog takes poor Dieter back to his jungle hell. It would seem that he never really recovered, keeping extra reserves of food and going back over the death of his beloved comrade, who was beheaded by pro-Vietcong villagers. But this isn't the real message of the film. Herzog wants to tell us that, somehow, people do survive. They are wounded, but they go on. For him, this is far more important than whether the war was a good idea or not.

In an astonishing final sequence in an aircraft graveyard in the desert, he tells us he's in 'pilot heaven'. Many I know found the film repulsive in its casual acceptance of actions that cause death or mayhem, but I'm sure that Herzog also wants us to think of bravery and recklessness. What propels young human males towards danger? Of all Herzog's films, and aside from his early fictional masterpieces, such as *Aguirre, the Wrath of God*, *Little Dieter* was his most poignant. It's hard to watch it without thinking of the more than one million young Germans who let themselves be driven to death by a psychopath. They weren't all criminals; most of them didn't get to fly, but some did. What are we to think of them, and Dieter? Herzog tells us that at one viewing, a television executive had to leave the room because he felt sick. The film never received its due – mainly, I suspect, because those who programme at festivals aren't sympathetic towards the admiration of the US military expressed by Dieter. I felt exhilarated. In its own modest way, Dieter's life seemed to describe post-war Germany, and I was grateful to Herzog for this truth, however he had chosen to wrap it. 'If so much is invented,' asks the critic Ian Buruma, who admires Herzog's oeuvre, while retaining some doubts about his inventions, 'how do we know what is true? Perhaps Dengler was never shot down over Laos. Perhaps he never existed. Perhaps, perhaps.' Yes, but Dengler did exist, he did suffer, and Herzog captured his experience.

As I watched Herzog's films, I found that I often agreed with him – not with his methodological musings, but with the often unacceptable truths that he was able to convey to my rather stoic Anglo-Saxon self. I didn't want to, but Herzog, drawn towards darkness and reluctant to let go of what he had found, like a prized dog, had brought it back for scrutiny. In *Grizzly Man* (2005), he introduces us to Timothy Treadwell, who died in 2003 with his girlfriend Amie Huguenard, eaten by a grizzly bear in the Alaskan wilderness after having spent thirteen summers living with bears. The film's subject is among the most moving of Herzog's recuperations from the chaos of life. He doesn't like Treadwell's ideas about the harmony and sanctity of nature. In his view, humans are different from animals. One should strive to comprehend them, and not, as Treadwell did, idealise them. Many of Treadwell's views – about the remarkable aspect of piles of bear shit, for instance – are ridiculous. But Herzog focuses only on why Treadwell held the views he did. It transpires that

Treadwell was needy, a failed actor, an ex-alcoholic. He did love these huge animals and liked being around them. It's intimated that this love was born out of a sense of hopelessness, and that by the time he and Amie were attacked and chewed into pieces, he wanted to quit humans. The story is told with great brio, but with compassion, too. Among the many tapes of Treadwell's bear and fox encounters, containing the most naive ramblings to camera, is the final one, recorded with a cap on the lens, which captures the couple's last moments. A pathologist tells us what the tape reveals about their appalling deaths, but Herzog, after listening to it, tells Treadwell's best friend that she must destroy it and never listen to it.

Herzog's work still elicits controversy, and there are many who don't admire it. A friend tells me that he also thinks that Herzog finds Treadwell merely foolish, and that his expressing his admiration for Treadwell's boldness is fake. I'm not so sure. Herzog's extraordinary narrative sleight of hand deals out the details of Treadwell's end with the skill of a practised card sharp. But he has to do this, otherwise we'd be bored by Treadwell. Many of his films are meditations on what we learn about man through nature. An Alaskan anthropologist talks about the 'line between bear and human' that one mustn't cross. But humans are always crossing lines – that is what they do, out of curiosity or compulsion. The really significant truth of Treadwell's story is that the Disneyish, 'sentimentalised view' of nature, in which perfection belongs to animals and not to rapacious and cruel humans, is not just wrong, but lethal. 'Here I differ from Treadwell,' Herzog says. 'I believe the common denominator of the universe is not harmony, but chaos, hostility and murder.' In the bear's expressionless face and huge jaws, one can see nothing of that 'secret world of the bear' that Treadwell trekked into the wilderness to observe, 'but the overwhelming indifference of nature'. Werner is a pessimist and a sceptic, not a cynic. There are few people capable of giving us such bad news with so much eloquence. The worst is here around us, in any place we care to look. Do we want to look? Herzog asks us. Do we really want to look?

It took television many years to accommodate any degree of narrative sophistication. On television, as anyone will tell you, it is next to impossible to imply that what you are showing might not be true. Television is without perceptible style, but it insists, often misleadingly, on the notion that what it depicts is 'real'. Its narratives come concealed behind a bland, undifferentiated flow of images. Film-makers can choose to allow themselves to drown in the flow or they can attempt to use the non-idiom of television for subversive purposes. They can do us a service by showing how the images of television are at odds with reality. With persistence, it is possible to get us to see how disconnected our media-drenched lives have become. It was a film set in the early 1970s that seemed most bizarrely prophetic to the problems of contemporary reportage. At its largest, the Symbionese Liberation Army (SLA) boasted nine militants, most of them from the vicinity of Berkeley, California. Its communiqués invariably ended with the Buck Rogers meets Chairman Mao message 'DEATH TO THE FASCIST INSECT THAT PREYS ON THE LIFE OF THE PEOPLE'. But the SLA became more celebrated than the other underground groups that came into being in emulation of the Black Panthers. This was because of the kidnap of the heiress Patty Hearst in 1974. For almost two years, America hung on every rumour regarding Patty's whereabouts. Was she a victim of her kidnappers, or had she become a willing participant? The footage of her participation in a raid on a bank and photos of her carrying a machine gun while posing in front of the snakelike SLA emblem seemed to indicate that she had joined the struggle against capitalism, but her utterances ('Mom, Dad, I'm OK. I'm with a combat group that's armed with automatic weapons . . .') sounded over-rehearsed, drugged. In *Guerrilla: The Taking of Patty Hearst* (2004), Robert Stone never pretends to solve the Patty mystery. He's an ironist, illustrating the fatuity of West Coast revolution with Hollywood images of Robin Hood and posing the question of whether the idea of insurrection can mean much in a society such as California's has become. He's interested in the Berkeley waters in which the SLA swam to the surface. He sees the story, correctly, as the first instance of the taking over of media by terrorists – a phenomenon with which we are by now only too familiar, elegantly defined by the French theorist Guy Debord as 'the society of the spectacle'.

Patty's story continued to be the source of pop non-fiction, but few looked at the implications of the narrative into which she had strayed. Stone found much of his astonishing footage while it was being thrown out by cost-cutting TV stations. The hacks appear bemused by their own capacity to manufacture news out of nothing. They acknowledge the vacuity of their own work as they stand outside the Hearst mansion, while enjoying the picnic environment. 'We never discussed should we be doing this,' a newsman says. 'We were acting as messengers for the family and back again.' At Patty's behest, the Hearsts spent millions handing out food to the Californian poor. Superficially, the SLA accomplished nothing, but they sped into existence the media-drenched world in which we now struggle to stay afloat, where trivia and significance come hopelessly bundled. I sat behind

Patty, pardoned by Bill Clinton, when she watched the premiere of the film at Sundance, and I asked her what she thought of the film. 'It was interesting,' she said, and I believe she meant it.

Another person in revolt, not just against the stale habits of documentary film-making, but also the conventions of contemporary life inside and outside academe, is Errol Morris. He is genial, purveying wisdom through aphorisms and new–old witticisms. But there is a darker Morris, too, who wishes humans were otherwise. This is how he expressed his own view of humanity in a debate with Werner Herzog. Herzog was airing his views about *cinéma vérité* and postmodern dogma:

> WH: I think there's a new enemy out there that we should really start to tackle more violently and more viciously. I mean, with sucker punches wherever we can do it.
>
> EM: I think it's the same—
>
> WH: Do you think it's insignificant?
>
> EM: I think it's the same old enemy, really. It's ourselves. I'm very fond of telling people when they say that they would like regime change, for example, in Washington, that what we really need is species change. That the species itself is so impossible and so deeply degraded that one could well do with something else for a change. But I don't think the problem is with *vérité*, per se. There have always been oddball claims about truth-telling in cinema.

After meeting Morris, I wondered whether such apparent misanthropy wasn't a cover of sorts. One cannot attend many gatherings of doc-lovers without feeling the need to perform, and making docs of the kind Morris has – rich in iniquity, filled with human stupidity as well as eccentricity – must end up by darkening the sensibility. But no, Morris holds the bleakest view of the prospects for humanity. At least some of it comes from his early career, before he started making films: in his academic experience studying philosophy (which he hated) and the history of science, and his life as a private investigator. His remark about Herzog – that the latter supplies investigations into 'the meaning of meaninglessness' – applies better to himself and his own work. Like many who have skirted nihilism, however, he remains cheery and upbeat in person, pursuing his epistemological obsessions with gusto. Anyone seriously interested in images and the art of photography must go to his blogs on the subject or the book drawn from them, *Believing Is Seeing* (2011). From these it emerges that Morris, while being a formal obsessive, having grown up with all sorts of movies and spent a good deal of his student life sneaking in and out of film archives, dislikes the sloppiness of *vérité*. He feels that it is extremely difficult reliably to extract the truth from our surroundings, and not always pleasant when you do.

His earliest films investigate the macabre and random aspects of American life. By his own account, he stumbled into his first great film while looking into the record of a man charged with providing 'expert' advice in murder cases. *The Thin Blue Line* (1988) ushers in the by now familiar trademarks of crime TV: reconstructions, a bigged-up score (this one by Philip Glass), dizzying twists and turns that come with new revelations. But Morris is up to something different. He approaches the murder as a beady-eyed ironist. Randall Adams was passing through Texas on the way to California, when he found work in Dallas. He was about to start employment. There is no motive for his murder of a police officer, shot after stopping the car Adams was a passenger in. By contrast, sixteen-year-old David Ray Harris, who was driving the stolen car used for the murder, had a criminal record and would have wished to hide this from the police. But Adams's guilt was established by Harris's testimony and the presence of a number of highly unreliable witnesses.

As you watch the film, it becomes apparent that Adams (an intelligent interviewee, speaking from prison) is a highly unlikely murderer. Morris is really asking how it is that we make so many mistakes. This is a question rarely posed in journalism and film-making, and it resonates throughout his work. What can we expect from human creations, such as government or justice, when humans are so bad at uncovering the truth? The Dallas policemen aren't stupid or venal. They seem to be afflicted by locked-in errors. All the facts are before them, but they cannot make sense of them. As salaried officers, they feel that they are paid to get convictions, and that the twenty-six-year-old Adams can be punished with the death penalty. At sixteen, Harris (who was later convicted of another murder and executed, and who seems to have been abused by his father, who blamed him for the death of a brother) was too young for this punishment. Morris tells the story in fits and starts, with humour and many dog-leg digressions along the back roads of American police lore, thus stopping us from identifying with any version of the truth. *The Thin Blue Line* was acclaimed as a postmodernist masterpiece drenched in unknowability, but it now comes across as the work of a wise, old-fashioned sceptic.

Grand members of the American elite are habitually interviewed by their equivalents in television journalism, with somewhat predictable results. *The Fog of War* (2003) feels different because Morris is able to air his own views about public life, which are quizzical, drenched in scepticism. Can public figures really accomplish anything? If they do, isn't it largely by chance? And aren't their efforts often dogged? *The Fog of War* follows the career of Robert McNamara through World War II and the Vietnam War up until 1967, when he resigned (or was pushed out, as he half concedes, though even this fact isn't securely established) as secretary of defence. McNamara was the technocrat of Camelot, a personal friend of JFK and the man who, with JFK's widow, picked out the site in Arlington cemetery where the president would be buried. He stayed on, fatally for his reputation and the lives of millions of Vietnamese, to serve Lyndon Johnson during the expansion of the Vietnam War.

McNamara came from an idealistic generation that had grown up during the Depression. He came from a family that hung on to its middle-class life as a consequence of FDR and the New Deal. He believed in the power of government to do good, and this never seems to have left him, even as he summoned up more young men and sent them into the quagmire of Vietnam, colluding in falsehoods about the progress of the war as he stoked the flames of failure. He had worked with the notorious Curtis LeMay on the logistical aspects of the bombing of Japan during World War II, and he was also a highly successful chief executive of the Ford Motor Company. However, he was ready to condemn the conduct of the Vietnam War. Prodded by Morris, McNamara seems alternately contrite and defensive. The film is cast as a series of lessons. The fascination of Morris's film doesn't come from the uncovering of McNamara's views, which were already well known, nor is any great degree of wisdom imparted by these lessons, many of which seem banal. McNamara talks a lot about how one can never fully be aware of what one is doing – a theme that clearly appeals to Morris:

> Lesson #11: You can't change human nature.
> We all make mistakes. We know we make mistakes. I don't know any military commander who is honest who would say he has not made a mistake. There's a wonderful phrase: 'the fog of war'.
>
> What 'the fog of war' means is: war is so complex it's beyond the ability of the human mind to comprehend all the variables. Our judgement, our understanding, are not adequate. And we kill people unnecessarily.

In the film, the former Vietnamese foreign minister tells McNamara that he (and the American elite) ought to have known that the Vietnamese were primarily nationalists. They had always resisted the Chinese enemy. McNamara never really addresses questions such as these. Historians don't like counterfactuals, he explains. He believes things might have gone differently, but won't say how. 'Who knows?' he asks. 'Well, I knew certain things. I'm very proud of my accomplishments and I'm very sorry I made errors.' You might feel, as a casual observer, that this isn't really good enough. One can certainly know in hindsight how wrong McNamara's policy was, and maybe Morris could have pressed him harder. Earlier, McNamara has told us that he and LeMay could have been tried as war criminals if the Japanese had won the war. McNamara remains charming and approachable; he isn't evasive. He seems the perfect example of what Noam Chomsky called the 'American Mandarinate'. It's interesting to see a film in which uncertainty is the guiding editorial principle, rather than moral outrage. One can feel this, while wondering whether there isn't something missing from Morris's urbane investigation into the nature of war.

In the film, McNamara is filmed head-on by means of the interrotron, a device Morris invented:

> Teleprompters are used to project an image on a two-way mirror. Politicians and newscasters use them so that they can read text and look into the lens of the camera at the same time. What interests me is that nobody thought of using them for anything other than to display text: read a speech or read the news and look into the lens of the camera. I changed that. I put my face on the Teleprompter or, strictly speaking, my live video image. For the first time, I could be talking to someone, and they could be talking to me and at the same time looking directly into the lens of the camera. Now, there was no looking off slightly to the side. No more faux first person. This was the true first person.

But in Morris's films there is no gain in intimacy. Instead, the subject seems isolated, pinned to the wall by the interrogation. It's hard to be certain whether this is the consequence of Morris's own cold eye or the presence of a video screen separating subject from interviewer. The same feeling of remoteness characterises Morris's *Standard Operating Procedure* (2008), which describes the notorious photos of the Iraqi prisoners who, wearing hoods and with panties placed on their heads, were piled on top of each other and forced to masturbate. This is, as the *Guardian*'s reviewer Peter Bradshaw said, 'the grimmest experience imaginable'. Morris isn't interested in judging; he just wants us to ask why these very young, poorly educated, bored Americans did these things – a question to which there is no answer, except that it wasn't their fault. But one can push a level of detachment too far. Morris wants us to know that images by themselves, while not meaningless, express only a part of what they seem to describe. The famous snap of a hooded man attached to wires and standing on a crate was a mock-up and a performance of sorts. To some degree (how much is never clear) the Iraqis were participants in their jailers' games. I can recall feeling that Morris's photographic interest was a divagation from what should have been the principal theme of the story, which wasn't the sad exploits of Sabrina Harman, Lynndie England et al., but the phenomenon of torture being freely exercised by the US military.

Morris's work exposes the phenomenon astutely described by Shakespeare as 'the dyer's hand'. What happens to you after intense exposure to much of the worst of the world? Cynicism is a Morris trope, and it is on ample display in *The Unknown Known* (2013), his study of Donald Rumsfeld, another member of the Mandarinate. Rumsfeld began his career working for Nixon and Ford. He was summoned back to Washington in order to supervise, catastrophically, George W. Bush's Iraq War, before being sacked. Unlike McNamara, Rumsfeld isn't apologetic. Sounding like the ultimate country-club wiseacre, his recourse is the great number of emails (he calls them 'snowflakes') that he wrote to defence department underlings and other members of the Bush administration. Apart from conceding nothing, Rumsfeld displays a charmless, patronising habit of omniscience. His notorious remarks about known knowns, unknown knowns, known unknowns, etc., seem no more than cracker-barrel mottoes.

It's said that an age gets the artists and chroniclers it deserves, and the flat, disengaged quality of a Morris narrative is recognisably of our time. How far can one get with films that offer no conclusions? Narratives like this are no different from ordinary journalistic ones, which is the same as saying that some unreliable narrators are more interesting than others. Liars or obfuscators come in many shapes or forms. It is possible that Rumsfeld believed he was being candid, but more likely is the possibility that, bored in retirement, he enjoyed jousting with Morris. Morris's Rumsfeld encounters provoked a memorable assault from David Thomson, film critic of the *New Republic*:

'Documentary' is one of the fallacies of the modern age.
Yes, the movie audience will say that many of the best films
are docs, so let there be more. They are good for us. But any
documentarian will tell you that their work relies on funding,
access, and keeping their noses clean. It is actually more likely
now that fiction will stick its finger in raw wounds. If you
want a thorough exploration of any topic, go for a book,
or several books. Our war machine long ago got a grasp on
controlling combat footage fit for the public. A few cell
phones in Abu Ghraib broke free of that control, but such
errors will be contained. Meanwhile 'documentary' is a word
that needs to go alongside 'justice' (they both fascinate Errol
Morris) in that you can get what you pay for, what you are
determined to obtain through due process . . .

I don't think this is entirely fair. One might conclude instead that Morris's technique of letting his subjects talk and then contextualising their speech through elaborate montages wasn't right for

Rumsfeld. He might have got further if he had interviewed some of the many people who believe Rumsfeld to be a war criminal. If he had done, however, Rumsfeld might well have not agreed to be in the film.

But that is not to say that Morris's methods are in any way ineffective. In *Tabloid* (2010), he uses them to great effect in the story of Joyce McKinney, who pursued a Mormon to a hotel in Britain's West Country, chaining him to a bed post. McKinney's exploits became an obsession of the British tabloids, which as usual were locked in a circulation war. The Mormon caper is one of those great British journalistic events in which truth never figures extensively. By the end of the film, you know less about what McKinney did than you did in the first five minutes. Morris is gregarious and affable, but pugnacious when it comes to defending his methods. He wants to tell us that making up stories is what humans do. '"Nice person" is the ultimate oxymoron,' he explained to me cheerfully, when I interviewed him after a screening of *Tabloid*. I couldn't really tell if he meant it. I watched Morris's film during the week when Rupert Murdoch's phone-hacking, tabloid vision of politics in Britain was finally called to account. The film seemed both an exercise in nostalgia and a warning: this is what happens if you take fictions too seriously; at the very least, you become a prisoner of them. You may in time come to be held in thrall by their power, by the dark reach, powerful but illusory, of the Murdoch empire. This is Morris's ultimate message, playfully delivered. Beware, he tells us. Beware of ourselves.

Within British culture, Adam Curtis is the most serious investigator of uncertainty. He started off his career teaching at Oxford and got bored. His media debut was a film about a dog that was supposed to sing Scottish songs:

We set the camera up. The owner dressed up in his kilt and started to play the bagpipes. The dog refused to sing. It just sat there looking at me just saying nothing. It just sat there with a really smug look on its face. This went on for about two hours ... We ran a long close-up shot of the dog's face with the sound of out-of-tune bagpipes. It was quite avant-garde, but the audience loved it ...

Curtis's films are nowadays carved out of the gigantic archive of the BBC's unused footage. He's most interested in its store of material dumped overnight from satellites, which often contains bizarrely illuminating, interstitial material. Seemingly born into the BBC, with an impeccable sing-song Oxbridge accent and the capability of disguising radical ideas within a patina of stylishness and a bemused lack of dogmatism, Curtis has developed his own idiosyncratic approach both to the use of archive film and the entire idea of reporting. He trained as a psychologist, and his films make a point of always following the route no one else is bothering to take. Although his narratives appear to be rooted in history, this is an illusion. His real subject is the difficulty we have in knowing anything at all. He likes to say how much he learnt from popular television, and his narratives are always highly watchable, even if you don't agree with them. Curtis's strategy is to coddle audiences, making them feel comfortable with his own, distinctly bleak vision. Like many English intellectuals, he balances a dystopian view of the world with great charm, and in his own, understated way is as great a pessimist as George Orwell.

In *The Century of the Self* (2002), Curtis looks at the private, as well the public, lies of the twentieth century. This is a big, bold, often witty look at the influence of the Freud family and their

ideas on the twentieth-century zeitgeist. The central figure is
Edward Bernays, Freud's émigré American nephew, though there
are walk-on parts for Anna, Freud's daughter, and the London
Freuds. Bernays took his uncle's pessimism about human beings
and converted the insight that mankind was motivated irrationally
into the pseudo-science of mass manipulation. On the grounds
that no one understands the world we live in, Bernays believed
that power should be handed over to an elite capable of standing
in for us. Because of the predominance of the US, that elite was
largely composed of those who worked for, or represented, the
interests of giant American companies. Their interest lay in creating needs among consumers. Over the decades, the requirements
of consumers and corporations became more refined, and the
tools for establishing who would buy which products were radically improved. This, Curtis contends, was the real revolution of
the last century, far more important than the pseudo-religions
of fascism and communism. But the rise of the new commercial
elite and their media servants threatened democracy as much as
the more overt threats of dictators. It resulted in the eclipse of
the public sphere, and its replacement by the rule of the private.
Everything came down to what you could figure out about who
consumers were and what they would buy. By the 1990s, these
insights had engulfed politics, and politicians like Tony Blair and
Bill Clinton were kept in power in the same way that companies
retained their consumers – through focus groups assembled to
tell others what they should think or do.

Curtis is a dazzling film-maker, and watching his films is like
being party to some elaborate game in which you see someone
jump from one rock to another in a fast-moving river, all the
while talking non-stop. You want to say, 'No, it cannot have

been quite like this,' but you can't. And anyhow, Curtis's donnish enthusiasm propels you. One can be sure that Freud would have had no idea that his American nephew would turn the notion of the unconscious to such vast commercial advantage, corrupting the Enlightenment rationalism enshrined in the American Constitution. One can remain uncertain that it all happened in that way, but these films remain wonderful, not just when you do agree with them, but most of all when you don't.

'I'm a journalist,' Curtis tells me in a Soho café. 'I'm really just a hack. I follow stories.' When I point out to him that journalists by and large don't trade in scepticism, that they don't come up with overarching views on reality, he shrugs. 'Let's just say I am lucky the BBC gave me the space.' Curtis's series *The Power of Nightmares* (2004) explored Islamism and the neo-cons from deep within the history of ideas, comparing both movements from the vantage points of their respective creation in Egypt and American think tanks in the 1950s. His series *All Watched Over by Machines of Loving Grace* (2011) does much the same thing, with similar provocative effects, setting the overweening utopian pretensions of the Internet against darker warnings about the destructive power of machines. Curtis has acquired the knack of constructing sequences out of apparently disconnected images, thus avoiding the clichéd illustrative style of television. As he told the *Observer*, he began by rooting around in discarded BBC footage:

> That kind of footage shows just how dull I can be . . . The BBC has an archive of all these tapes where they have just dumped all the news items they have ever shown. One tape for every three months. So what you get is this odd

collage, an accidental treasure trove. You sit in a darkened room, watch all these little news moments, and look for connections.

For *Bitter Lake* (2015), Curtis ransacked the footage shot by BBC cameramen in Afghanistan. He believes, radically, that just about everything is being left out in the accounts we hear about the world, that this isn't a media story, though it implicates all of us. 'Increasingly,' he announces, 'we live in a world where nothing makes any sense . . . Events come and go . . . those in power tell stories to make sense of the world, but the stories no longer make any sense.' At the end of his two-hour film, which Curtis conceived to be shown on the Internet rather than broadcast on television, he tells of 'a new story' to replace the old one. What he tells us is widely accepted, and surely correct: that the West (mainly the US and Britain) neglected to ascertain why they were getting into Afghanistan. Did policy-makers understand the history of Wahhabism? Did they clock the ultimate irreducibility of Helmand province, which had been the site of a massacre of British troops in the nineteenth century? Out of arrogance, they didn't, and they (or 'we', as Curtis would say) ensured speedy failure. As with Curtis's other work, however, there is a secondary, more powerful message embedded in the flow of beautiful images.

Curtis tells me he doesn't like fictions, but he is a master at unpeeling the skin surrounding contemporary mass lies. I once encountered an irate American national security intellectual, who wanted to know how the BBC had seemingly authenticated Curtis's work. Didn't I know that what Curtis said wasn't the case at all? I said to him that the BBC didn't work like that, but, I added, I thought Curtis took truth-telling very seriously indeed.

Even if you don't accept his views, they are worth taking seriously. In much the same way that Chris Marker appeared to be making films from the wreckage of Marxism, Curtis believes that Western liberalism is played out. It's no good persisting with the idea that all you need to do is set up a democracy, create a legislature and a stock market, and give lessons in the history of modern art (there is a bizarre, hilarious moment in one film, in which a young expat tells Afghans about the significance of Duchamp's urinal). Curtis makes it clear that the Russians, for similar reasons, were no more successful in Afghanistan.

'We don't know,' Curtis says, and indeed we don't. Elsewhere, his script makes an eloquent plea for us to avoid simplification. It does no good to force events into preconceived patterns. If we do, we end up perpetuating 'the emptiness and hypocrisies of our own beliefs', creating 'simple stories of good and evil'. What we seem to have instead, however, are even simpler stories of bruised misunderstanding, as if the failure of policy wasn't 'our' fault but resided either in stupidity or ungratefulness. On these matters, however, Curtis remains silent. For him, it is enough simply to have posed such questions.

For the Charlie Brooker show *Screenwipe*, Curtis made a masterly parody of Adam Curtis. He captured perfectly not just the donnish allure of the Curtis commentary voice, singing siren-like from the rocks, but also the borderline certitude that nothing can be known for sure. This position is widely held in our time, and along with the sheer beauty of Curtis's assemblages of images, it accounts for the cult status of his work. You can read these films as a warning, too; it isn't necessary to sign up to the Curtis presumption of unknowingness. In the end, it's a mistake to subject the films to extensive factual tests. One gets nowhere by picking holes in his arguments. If only we understood, he seems to say – politicians most of all, but the rest of us, too, since we collude in the circulation of half-truths through our mistaken attachment to politicians – we might be better off. Still, we won't understand. Even if we do, just a little, it won't always be clear to us that we do. So we can remain in the dark, or we can watch his films.

10 : Truly Global

In Wuhan, on the Yangtze River, pupils at the Evergreen Primary School are taught to understand democracy in *Please Vote for Me* (Weijun Chen, 2007), a benign update of William Golding's *Lord of the Flies*.

I hadn't been to Soweto, and I was standing near the end of a row of small apartheid-era houses. Beyond me lay a rubbish tip and the veldt, and to my left, in one of the small brick houses, Dumisani Phakathi's mother ran her minuscule food business, selling mealie meal and a variety of packaged foods. Meanwhile, her son went up and down the street trying to figure out what to put in his film. I'd given up on any coherent efforts to tutor Dumisani, or indeed to determine how his film would end up. But we had agreed on a title: *Don't Fuck with Me, I Have 51 Brothers and Sisters* (2005). This was literally true. Dumisani's father had criss-crossed the veldt in search of teenage players for a local football team. It was only after his death that his various families were apprised of each other's existence. And here was Dumisani, busy tracking down his siblings, one by one. It wasn't clear yet whether he would interview his mother, though he often talked about it. 'I'll decide when the time comes,' he said. In the meantime, he was interested in his own inability to settle down, and whether this was a bequest of his father's. As we stood in the road, I had a sudden acute sense of the indestructibility of South Africans. We were supposed to be working on a series covering the horrifying effects of AIDS in South Africa, and the post-apartheid government's failure to acknowledge that the problem existed, but Dumisani wasn't interested in such details – 'Other people can deal with that.' He liked to dress up in township-dude costumes and flirted shamelessly with the sober-sided Brits in the Blair-era High Commission in Pretoria. But he was sombre and outraged at the Voortrekker monument celebrating the vanquishing of the Zulu people at the hands of the Afrikaners. He thought as a Zulu, as well as a member of a tribe sired by a wayward football coach.

Months later, I sat in the midst of a group of fellow white Europeans, watching the mainly black South African film-makers respond to films they had made about their own country. Like Dumisani's, these were supposed to draw attention to South Africa's AIDS crisis, but like him, the film-makers had gone off and made their own films. Most of them were eloquent and touching; some, like his, were artful. You couldn't conclude that there was such a thing as an Africanist style of self-expression, but the films were somehow different. It seemed to me that their authors were busy reinventing docs, fitting them to their own purposes. I can't claim in any way to have been responsible for the internationalisation of docs, but when I returned to the BBC I began to wonder how this could be achieved. It was plain to me that films made by people in their own countries could be different in tone to those made by visiting film-makers. So far, however, authorship had largely been a privilege conferred by richer countries. There was a degree of snobbery about the way selected film-makers from far-off countries were paraded before Westerners. Reciprocally, Western film-makers were applauded for *dépaysement*, as if immersion in another country was so strange as to merit applause.

Overwhelmingly, what I wanted to see was the world that Dumisani was seeing, much more than listen to NGOs. We seem to be obsessed by 'issues' rather than the people and the truths behind them. I don't feel films succeed entirely in avoiding this, but they try. There aren't enough Dumisanis. The attitudes excoriated in a sharp piece by Binyavanga Wainaina still prevailed in film after film:

> Treat Africa as if it were one country. It is hot and dusty with rolling grasslands and huge herds of animals and tall, thin people who are starving. Or it is hot and steamy with very short people who eat primates. Don't get bogged down with precise descriptions. Africa is big: fifty-four countries, 900 million people who are too busy starving and dying and warring and emigrating to read your book. The continent is full of deserts, jungles, highlands, savannahs and many other things, but your reader doesn't care about all that, so keep your descriptions romantic and evocative and unparticular.
>
> Make sure you show how Africans have music and rhythm deep in their souls, and eat things no other humans eat. Do not mention rice and beef and wheat; monkey-brain is an African's cuisine of choice, along with goat, snake, worms and grubs and all manner of game meat. Make sure you show that you are able to eat such food without flinching, and describe how you learn to enjoy it – because you care.
>
> Taboo subjects: ordinary domestic scenes, love between Africans (unless a death is involved), references to African writers or intellectuals, mention of school-going children who are not suffering from yaws or Ebola fever or female genital mutilation.

To be sure, there were exceptions to the Western rule of self-removed half-concern tempered by sensationalism, but one must remember that all Western views come from Western politics, and 'foreign' subjects will always retain some of their exoticism. However, many journalists have broken with these rules. The work of Norma Percy and Brian Lapping allowed one to enter the reality of Balkan politics, in *The Death of Yugoslavia*, or Russian intrigue, with *The Second Russian Revolution* (1991). I could point to Kim Longinotto's remarkable work. But I remained surprised by the paucity of work in which film-makers followed in the path of Jean Rouch. We might want to enter societies somewhat different to our own, but somehow they remained recast in a Western image, as if docs and their makers, doomed to non-immersion, could only rarely do more than I had done with Dumisani, standing at the end of the road. I sense that this remains the case with the many exploration shows on television. They may purport to take us out of our suburban or inner-city comfort zones, but they merely redraw the boundaries slightly, giving the illusion that we crossed them.

I was embarrassed, too, by the poor take-up when the BBC did venture outside familiar terrain. In one of my favourite films, *The Emperor's Naked Army Marches On* (1987), Kenzo Okuzaki drives a small van plastered with slogans around Japan. At first, in his World War II-era uniforms you might take him for one of the many Japanese nationalists. But you'd be wrong. Okuzaki has his own personal mission: to uncover instances of cannibalism that occurred in the closing weeks of the 1945 campaign in New Guinea, in which he served and in which, out of the entire 36th Engineering Corps, only thirty survived. He tells us that he has served a prison sentence for murder and once fired four pachinko balls at the emperor while he stood making a speech on the palace balcony. For the film's director, Kazuo Hara (helped by the master, Shohei Imamura), Okuzaki's degree of derangement isn't important. Forty-one years have passed since these vile acts, but the point is that the facts remain unknown. Were two soldiers shot because they deserted – after the war had finished – or were they murdered to give officers something to eat? And what about the murdered sergeant? We never get the answers to these questions. What the film reveals is a society too blocked and reticent to confront such horrors. And Okuzaki, obsessed by the past, comes to seem sane by comparison with those around him. He wants to bring the ghosts of those murdered to rest, but you come to feel that, given supernatural powers, he'd perform a vast act of exorcism on Japan itself. By the end of the film, he's in prison again for twelve years, after attacking the son of the non-commissioned officer he deems to be a culprit. We are told that he is content, and that his mission is at least partly fulfilled. Alas, few people could be induced to watch this masterpiece. I could kid myself into believing that this was a consequence of the BBC's poor efforts at promoting such films, but I knew the real reason. Films like this would always remain in art houses. Even with the Internet, they'd remain the interest of a happy few in Britain who wish to find out about places other than the US.

Meanwhile, a slow change in attitudes was perceptible, partly but not wholly caused by the opening up of the world and the free availability of cheap filming materials. In *Gulag* (1999), Angus MacQueen captured the remnants of Soviet horror as they receded from view. We tend to think history happens in straight lines. One model is the straightforward one of progress from the nineteenth century, whereby things inexorably get better; the other (beloved by journalists) registers the sheer awfulness of much of the world, while nonetheless asserting that with diligence and courage, things can be improved. MacQueen went to Russia in the Yeltsin era, when, post-glasnost, it was possible to imagine that enough could be known about the Soviet past to alter the way in which Russians viewed their own history. Such hopes have been dashed by the long reign of Vladimir Putin, in which Soviet communism and Stalin have been rehabilitated. But MacQueen's impassioned, three-hour-long, diary-style film *Gulag* remains, and with it the story of millions of deaths and wrecked lives can be recalled. He follows the Gulag experience, from arrest through shipment to Siberia to final release. There are many heartbreaking interviews, the best from the seventy-something women who talk freely about working in sub-zero temperatures and being raped by guards. The guards and super-visors give their side of the story. 'Prisoners were the only solu-tion,' the NKVD deputy supervisor in charge of seven factories in Norilsk explains in a bland, matter-of-fact way, as if there could still be no real argument.

What else was to be done? I began to think that it might be possible to upend the tradition of well-dressed Englishmen get-ting on and off trains. What were our real transactions with the less fortunate parts of the world? Didn't we baulk at inequal-ity? For every hundred well-meaning films constructed out of guilt, there were few that touched on such half-taboos. But I came across film-makers eager to break with such traditions, and indeed protagonists to whom wooden styles of non-encounter were alien. The world of 'globalisation' is sleek and optimised within the corporate sphere. The films that expose these flaws and the corruption of this system are often not welcome, rare as they are.

Fireworks had ushered in the new century, but in June 2000, in Rio de Janeiro, the public were traumatised by a bus hijacking that took place outside the Jardim Botânico, in the centre of the city. Television cameras were on hand to record proceedings, which lasted several hours into the evening, ending with the killing of a young female hostage and the asphyxiation of the hijacker in the back of a police car speeding away from a lynch mob. In *Bus 174* (2002), José Padilha fashioned his narrative out of these facts, but his real subject is the barely contained violence of the city. Padilha is now Brazil's most successful director through his fictions. *Elite Squad* is Brazil's most-watched film, and the series *Narcos*, based on the reign of Pablo Escobar, a Netflix international blockbuster. His bus-hijacking film asks an apparently simple question: not why crime is prevalent in Rio, but, more provocatively, why violence has, seemingly ineradicably, become part of society.

Bus 174 begins with aerial shots showing the magnificence of Rio and identifying the slums that lie amid the mountains and great beaches. Subsequently, the focus is kept tight on the short, brutish life of the hijacker, twenty-two-year-old Sandro do Nascimento, and on the police haplessly clustered around the bus. This is contemporary realism with a vengeance, with nothing omitted. The strength of the film comes from Padilha's aversion to any form of moralising or easy answers. 'We only see what we want to see,' observes a sociologist. Sandro wanted to be no longer invisible, playing to the television cameras in a quest for a 'moment of glory'. He never knew his father, and his mother Clarice was murdered before his eyes in her shop by three robbers. He had no education and went from reform school to Rio's horrific prisons. When he was living on the streets, his friends were killed in a police shoot-out. He was adopted informally by a second mother and his life suddenly seemed to be worth something, but he drifted out of her care, back onto the streets. Did he have any sort of a chance? He concluded that he didn't, and this, along with the copious amounts of glue sniffed, accounts for his otherwise purposeless attack. 'It's all violence, isn't it?' his aunt explains. Over black, after the killing of Sandro, a chorus of voices tell us that society would like the Sandros to disappear. 'Who will stand up for Sandro?' someone asks in anger.

I became fixated on the billions of anonymous Sandros throughout the world. Who would find them and give them their voices? I wondered if this was what docs should be doing. Without a system, films like Padilha's would never find an audience. And, I reflected, for the first time in my life I was in a position to do something that would secure viewers around the globe. So, with friends, I developed two ambitions for television. First, I wanted to see whether it would be possible to show enough films in countries undergoing the stress test of globalisation, or further conflicts, to enact change. Second, I felt the time had come to devise a system for the global distribution of docs, so that the notion of people talking to each other via the documentary form would become a matter of routine. There were truths in these independent views from different cultures. I started with South Africa, China and Israel. But South Africa had taught me a lesson of sorts: much as people like myself would wish to create docs out of nothing, their survival depended on some sort of local support. If broadcasters did not sustain film-makers, they couldn't survive. Corrupt, highly censored broadcasters were surely better than none at all. But South Africa told me that this wasn't the case. The SABC, which had been the mouthpiece of apartheid, succumbed to corruption in a spirit of inertia. I could literally see wads of money changing hands in return for commissions. South African docs would have survived the onset of political correctness, but the bankruptcy of the SABC finally killed them. I wished for more resources and, not having them, began to work with colleagues from Europe and North America. With them I began to dream up plans. In the meantime, I went to Israel and China.

In 2008, I was driven around the Palestinian West Bank in an armoured jeep. My guide wanted to show me the sheer extent of the means used by the Israeli army to separate settler communities from the Palestinian Arabs surrounding them. He had given small cameras to the Arabs, enabling them to record the attacks to which they were subjected. Since the cameras had arrived, he pointed out, the number of aggressions had diminished. In this small, functional way, we could learn to use media in a radically different style. Each year I'd go to Israel, where I'd listen to the anguished testimony of Israeli film-makers. They were aware of how little they could do about the drift of their country away from any settlement with the Palestinians. It was hard for them to meet Palestinians, let alone show any degree of identification with them. On Israeli television stations, the Palestinians were now shown as an external threat, as if the land still occupied by Israel had nothing to do with these people.

I watched Emad Burnat's *Five Broken Cameras* (2011), which chronicles the village of Bil'in. He'd started by wanting to make home videos, but became the village's witness to the building of what Israelis now called the 'separation barrier'. As one camera after another was broken by the Israeli army, against the misgivings of his family Burnat went on filming. He was badly injured in a car crash and his best friend was killed. Ultimately, the Israeli Supreme Court ruled against the placing of the barrier, but this meant that the wall was built further away. No restitution was made for the olive groves ruined by the bulldozers. But Burnat's filming, assembled in collaboration with an Israeli film-maker and a French editor, told a far richer story. The villagers weren't politicised and didn't admire local Palestinian politicians. They wanted to be left alone, but they were trapped. The same was true of the Israeli soldiers, alternately bored and angry. No one benefited from the skirmishes; there were no heroes. Burnat was modest about his achievement, but there was no reason to be. *Five Broken Cameras* revealed more about the pitiful aspects of so many years of occupation than any number of news reports.

But there was a downside to such efforts at jointly describing the long-lasting dispute over the future shape of the area. The aborted Oslo accords didn't lead to a settlement. It became more difficult for Israelis and Palestinians to work together, even in the areas of the West Bank still occupied by the Israelis. When Israel withdrew from Gaza and the statelet fell under the authority of the Islamists of Hamas, Israelis couldn't go there. Palestinians ceased to want to work with Israelis, and the Israeli government didn't encourage contact. Western broadcasters had to choose between Palestinian films and Israeli ones. The former were mostly nostalgic pieces of agitprop that didn't criticise the increasingly inept Palestinian authorities. For their part, Israeli film-makers became more critical of their society as the years passed and the impulse towards any kind of mutual understanding stalled, then became extinct. As they raked over the near past for answers, they produced extraordinary films. But there was a negative aspect, too, when these films were shown inside and outside Israel.

The Gatekeepers (2012), for instance, presents a small parade of retired Jews dressed in a variety of leisurewear, none of it especially becoming. It turns out that they ran the Israel Security Agency (Shin Bet), and in Dror Moreh's study of the ethics of terror, they tell us what they did. Predictably, these men disdain the 'binary certainties' of politicians eager to appease anxious electorates. But that's only one of the discoveries we're invited to witness. They want to tell us that they did a good job infiltrating Arab communities and, when the technology was available, used mobile phones instead of bombs to kill Arabs. At first, these old men sound like drudges from a le Carré novel – suburban George Smileys, mildly startled to find themselves being interviewed. Under Moreh's astute questioning, however, they reveal that they laboured in the dark. There was no strategy when it came to dealing with the million-odd Palestinians under Israeli control after 1967. To begin with, operatives learnt Arabic and befriended the natives. But this was frustrating: 'The rabbit goes underground; the dog can't find it.'

These are old men's words, and it's clear to the film-maker that the time for such regrets is long past. What matters is that they went on killing, making possible the criminal state actions evident in the concept of 'targeted assassination'. Ultimately, the strong will indeed do what they can to those under their power. 'We've become cruel,' one of them says, closing the film. Moreh's masterpiece gives, in full and without flinching, an account of the degradation of Israeli life under the circumstances of occupation. No one, it is implied, can escape the consequences of violence exercised by the state in the name of its citizens. To their credit, these honest men don't try. This is something about which Hannah Arendt had much to say when visiting Jerusalem to cover the trial of Adolf Eichmann. *The Gatekeepers* gives meaning to the notion that evil can be banal, but its arguments stretch outwards to the rest of us. Who's to say that in the terror wars, we aren't collusive bystanders?

Just as devastating, in a different way, was *Censored Voices* (2015), in which ex-kibbutzniks recount their version of the Six Day War, helped in their memories by a number of hidden interviews made by the author Amos Oz in the first days of triumphalist peace in 1968. The young warriors of the Israeli Defence Force hadn't regarded themselves as heroes; they had hated what they saw as not just a defence of their country, but a war against Arabs. *Censored Voices*, like *The Gatekeepers*, is a truthful telling of a history of Israel that is different from the official one.

Many of those who complained about the BBC's coverage of the conflict between Israel and Palestine didn't want the Palestinian side to be depicted at all. They objected fiercely to films such as *The Law in These Parts* (2011), which describes how Israeli judges in the military tribunals bent precedent in order to legitimise the settler movement or excuse the excesses of the IDF. It was impossible to 'balance' such films, and the BBC was obliged to respond to complainants, as those who wrote in weren't happy. There were many, as I discovered, who didn't care about the plight of the villagers of Bil'in. I was made aware by colleagues that the British public might have become overexposed to the conflict between the Israelis and Palestinians. Did we really want to know so much about this subject? I went on arguing that we did, while aware how marginal my own position, and those of my Israeli friends, had become.

It might be easier to get documentaries shown globally if broadcasters clubbed together. Showing them within the context of a contemporary theme might make them more palatable for audiences. I began to work more closely with colleagues, and we came up with the simple idea of asking, 'Why?' This could refer to why certain abuses existed or, conversely, why something wasn't wholly bad. Efforts such as *Why Democracy?* (2007), its successor *Why Poverty?* (2012) and *Why Slavery?* (2018) travelled around the world, reaching very large audiences not just in the Western countries that showed documentaries, but in many places that, up until then, hadn't. Such projects were difficult to organise and time-consuming, but they brought closer the dream of docs being shown globally. They also seemed to repudiate the idea that local audiences didn't care about the rest of the world. I liked the way in which these films found their way into the cracks in the world's media. They existed in countries where they weren't publicly shown, via the Internet or on pirated copies. In this sense, my own somewhat subdued feelings of militancy were satisfied. I enjoyed seeing the raw material of films being smuggled out. I felt that if we could make such initiatives work, they might somehow be transformed into a coherent and lasting way of showing documentaries globally.

In 2005, I found myself in the basement of a Beijing hotel with thirty-odd Chinese film-makers. I was in town with a colleague to find a film about democracy, in a country where it didn't really exist or was very tightly controlled. The best project proposed an experiment. The film-maker, Weijun Chen, would create a democratic election among nine-year-olds in a school, not in Shanghai or Beijing, but in Wuhan, on the Yangtze. This is how the remarkable *Please Vote for Me* came into existence. Meet the first candidates standing for open, non-Communist Party elections in China. They are from the Evergreen Primary School in Wuhan. When Mrs Zhang, the teacher, tells her pupils about democracy ('very different from before'), they appear nonplussed. However, they learn rapidly. Welcome to a democratic primer – 'How to Get Elected While Wholly Lacking Scruples', it could be called – or what appears at times to be a relatively benign update of William Golding's *Lord of the Flies*. Our outsider candidate is Xuo Xaiofei, the daughter of a single mother who confesses that she cannot support her beautiful girl adequately. Warm to the bumptious Mao lookalike Cheng Cheng, even as he tries to bend the system, disrupting his rivals' efforts. See how, ultimately, democratic practices favour the incumbent Luo Lei: his father is the local police chief and is ready to offer free rides on the Wuhan Wheel.

I met Weijun Chen in Beijing. He'd made *To Live Is Better Than to Die* (2003), an exposé of the Chinese government's blood-donor programme, which had spread AIDS, destroying many families. He is a clever film-maker, with the instincts of a tabloid journalist. *Please Vote for Me* was shown globally as part of the *Why Democracy?* series and has been used as a teaching aid at the Harvard School of Government, as well as at the UN. It was broadcast in more than twenty countries. The reporter Jon Snow told me how he had been in a Singapore hotel, putting on his trousers, when it was shown on BBC World News. Twenty minutes later, he found he still hadn't put his second leg in. Never officially shown in China, it was nonetheless a runaway bootleg success, selling over a million copies.

Another film-maker I met that day in Beijing told me about a film he was making, and then left rapidly. Zhao Liang was a video artist. He seemed shy, slight, keen to get away, even as he talked about the film he'd been making for eight years, which was about petitioners who flocked to Beijing in search of redress for offences committed by officials. An interpreter explained that he was indeed frightened. 'He thinks there are police spies here,' the interpreter explained, pointing at the room filled with film-makers. When I finally watched *Petition*, I understood his precautions. The film describes an anomaly in China: a court dating from imperial times that enabled those whose lives had been ruined by callous officials to post their grievances to a central office. Nowadays, the court (which moved online prior to the Beijing Olympics) resembled a run-down post office. Zhao filmed petitioners who inhabited a slum surrounding the court, many of whom had been there for seven years. He was interested in what waiting had done to them. They were desperate, sometimes violent, close to killing themselves. Officials from local parties didn't like it when petitioners made their way to Beijing, and Zhao had filmed thugs coming to get them and bundling them into cars. The film would have met with the approval of Orwell and Kafka. It showed, in great detail, the total absence of a human rights culture in China. In its strongest passages, Zhao depicted how the waiting had made these petitioners into crazed shadows of themselves. The film was shown at the Cannes Film Festival, and immediately banned by the Chinese authorities. According to the *New York Times*, Zhao was visited shortly afterwards by Chinese officials. They told him that they knew he was broke because of *Petition* and offered to commission a film for showing in China.

'When you're working in China, there's a grey area that you have to navigate well,' Zhao explained to the *New York Times*. 'I think that a work has to have an audience . . . The meaning of a piece of work has to be acknowledged by other people. It has to influence other people.' But he also said that he had been forced to make cuts in order to get his second film shown by the censors. His next film, *Behemoth* (2015), was made outside the system. With its snippets of Dante in Chinese, it lingers in long takes over wrecked landscapes, half-abandoned industrial plants and deserted, unoccupied new towns in Chinese Mongolia. *Behemoth* isn't always easy to watch, but it provides a wrenching vision of the ruin of Chinese nature in the pursuit of economic growth. Zhao's target isn't capitalism or indeed the Chinese Communist Party. He sees the industrial world as a beast, but this beast is us. We are responsible for the end of nature. In the opening and closing scenes of the film, a tiny naked figure is seen against the monstrous gash in nature. It's an image for our times.

It's said, though no one really knows, that the Chinese authorities employ more than thirty thousand censors on and off vast campuses. Documentaries receive due attention, along with the remnants of newspaper reporting and online blogs or tweets. When Chinese films receive prizes, even if they are controversial and will never be shown in China, officials attend the ceremonies. They don't seem unhappy to see such films made and tend not to hinder the efforts of members of the Chinese diaspora. In Taipei, CNEX, a Taiwanese non-profit organisation, has funded many films that cannot be shown on the mainland. But this picture becomes different when the films somehow get through the cracks. Film-makers receive visits from officials, who take them out for a coffee and a talk. The maker of *Please Vote for Me* received a few such visits from the authorities, who suggested that he had worked unauthorised for foreign non-profit organisations and might not have declared his income. In 2016, I watched the film-maker's latest work, which describes how babies are brought into the world in a Wuhan hospital. Much of the film consists of what one sees in peak-time medical shows on Western TV, only the proceedings are more frenzied. More interesting is the message that is repeatedly conveyed through conversations between doctors and orderlies and the hapless relatives of the women giving birth. In one conversation, an orderly says that 8,000 yuan 'isn't enough for two babies'. The father has to go back to his village to find money for his offspring, and when he can only get a short-term loan from the villagers, is obliged to put his two newborn daughters up for adoption. Taken as a whole, the doctors of the hospital don't seem aware of the Hippocratic oath, and the film appears a terrible indictment of the lack of free medical facilities in China. Why should poor people be obliged to fund the birth of their children out of their savings? What is good about a system in which medical care is interrupted while the doctors or their representatives haggle over the price of plasma?

The film was to be shown in Chinese cinemas and on state television. Its message, which was unexceptionable, was that things should change. I was sure that the film-maker, left to his own devices, would have produced much the same film. But it was also part of the overall Chinese project of roping in film-makers and limiting their independence. A film about medical deficiencies was made because the government agreed with the message and the doctors could be enlisted in the enterprise. The enlightened bureaucrats of China thought it was time to do something about the state of Chinese medical care. As we know in the West, however, there is always a price to pay for such interventions.

Docs were now seen all over the world, but a sense of unrealised potential remained. Working with colleagues, I helped set up a means of remedying this. The *Why?* films, shortened for the requirements of a news channel, were shown on the BBC's World News service, and then sold at rock-bottom prices, or distributed free if the recipients couldn't find the money, to public broadcasters globally – in Argentina, Colombia, India, Vietnam, Mongolia et al. The scheme was perilously short of money, and disarmingly simple, and I suspect that many of the funders we approached, begging for money, couldn't figure out why it hadn't occurred to anyone before. But it was clear that audiences happily consumed these docs. In sophisticated markets they were taken for granted by now, but in developing countries millions watched each film, and they didn't seem worried by the fact that many of them were demanding, came with subtitles and posed questions to which there were no ready answers.

It was possible once more to indulge in the old dream of free media connecting people globally, and in 2014, one film seemed to offer hope to this end. *Democrats* was the work of the Danish film-maker Camilla Nielsson, who had trained as an anthropologist. It recounts the improbable story of the creation of a new Zimbabwean constitution through the struggles of two politicians, Douglas Mwonzora, from the ruling ZANU-PF party, and Paul Mangwana, from the opposition. They know that their assignment is either an insult (because the constitution will never be ratified) or a trap set by the country's brutal eighty-something-year-old dictator Robert Mugabe as a means, to put it bluntly, of getting rid of them. Despite Mugabe's fall, lawyers continue to argue over the merits of democracy, and Nielsson's film remains painfully relevant. Its scenes show rallies, rigged ballots, briefings and counter-briefings. They look as if they might have been scripted, as Zimbabweans painstakingly recreate either the Magna Carta or the invention of the American Constitution. Here are plots and treacheries – enough, indeed, to fill an entire fictional series. In the end, however, the two men get to like and respect each other. They may never manage to introduce democracy, but they never really thought that would be the outcome of their efforts. They come to treat each other as friends and colleagues. That seemed to be where we had got to with democracy in the world, and it seemed appropriate that many millions of people would get to understand this unfinished, always threatened project.

11 : Cracks in Everything

The Lumière brothers' first documentary, *La Sortie de l'usine Lumière à Lyon* (1895). They declared 'the cinema is an invention without any future', yet their staff look well dressed and seem happy in the sunlight.

Throughout my career in docs, I've seen films born both in years of corruption and years of truth. Truth is not just the concern of obsessed medical practitioners and politicians; its impact is everywhere. Increasingly few of us believe the news, and daily I see more lies appearing.

The cracks are everywhere, sometimes dangerous, sometimes opportunistic. What is 'true' is currently impossible to spell out categorically; you can't easily understand it, let alone oppose it. With the rise of 'fake news' – lies passing as fact – docs now seem to stand ever further apart from the mess of the news media. They are different. They remain on their truthful perch, albeit precariously. Docs, and the factual tradition, matter. In the current landscape, they are as important as current affairs reporting. The best ones look at the chaos around them. We all need some black-and-white clarity to the mess that surrounds us.

In France, this clarity is typified by Daniel Sivan's film *The Patriot* (2017), about an Israeli hacker called Ulcan who had publicly attacked anti-Semites. Ulcan somehow escalated the situation to involve Belgian politicians and a French hate-jokester called Dieudonné M'bala M'bala. The comedian rewrote an old French pop song and called it 'Chaud Ananas' – hot pineapples – which, in French, sounds like '*Shoah nanas*', or 'Holocaust floozies'. The comic's fans were overwhelmingly young, white and male, and they carried French-language, pineapple-covered signs ridiculing the Holocaust. They gleefully performed the '*quenelle*', an inverted Nazi salute, unimpeded by French law. Sivan, a talented film-maker and reporter, was fascinated by the bizarre contradictions of the story. Ulcan, the hacker, first attacked the bank accounts of anti-Semites, before involving leftish French journalists in anti-Palestinian circles. He told the parents of one journalist that their son had died in a car accident – news that upset the father so much that he dropped dead from a heart attack. The hacker then fled, a fugitive, to Israel, followed by the French bringing fifty charges against him and attempting to have him extradited. Despite all this, Ulcan continues to post on the Internet, a hero in Israel. The question at the core of the film is: is Ulcan a real patriot or a real criminal? Many people don't want to see the growing problem of anti-Semitism in Europe and the US, and the film hasn't been broadcast in France or Germany. But I find this story so strange and compelling. What became of the journalist with the dead father? Is anti-Semitism growing into more than a cult once again? With our 'new' belief in 'fake news', we seem to seek out difficult truths. Where can we find a 'true' sort of news?

There is a battlefield, somewhere between falsehood and verity, and it works the seam of propaganda, distraction. It's something different and not immediately visible. It's easy to see the lies, but we cannot see part-evasions and entertaining non-truths. You cannot be too serious, or you'll soon be worn out. A German artist, Mario Klingemann, released a YouTube video featuring the image of a twenty-something French chanteuse, Françoise Hardy. She is heard speaking off-screen to a presenter about the 'alternative facts' offered by President Donald Trump's former press secretary, Sean Spicer. In reality, Hardy is seventy-three years old and the voice we hear belongs to Kellyanne Conway, counsellor to the president. A generative adversarial network (GAN) splits the conversation with the recording of Hardy. It's a bizarre joke, aimed at fans of old intellectuals, and it makes Conway's fibs seem even more ridiculous. Can you distinguish the voice and the image? Do you care or not? Most totalitarian artefacts use lies. 'We think that AI is going to change the kinds of evidence that we can trust,' says a boffin working for Google at the non-profit research company OpenAI. What should we think about 'reality'? What did Susan Sontag see in the 'shady commerce between art and truth' but words and images?

A bizarre shift in the world seemed to have occurred, and it happened almost overnight. It made me think of Virginia Woolf's observation that on a certain morning, everything was different. Woolf was talking about the impact of modernism, but this current cultural upheaval seems both bigger and more threatening. I thought over and over again of the uncertainty and insecurity in the world, and I reacted in different ways. Sometimes I read old books for anchorage, sometimes I dipped into the new. Most of the descriptions of films in this book were affected by this discovery. But I also found myself wondering how to describe the new reality around me, how to live with it. I was tempted to say that everything I saw was too big to deal with. Then I would retort that to give up on the prospect of handling anything was to admit defeat. If the new uncertainty seemed too big to define, I focused on its components. Anger was one of them, and hatred. Confusion (about things we had to accept, such as the heating up of the planet) was another. There was a mistrust both of institutions and of the individuals who told us what was happening, which bled into a mistrust of democracy itself. Accompanying all these things, defining them even, were the ways in which we'd come to understand them. Not so long ago it had been possible to entertain the notion that what we called 'the media' was a flawed engine of enlightenment, but such notions appeared hollow now, as the means by which we understood anything were themselves swallowed up.

Had similar changes occurred to people in the past? As I thought of Woolf's dictum, I pored over the twentieth century. I wondered about waking up to the Wall Street Crash or discovering that Adolf Hitler had come to power. I told myself that such things shouldn't be affecting me, a citizen of a relatively rich part of the world who lived in a settled democracy, and yet I found they did. They didn't stop me working, but they seemed to make my own work harder. How was I to describe these levels of uncertainty? At the same time, I was astonished by the fact that others experienced similar feelings. Uncertainty wasn't an epidemic, but it was something more than the occurrences – financial, political, media-inspired – that passed through our collective consciousness. Something told me that it was going to become more intense.

Meanwhile, documentaries were everywhere. It seemed perverse to say that they weren't performing as they should, or that they were hard to fund and made those who sought out difficult subjects live on the edge of penury. Somehow they and their makers did survive even the lack of interest from broadcasters. If you wanted to make another doc about white rhinos, you could find a rich liberal capable of funding it. The same was true in relation to a film praising Ronald Reagan, or even attempting yet again to establish the veracity of *The Protocols of the Elders of Zion*. Documentaries appeared in sliced-up or half-corrupt versions on

YouTube. They were immediately pirated and released on clandestine sites. In some crucial respects, they had become part of our lives, edging out older genres such as investigative reporting. I didn't feel that there was a price to pay for this triumph; to me it seemed that their arrival at the party was long overdue. And yet for all the distinctiveness of docs, for all the vividness they brought to contemporary media, there were problems of definition similar to those that had dogged them when they were still obscure. Were they really important? How could they be made more so? It was time to look again at the question of what documentaries were and what they did. But I was determined to approach them not so much in terms of their own history, but with regard to what role they might play in the new, troubled media that lay before us.

Each time I watched a new documentary, I could see the real possibilities of independence. At the BBC and other stations internationally, however, documentary film seemed occasionally to be sunk in a post-Grierson torpor. There were endless surveys of British institutions in which the only discernible point of view was that such series should continue to be made – about herring fishing, the Church of England, posh hotels, etc. People did watch them, and they were well made, but they were very dull. I wanted more views, but more important was the freedom of reporters to see and say whatever they liked. I wanted to see programmes capable of changing the way we lived, but I didn't feel such efforts should be prescriptive.

Travelling, I'd come across extremes of media dysfunction, but I'd always see something that contradicted my worst expectations. In Gaza, for instance, I encountered a parody of state-controlled media in a tiny house by the sea, from which four hours of Hamas propaganda were pumped out each day between electricity outages. I caught a gleam of inspiration in the station manager's eye. I saw the same gleam in the eyes of a Chinese producer who circulated fake or highly doctored news items sponsored by food manufacturers. These were heavily crafted to satisfy the censors, but they reached over two hundred million on the Internet. Alongside such efforts at conformity, however, I'd meet film-makers who were willing to risk their necks in search of something better. Why spend two years following a Chinese mayor as he pulled down half a city (*The Chinese Mayor*, 2015)? Why not? And why interview, again and again, the racist thugs of Israeli football (*Forever Pure*, 2016)? Why immerse yourself in such horror, if not out of a desire to combat its consequences?

George Orwell was always among my most-loved twentieth-century British writers, and I knew that he had based *1984* on the BBC before I discovered from his diaries and letters that this was indeed the case. I often think about the first days I spent at the BBC, in far-off 1972. The offices and newsrooms were ramshackle, consisting of defective typewriters, bad chairs covered in olive-coloured material, cream walls and brown carpets. Drinking at lunchtime was tolerated in light of the astonishingly long, often punishing hours we all worked. I'd been approved as a suitable recruit by a tweed-suited, middle-aged pipe-smoker, who was pleased to register my lack of radical connections, while tut-tutting over my apparent inability to comprehend the nature of the vocation that awaited me. I was telling him that I was interested in investigating the nature of Irish republicanism, a force that seemed then to be threatening the foundations of the British state, when he drew me up mid-sentence. 'When you work at the BBC,' he advised sagely, 'never say what you want to make programmes about. Just say you work at the BBC.' I did manage to make a film about Irish republicanism, but only forty-odd years later, by describing the life and martyrdom of Bobby Sands, who starved himself to death for the cause (*Bobby Sands: 66 Days*, 2016). I suppose this proves the adage that one must always stick at things.

I believed in what I did. I loved the way I could get an interview done in Mexico City with the distraught wife of Salvador Allende, after the latter had died in the coup. I loved the illusion of the world passing through my own partial consciousness, imperfectly refashioned. My illusions were shattered by the BBC grandee I loved best. He was a war hero from the navy, a liberal campaigner, married to a film-star ballerina, but he'd retained a degree of apparent diffidence that covered so much sharpness. I envied his rumpled good suits and, more than that, the way he could move from the appearance of seriousness to a happy-seeming diffidence and self-removal. He'd take my scripts and seem to mark them. 'Good,' he'd say, as if I were still a pupil, while he eliminated anything that was over-certain or dogmatic. 'It's always best to qualify things a bit,' he explained. One night I plucked up courage and asked him whether he thought that what we did mattered. 'It does pay the bills,' he said.

Eventually, I learnt that the BBC didn't always appreciate the programmes that I really liked. I'd never be told what was wrong with them, merely that I should strive to be 'balanced'. I'd discuss this with friends, including the redoubtable Christopher Hitchens, who despised all restrictions on free expression. 'You can't really want to stay at the BBC,' he would tell me. Meanwhile, I read. I knew about Orwell's travails at the BBC. He'd described it as 'a cross between a girls' school and a lunatic asylum'. He said that he had never met anyone in India who had actually listened to any of his programmes, and felt that the BBC had been broadcasting on the wrong wavelength. 'Two wasted years,' is how he described his time there. Nonetheless, he was sad to leave.

I watched *HyperNormalisation* (2016) on the sixty-second floor of a Shanghai hotel that overlooked a place entirely given over to the act of shopping. At close to three hours, made for Internet viewing, this was Adam Curtis's ultimate expression of perplexity to date, a massive blog of his life and times constructed from BBC outtakes and filled with forgotten or overlooked material ripe for harvest. 'We live in an extraordinary time,' he begins. The time, he believes, is so far out of joint that we don't understand it, though he did – enough at least to be able to explain what it is that we don't understand. Curtis begins in New York and Damascus, where Assad Sr decided he detested Americans because they had divided the Arab world in two, and Curtis's deft editing unleashes a pattern of grand, perverse statements. Here is Patti Smith; there are lawyers squabbling over a bankrupt New York; here is Jane Fonda; and there are the Ceauşescus being executed. The subtext to all this is Curtis's much-announced dislike of American stupidity. But as we clamber on to the Internet age, smart things are said about the sheer reach of the machines watching over us.

I liked the worrying side of Curtis. He was an old-fashioned English dystopian and he cared about our liberties. I was sure that he was right about us needing to meet the complexity of the world head on, but I felt that this film didn't quite do this. The real problem isn't that Curtis is incorrect about the state of the world, but he is acute in his analysis of the contemporary evil of what Stephen Colbert calls 'truthiness'.

'I like to come from the outside,' Curtis told me. 'I think we need to puncture the bubble of the liberal world. Here are all these people saying, "We've got to change the world." And the one thing that is certain, if you look back at the last fifteen years, is that "we" haven't changed the world. Films try and fail to do this: go to any festival, see how many films are built on the cliché of changing things. There has been a massive shift to the right. Nasty people are in power. Inequality has grown. Technology has shifted power to the powerful. Finance has taken precedence. Liberals will say that this is all terrible, but the truth is that they don't want to deal with the complexity of the world. They'd rather retreat. It's what I call "Oh dearism" – "Oh dear . . . oh dear . . . oh dear . . ."'

I asked Curtis what he thought we should do. He talked about a 'new story' being needed. But where was the new story going to come from? He began to say that it was hard to think of any world-changing without a collective idea. Then he gave up on this line of argument. 'I'm just a journalist. It's not my job to come up with it. But you can find stories in the midst of chaos. You open things up by dissolving certainty. You can have moments of clarity. And that's what I call proper journalism.'

The most successful agitprop film of recent years was Al Gore's *An Inconvenient Truth*, which took $49 million around the world at the box office, won two Oscars and finally restored Gore to public life. Stylistically, Davis Guggenheim's film was neither original nor executed with great flair; it was a lecture, filmed on separate occasions. It should be seen as a predecessor of the TED lectures, but it was nonetheless highly effective. Gore presented what he considered to be the facts surrounding global warming with flair, and in a spirit of desperate cheerfulness. He was impressive because (as the film reminded viewers, with sequences of its protagonist getting on and off planes) he had taken the trouble to find out about climate change. This wasn't a cause that was being strategically espoused but a lifelong fear, and Gore's conclusions went way beyond the sonorous expressions of concern we have come to expect from politicians and newscasters:

> Each one of us is a cause of global warming, but each one of us can make choices to change that with the things we buy, the electricity we use, the cars we drive; we can make choices to bring our individual consumption of emissions to zero. The solutions are in our hands, we just have to have the determination to make it happen. We have everything we need to reduce carbon emissions, everything but political will. But in America, the will to act is a renewable resource.

It would appear, superficially at least, that the appeal was effective. Sixty-six per cent of viewers who claimed to have seen *An Inconvenient Truth* said the film had 'changed their mind' about global warming; 89 per cent said it had made them more aware of the problem. Three out of four viewers said they had changed some of their habits as a result of seeing the film. It appears to have offended those who resented the rehabilitation of Gore or didn't take global warming seriously. George W. Bush said he hadn't seen the film. Oklahoma's Republican senator Jim Inhofe said he didn't plan to see the film (in which he appeared). Bizarrely, he compared the film to *Mein Kampf*. 'If you say the same lie over and over again, and particularly if you have the media's support, people will believe it,' Inhofe said. In Britain, as a consequence of a court case brought by Stewart Dimmock, a lorry driver and activist, the film was found to contain nine 'errors' – i.e. *instances*, legally defined, where Gore was thought to have departed from mainstream scientific views. But the judge didn't condemn the film, suggesting that Gore had throughout his argument done his best to be accurate and declining to deny the film access to schools, as the plaintiffs had demanded.

But I wonder now whether Gore's film ever reached beyond those predisposed to agree with him. The bubbles of contemporary culture are larger than we care to believe. I wouldn't have said this five years ago, but one might now think of the BBC as a liberal bubble-in-the-making. This isn't so much a consequence of what the BBC does or doesn't choose to show. It has more to do with what people select, or indeed what is selected for them by the algorithms of powerful corporations. I was convinced that *India's Daughter* did break out of the liberal context in which the discussion of rape in India took place, and I remain so – not least after speaking to a film-maker working in India when the film went online after its banning by the Indian government. He told me that the local police, taking him for a BBC employee, had rebuked him and restricted him to the hotel where he was staying. When they viewed the film, however, they concluded that it wasn't a foreign-originated insult to India. They appreciated the film for what it was. But such crossovers from one audience to another may become harder as both governments and big companies become more adept at localising audiences and restricting them to what they are certain to agree with.

To the film-maker Eugene Jarecki, the new disorder of the media meant that one lived in a 'permanent waiting room', in search of whatever would make a film come alive and not get lost. 'Each film really is a flight into the unknown,' he told me.

'One doesn't know how it can be made to fly or where it will go. There isn't really a system any more, there are no valid predictions related to how a film will do. And that makes it hard to plan, and it's very time-consuming.' Jarecki's 2012 film *The House I Live In* is a bold mix of essay and reportage, linking punitive sentencing for trafficking or possessing drugs with the historic imprisonment of black Americans. Jarecki explains that the sentences handed out were part of the marginalisation of American people of colour, a pretext for continuing oppression. He interviews many prison officers and judges throughout the US who agree with his analysis. Jarecki tells this story in part through the experiences of the woman of colour who brought him up when she worked as the family nanny. The film won a major prize at Sundance but, as Jarecki admitted, 'It did nothing in cinemas.' Undeterred, he sought other means of showing the film. He went to 'prisons, state capitols – anywhere I could find prisoners, judges, law enforcement officials, cops, all the people depicted in the film who would understand what I was saying'. For these screenings, he made a shorter version, and he would be present. The venture was funded by several non-profit organisations, including the prestigious and very liberal Ford Foundation. 'It took over a year,' Jarecki said. 'I had to organise it all myself. But it was worth it. I think the film really did bring people round to thinking differently about punishment. I hope so. I wanted to save my film because I felt it had a lot to say. But would I do it again? That's a difficult question to answer.' When I talked to him later, after the election of Donald Trump, his views were bleaker. 'I think we all need to think again,' he said. 'We've been in a place where gentleness and truth seemed to mean something. In ten years' time, we'll look back when things are far worse, and our children will say: "You might have noticed all this." I'm afraid I'll just have to say: "I didn't think it would get that bad."'

When I asked what should be done, Jarecki talked about the vanishing of journalistic standards. 'It's a real problem,' he said. 'How do we now reach many, many people without resorting to fake news and propaganda?'

The journalist in me craves sharpened pencils and cameras taken in the hope of finding out what's going on. I may be annoyed by the worthiness of the genre and joke about the way in which documentary film-makers behave like mendicant friars, wandering around the world in search of misery. But docs have some connection with the journalistic culture from which I come. The connection exists even in art-house films. Docs require transactions with reality, but they also do things beyond the scope of even the most sophisticated news reporting. This is what documentary-makers call 'watching'. News doesn't watch, it summarises. Documentary film has the power to enter the lives of others. It might alter the lives of those who watch it as surely as it does the lives of those it depicts. I'm affected by the fragility of documentary film. The insights that films provide are fleeting, temporary and contingent, but they remain valuable for these reasons.

Sometimes the funding of a film becomes more important than what it is supposed to say. Often I feel enraged by the non-system of documentary films, and the fact that so many of the best ones never quite got made, or if they did, never wholly fulfilled their potential. But I don't get discouraged. Each week, or at least each month, another small miracle is on display. I really do learn from them. Films are more immediately engaging, more overpowering than the endless non-fiction articles I consume, partly in order to find good subjects for these films. There is surely an empathy deficit in the world, a deficit that documentaries help fill, and not always in a small and insignificant way. Like poetry, in Auden's formulation, they make nothing happen. They make the world more tolerable, because understanding is always best. And perhaps they can, like the best writing, prepare us for change. Is that all one can hope for?

But documentaries were also affected in the same way as print journalism. First, the old system of transmission was stretched to breaking point. It no longer became sensible to think of a film appearing once or twice on television and then disappearing, bar the odd prize-winning lap of honour. You could watch films when you wanted on the Internet, wherever you wanted, if the connection was okay and you weren't interrupted by a hostile government. Films could be made by anyone, because the technology, which had become cheaper and cheaper, was matched by distribution systems that were free. Some saw this as democratisation; others as a series of new markets stretching almost to infinity. Journalists, by and large, were impoverished by the free global distribution of their work. It wasn't clear whether documentary film-makers would go the same way. At the very least, they would be obliged to modify not just the way they worked, but most likely the kind of films they made. It wasn't clear how the new Internet culture would respond to long films. It was thought that a preference for short things would emerge. In any case, what my former BBC boss Mark Thompson, now running the *New York Times*, called 'the permanent earthquake of media' had begun, except that, unlike an earthquake, it imposed new structures on the landscape, even as it destroyed many of the old ones.

It seemed important to meet those associated with the idea of cyber-utopia. There were right-wing voices among the new

West Coast crowd of billionaires, many of whom didn't believe in paying more in the way of taxes than was strictly necessary. But for most of them a belief in the perfectibility of man had gone hand in hand with the accumulation of great wealth. I spent an afternoon in a New York hotel with Jeff Skoll, one of the creators of eBay and the begetter of many consciousness-raising films, fictions and documentaries. Skoll talked about the world as a series of problems that could be approached in the style of a start-up, one by one. Things could be changed for the best. There was no need to panic, because technology and liberal ideas would save us all. Skoll enumerated the many projects he'd completed or was involved in. At the time I met him, he was working on a film that anticipated the creation of a Palestinian state – and I found that I didn't want to tell him that such expectations might prove premature. Skoll was Canadian-born, friendly and modest, and it took him more than an hour to finish his Diet Coke. I had never met anyone like him: no one quite as rich or earnest or single-minded; no one quite so confident about the future. Afterwards, I told myself that my own fears were groundless; there really was a new wave of enlightenment sweeping the world. Companies like Amazon and Google made money, but they did good, too. We had to believe this. But even as I thought this, I realised that no, nothing could be so simple. I wanted to believe in the world according to Skoll, but found I couldn't.

I began to wonder what place documentaries would occupy in what appeared to be this new disorder. Superficially, they flourished, most of all in the US, where it was usual to find among the list of credits private investors big and small, and foundations. A boom in funding for documentaries that could be said to have changed the world had occurred. Could one measure the impact of a single film? Why not? Could one ever know how some good cause had been advanced by so many screenings? Wasn't there a risk that amid the appropriation of films by those concerned with campaigns, the films would lose their autonomy, becoming indistinguishable from the campaigns they existed to promote? I could quibble about all of this, and I did, as indeed I might about the glut of West Coast liberal causes on display each year at venues such as Sundance. There was a price to pay for documentaries being owned by the wealthy and liberal. I could make lists of subjects that wouldn't be touched in this world. In some respects, liberal docs inhabited a world as strict as the Indian caste system. The left-behind failed to interest, especially if they were white. Poor people tended to show up in these efforts as props, thus worthy of somewhat patronising attention. There was a distinct shortage of films about failure, unless this could be wrapped up in the mantle of minority rights and thus sanctified. Minority rights became the way in which such films were obliged to address contemporary inequality.

A film I loved, such as *Grey Gardens*, wouldn't get any attention in the contemporary environment unless it could be depicted as a remedial work focusing on middle-aged alcoholism among the leisured classes of Long Island. Not just humour, but depicting the world for the hell of it or merely because it seemed a good idea was becoming rare. It became usual, at lavish pitches attended by NGOs and their funders, to speak of 'social change', as if anyone really knew what that implied.

The most bizarre aspect of world media appeared in the contradiction between the extreme sophistication of the means of communication and the way in which simpler messages were now needed. This was commonly acknowledged, and usually attributed to the short-form neo-telegraphese of social media. The solution was for intelligent people to arrange the facts in the right order; that way, enlightenment would ensue. But no one really believed this any more. People were opposed to 'experts' of any sort. They wanted to make their own minds up – or they were happy to have made up their own minds already.

In London, I met the English–Ukrainian writer Peter Pomerantsev. He'd spent a decade working in Russian television and had witnessed the steady elimination of any notion of factual accuracy, or indeed any pretence that 'reality television' should conform to even basic levels of truthfulness. This wasn't startling, but Pomerantsev suggested that the Kremlin had learnt from these casual lies, transforming them into a new system of censorship. Pomerantsev had an urbane, public-school manner. I imagined meeting him in the context of a teenage debating contest, or finding him quietly reading Dostoevsky, leaving others to battle it out on the playing fields. His book *Nothing Is True and Everything Is Possible* described a decade spent concocting fake stories for the Moscow media, but he'd never quite succumbed to cynicism. Instead, he'd become an expert in the contemporary growth industry of the manufacture of lies. 'It really is like this,' he kept saying, in what appeared to him to be a vain attempt to reproduce his own surprise at finding out the dirty secret of Russia's post-Sovietism. 'Stalinism trafficked in lies – the biggest lies,' he explained. 'However, there was some notion that these lies were in fact truthful statements. People had to believe in them to get along or stay sane, or maybe they just did. Now there's an official encouragement of falsehood. People in power have figured out that it's better not to seem even to tell the truth. You can just say your opponents are always lying. You don't have to claim the truth for yourself; indeed it helps if you don't, because that might invite some sort of scrutiny. So you allow people to live in a continuous state of contradictory realities. The idea is that they will give up on truthfulness. And that's the same as wanting to be ruled.'

I asked him whether Orwell would have understood this. 'Oh, definitely,' he said, smiling. 'It all comes out of Orwell. But it seems more dangerous in some respects than the system Orwell described. He describes the abolition of objectivity, which implies its existence. Now we're seeing the notion that it never exists, anywhere.'

In 2016, it became apparent even to the least attentive that the situation described by Pomerantsev wasn't confined to Russia. Things that weren't true but might have been, and which were somehow believed, were everywhere. Perhaps one could look again at how films did affect audiences.

I was surprised by how much film-making took place within what were called 'silos' – enclosures of the film-makers' creation. The media guru Ethan Zuckerman described non-fiction film as 'broccoli farming'. He meant, less than flatteringly, that large numbers of films were being made without too much thought as to how they would be consumed. How much earnestness did the world need? I found the argument somewhat unfair, because one couldn't know how many exposés of injustice the world needed, just as one could never gain any definitive insight into the world's demand for overpriced handbags. However, month by month, one might entertain the illusion that the formless oceans of Internet space would soon be populated by films that were never watched.

So one should think even now about the kinds of films capable of reaching audiences. For the Oscar-winning Alex Gibney, this means the artful creating of 'combos' – large-scale nutritious creations, with properties that would appeal to many different types of person. *Going Clear*, his 2015 investigation into the Church of Scientology and its cultists, fulfils all these criteria and shows it is possible to combine raw sensation with intensively researched investigations. A similar effect is apparent in *Cartel Land* (2015), in which the film-maker Matthew Heineman inserts himself into the gun battles between the Mexican Federales cops, vigilante civilians and the drug barons. Suspenseful, sickening in its detail, the film establishes beyond argument the connection between extreme violence, extreme corruption and the trafficking of illegal drugs. But it is also a story told in the American tradition of personal exposure, from Stephen Crane through Hemingway to the New Journalism of the 1960s. It shows that there is still a journalistic tradition to be mined for contemporary success.

I asked Gibney where he now stood with respect to the impact of his own films. He said that based on the feedback he'd received, two of his films had 'hit the zeitgeist'. One of them was his investigation of Scientology, which had been viewed by over twenty million people. 'Did it destroy Scientology? No. Did it cause the IRS to rescind the tax-exempt status of the religion? No. Did it end Tom Cruise's career? No. So for many activist groups that would make it a failure. And they might well ask: what was the political impact?' As Gibney said, *Going Clear* did comfort the afflicted 'former members of the church' and afflict the comfortable – 'the church has lost members and clout'. But more than that, it made people think about how we can all be locked up in a prison of belief.

But Gibney also thought another film had really 'changed minds'. This was *Taxi to the Dark Side*, the film that won him an

Oscar. It has reached fewer people, but its rigorous exploration of the ways in which the military establishment had come to rationalise the widespread recourse to torture in Afghanistan and Iraq had created a 'sacred space', allowing 'different kinds of people' to engage with the story. Gibney was proudest of the fact that the film had become required viewing at army training schools.

If the Internet appeared to privilege the short attention span, film-makers and funders were responding by offering bigger portions. In 2016, an eight-hour biopic described the troubled American reality in pitiless detail: Ezra Edelman's horror-filled O. J. Simpson story, *OJ: Made in America*. The eight parts leave no doubt about OJ's guilt in the battering to death of Nicole Brown, his wife. But Edelman also links OJ's life to the wider goings-on within US culture. We're told about race and economics in college football, the non-presence during the 1970s of people of colour in advertising – OJ was always surrounded by whites in his Hertz ads, so that he appeared to be white by association – the racism of the LAPD and, most serious of all, the annexing of judicial procedure within the narrative of black grievances that came to dominate OJ's first trial, enabling his acquittal. OJ's calamitous life has surprises everywhere, from the revelation that his father was gay through to court footage of the hapless defence, in which it was revealed that black female jurors resented OJ's marriage and felt no particular sympathy towards his murdered white wife. Narratives encompassing the wider American picture tend to evoke pathos, but OJ was an opportunist, indifferent to the plight of fellow African Americans. Although the film-maker insisted that he had no social or ideological interest in the OJ story, twenty-one years after the first trial it's clear that nothing much has changed. African Americans are still courted because they are flattering to powerful white men, then thrown away, as OJ was, when he attempted to recuperate some mementoes of his that were being sold in Las Vegas and was tried and finally found guilty, but on a few unconvincing charges. He was corrupted by money and fame, but some splinter of inadequacy in part explains his violence.

The new docs must be crafted, exhaustive and somehow immersive. Andrew Jarecki met David Friedman when the latter was performing as a clown for his children. In this roundabout way, he became aware of the mystery of the Friedman family, from Great Neck, Long Island. Not just David's father Arnold, but also his brother Jesse pleaded guilty to multiple charges of the rape and sexual abuse of young boys. The offences were supposedly committed during computer lessons given in the family's living room, but no evidence was supplied beyond the erratic, often coached testimony of the young computing students. From this raw material and remarkable home videos came Jarecki's *Capturing the Friedmans* (2003), a film rich in ambiguity and uncertainty that also offers a view of banal, suburban, middle-class Long Islander life. It's clear from the beginning that something is very wrong with the Friedmans, but the charges always appear far-fetched. Some of the answer seems to stem from the abused childhood of Arnold, who as a kid had sex with his brother and who now seems permanently remote, absent not just from his family, but from his own life. Encouraged by his wife, he pleads guilty to the charges and later, when it's evident his strategy has failed totally, kills himself in prison. He had intended to spare his son Jesse from similar charges, but when these are brought, he too is encouraged to plead guilty by his mother (against legal advice) and is sent to prison for thirteen years. In the end, many things remain uncertain, and this grounds the film in everyday reality, saving it from joining the run-of-the-mill crime-exploitation programmes on American television. It's clear that Arnold was a paedophile who collected child pornography and had sex with boys, but it's far from certain that he committed the offences of which he was found guilty. Jesse's guilt seems wholly improbable. The film is paced admirably, like a thriller. In his conscious pursuit of ambiguity regarding the Friedmans, with their oddball marriage and strange family rites, Jarecki never loses his compassion for Jesse, who didn't deserve to witness his own life being ruined and who remains a touching, dignified presence, still striving to insist that he never did anything wrong.

Laura Ricciardi and Moira Demos spent ten years between Manhattan and Manitowoc County, Wisconsin, making their first series, *Making a Murderer* (2015). It's clear that they had no expectation that the ten-hour documentary would have the impact that it did, causing hundreds of thousands to petition the White House to secure a pardon for, or at least a retrial of, Steven Avery, its protagonist. Avery spent eighteen years in jail after being convicted of rape. He was freed after DNA evidence incriminating an overlooked suspect came to light. He was later rearrested and found guilty (along with his nephew, in a separate trial) of murdering Teresa Halbach, a photographer who had taken photos for him in the family car-wrecking yard. The film-makers believe that Avery isn't guilty, and their perspective comes from Avery's brilliant defence lawyers, who dominate the investigations and proceedings. More important than whether Avery is or isn't a murderer is what the film painstakingly reveals about the slipshod practice of justice in Wisconsin. The prosecutor and the police were always convinced that Avery was guilty.

They never looked for other suspects. The interrogation of Avery's nephew Brendan was conducted without the presence of a lawyer, and the film shows him being pressured during the interview. (The fourteen-year-old Brendan later withdrew his confession, claiming that his interrogators had given the impression that if he cooperated, he would be allowed to go home.) The judge, too, believed in Avery's guilt, with much time given to Ms Halbach's family, who were understandably convinced of Avery's guilt. It seems unlikely that any jury could have approached the evidence without being affected. The Avery family were outsiders. They weren't liked, and their acres of wrecked cars were considered an eyesore; they were true contemporary outlaws. Prosecutor Ken Kratz played on these local hatreds to a shameless degree, turning the question of individual guilt into a moral crusade. The surface message of the film is that we should be careful how we treat our systems of justice. It's hard not to feel at the end of this 'howdunnit' that the behaviour of the police and the prosecutor was seriously flawed. But the film would be more powerful still if the film-makers had displayed a greater lack of certitude. However, that would most likely have made the film less appealing to those who flocked to Netflix for outsize helpings of true crime. *Making a Murderer* was indeed a combo offering.

This current era of changing tastes can be seen both on the Internet and at film festivals via the rise of short-form docs. I've tried to make shorter films that focus in on single ideas, with audiences seeming to like simple scenes. Some of these films are interesting, and a few of them pack a punch, though with the ever-growing mass of online material, it is hard for viewers to find the truly wonderful ones. Yet the lack of impact that some of them have remains remarkable. It is a new art, and one that is evolving quickly, but so far the attempts by the *Guardian* and the *New York Times* to create short docs don't come up to the standard of the arguments to be found in their written pieces. Short films by NGOs are didactic and similar to the flat and often dull pieces of information found in pamphlets. On sites like YouTube, it appears viewers are looking to each other for innovation, and it is there that the best, most-viewed short docs are to be found. I hope that longer docs will survive, too, if only so that my conservative taste in films continues to be met.

The idea of handing over authorship to those whom you have decided to make a film about is almost as old as the idea of making a documentary. Rarely, however, has it been used to such good effect as in *Exodus: Our Journey to Europe* (2016), an account of the attempts of refugees to get to Europe. Although the filmmakers dutifully distinguish between 'economic migrants' (from poorest Niger via Burkina Faso and shattered Libya) and asylum-seekers (from Syria, but also, less acceptably to the authorities, Afghanistan), they focus rightly on the desperation, courage and ingenuity of newcomers. The film was attacked somewhat predictably for being PC and representing the BBC's soft-touch liberalism. It is so startling because it doesn't treat its subjects as objects of concern. They are genuinely, astonishingly empathetic: one could have watched many news stories featuring boats and near-drownings, or trucks abandoned with their cargoes, and still feel freshly outraged at what these migrants must do to cross borders. Much of the freshness comes from the ingenious use of the phones given to them. Smartphones are GPS-rich, meaning migrants are less likely to get lost; they also allow groups to keep in touch via encrypted technology; and they provide a means for calling the families left behind. But they also provide much of the footage, allowing the viewer to enter trucks as they leave a Danish port for Britain or witness the moment when a character bearing a faked passport is finally allowed onto a plane, which takes off and enters UK air space.

Gracefully filmed, *Last Men in Aleppo* (2017) tracks the efforts of the 'White Helmets' in the wake of Russian and Syrian bombing raids. Culled from hundreds of hours of locally shot footage, Feras Fayyad's masterpiece tells the story of the four-year-long siege of Aleppo through the volunteers who, raid after raid, pull bodies from the wreckage. One can sit through these brutally long takes and get some idea of what it must feel like to be pounded into submission each day, refusing to surrender. The film's heroes, Khaled, Mahmoud and Subhi, are never sentimentalised in their sense of solidarity as they pull out body parts, hiding from those rescued the cruel reality that their loved ones died in the rubble. 'All dignity is dead,' observes the young Mahmoud, crying out at the lack of support from the Arab states and the West. Surely he's right. 'Some people prefer to die than to live in refugee camps,' Ahmed says, 'but Aleppo is my city.' Shortly afterwards, he, too, is buried under the rubble, dead. Meanwhile, *City of Ghosts* (2017), a series of dispatches from Raqqa, tells of the efforts of citizen reporters to expose the civil war and the Isis occupation and murders in Syria. The two films are eloquent and beautiful, not merely a list of atrocities. They are made more painful by the failure of the West to do much in Aleppo, or indeed in the war against Isis. One can respond to them as audiences must have reacted to films of the stricken Spanish republic of the 1930s, or American audiences to the many wrenching depictions of the 1940s London Blitz. 'What do you want us to do?' asked a bemused and shocked member of the audience after the premiere of *Last Men in Aleppo*. I didn't think it was a dumb question. What we choose to do won't, it would seem, depend on our governments, who for the most part are inclined to do nothing in the face of conflict-averse public opinion. But there remain things that we can do, and ruthlessly, stubbornly brave films show us what these might be. Or if that is too complicated, they can simply depict the ways in which human beings endure conflict or are ennobled by it. The very young film-makers were at pains to stress the modesty of their undertaking. No, they didn't wish to supply a message. They aren't dealing with 'policy' towards refugees. Because of these self-imposed limitations, their films will reach more people, 'opening a chink', as the directors Feras Fayyad and Matthew Heineman say.

I watched these three films as if they were the first documentaries I had seen. We don't know what to do about the people striving to come to Europe, but after viewing *Exodus*, we know what they want: to be treated as humans, as the schoolteacher from Aleppo says, speaking in fluent and graceful English that puts our own diffident mumblings on the subject to shame. You could say that the films merely tell us about exile and desperation, but that would be an understatement. What they really say is: 'This is what it means to be human.' What they really ask is: 'What do you mean to do about that?'

There will continue to be big films, and many smaller ones, too. Audiences will find what they want to find. Mostly, what I sensed in what seemed to be a darkening time, filled with danger and resistant to so much of what I believed in, was that one must go back to what was best. 'Simplify and exaggerate,' was what you were told as a young reporter, but I felt that one must dump the second of these injunctions. Stories were what I had watched in doculand, but I'd never been able to figure out what made a story good, and what didn't.

Much of what we think of as analysis is, in fact, narrative. 'Narrative must never violate or embellish truth: it should be its most powerful vehicle,' says journalist Matthew d'Ancona. We live within time, think within the limits of time. Stories have the same relation to truth as the least linear utterances. I'd been drawn to documentaries because they were in every sense partial and provisional. They changed what they described, often magically. No one should ever think that something constructed out of momentarily understood reality, however hard it was worked on, was the last word on anything. And anyhow, who cared about last words? Who needed them? What really mattered were the cracks in everything.

'Mum,' says a teenager soldier in Peter Jackson's *They Shall Not Grow Old* (2018), 'we will be in the pictures!' Carefully lip-synched and colourised for our day, the Tommies look surprised at their on-screen incarnation. Using computer technology, footage made at between ten and eighteen frames per second is converted into twenty-four frames per second, in a documentary described by Mark Kermode in the *Observer* as 'a time machine'. It was almost impossible to take bulky cameras into the trenches, and yet here pale, aghast boys describe a World War I battle – the lice, the ill-cut uniforms, the latrine, the disgusting cold food, card games and shell shock. Blinded after a gas attack, soldiers are seen shaking together; beside the sandbags you can see fearful German fighters. Some one hundred hours of film and six hundred interviews made by the BBC and the Imperial War Museum were viewed and listened to by Jackson and his editors. 'I just wanted to make sure that what we were seeing was real,' he says. The young people were real. You could see that they were real. This is what a documentary can do.

Each year, I'd go to the ramshackle, peeling, beautiful city of Arles, trapped in the midsummer heat by the Rhône. Many of its churches were deconsecrated, the images of the Virgin removed, the godly inscriptions scratched out or replaced with the title of the *arlésien* secular associations that had replaced them. For three months each year, Arles is filled with photographic images. Not all of the vast array of photographs are interesting or momentous, but I was never bored. I found I went to Arles not to keep up with photography so much as to create a fence for myself against literalism, or the associated notion that there was any one way of depicting reality. The city had become a form of purgative. 'Be bold,' the images said. Or a bit less unsubtly: 'Unless you think of things differently, you'll end up in the multiple ruts of cliché.' Arles reminded me that empiricism wasn't everything. Just seeing the facts wasn't enough, though it might indeed get me through the rest of the year. And amid the large-scale retrospectives of well-known photographers, it was the small-scale, accidental discoveries that astonished me most. It was here that I encountered, in different years, the photographs from a Montreal restaurant where clients posed with a piglet; a collection of Germans posing with people in bear suits; and, most remarkably, the people (now extinct) of Tierra del Fuego, who daubed themselves in ochre and whale fat for their fertility rites, and for whom in 1921 a German priest had expressed such love that, in the style of an early Werner Herzog, he ended up not just commemorating the tribespeople, but entering their rituals.

Many of the Arles exhibits were crowded into giant, super-seded wrecks of SNCF railway workshops, and amid these half-ruins I came face to face with a screen on which images of a procession of workers coming out of a primitive factory were projected. They were hurrying, so this was most probably the end of a day, and they were dressed in a variety of outfits, some *soigné*, others close to rags. There were young girls and boys, busty women, skinny old men, and one could see clogs as well as shoes. No one, I noticed, looked at the camera. People hadn't been posed or directed, but they told their own stories. Watching them, you could want to enter their lives. I thought of the num-ber of times I'd watched documentaries in this way, looking not just for clues, but for something that would allow me to enter the lives momentarily before me. I watched the five-minute-long film three times, and I'm not sure when I realised that I was looking at the first experiment in filming photographic reality, made by the Lumière brothers in 1895.

In an adjacent shed were rows of chairs in front of three huge screens. Out of the darkness came the title, *More Sweetly Play the Dance*, by William Kentridge, and then another procession, shuffling slowly in time to a mix of fanfares, military music, funeral dirges, noises off and half-lost syncopations of post-apocalypse. Within the procession one could make out various figures. People held up trees or IV drips, or old firearms. There were huge tubas, a typist and an orchestra, a strutting military man and skeletons. Some of the figures were photographed from life; others came out of Kentridge's drawings. It was not easy, and surely misguided, to want to distinguish between the two. The procession, much like the Lumières' one, was radiantly real. Like all of Kentridge's films, the context was recognisably African

– the allusions to AIDS, starvation, dictators, etc. wouldn't be missed even by the least attentive. But it was possible to strip out the more obvious allusions and be witness to something different. It was the way that these figures slouched or tried to strut, the way they seemed called out of the sequence in which they existed for us, that stayed with me. I'd seen many of Kentridge's films, in which he recreated the brute capitalist past of his native city, Johannesburg, through the actions of the Jewish businessmen Soho Eckstein and Felix Teitlebaum; but this was somehow bigger, not just in scale, and it was less specific in its borrowings, dark and wholly truthful. You could enter these scenes, bringing to them whatever questions you had, and you might get an answer. I remembered how Donn Pennebaker had said that he was a watcher. Watching was what we had to do, and I watched. 'Pay attention,' I said to myself. And I did.

I watched what happened.

Afterword

British doctor Henry Marsh at work in Ukraine in *The English Surgeon* (Geoffrey Smith, 2007).

In the midst of writing this book, I was asked to do a talk in London about documentaries. In the audience were some Turkish film-makers. They wanted to make documentaries, but their government would not allow it. Freedom in Turkey was extremely limited; you really couldn't say what you wanted. Another member of the audience asked about the merits of making depressing films: could a film be both upsetting and entertaining? In response, I showed a clip from a film about brain surgery in Ukraine, *The English Surgeon* (2007), in which the British doctor Henry Marsh explains the perils of an upcoming operation to a patient. The film is tough, but the lives of the patients and the treatments they receive are engrossing, not at all depressing. Mid-sentence, I myself had a stroke. Suddenly, the world didn't make sense and I couldn't communicate any more. Throughout it all, I could see the footage from *The English Surgeon*. It really is one of the best films I have ever watched.

100 Docs

Nanook of the North (1922), Robert J. Flaherty
A portrait of Inuit people in northern Quebec.

Man with a Movie Camera (1929), Dziga Vertov
Avant-garde documentary set in the USSR.

Rain (1929), Joris Ivens, Mannus Franken
A rainstorm disrupts Amsterdam.

Man of Aran (1934), Robert J. Flaherty
An ethno-fictional portrait of pre-modern life in the Aran Islands.

Night Mail (1936), Basil Wright, Harry Watt
Follows the Postal Special train across scenic Britain.

Inside Nazi Germany (1938), Jack Glenn
A journalistic exposition of Nazi Germany.

Fires Were Started (1943), Humphrey Jennings
Propagandist docudrama about Britain's firefighters during the Blitz.

Moi, un noir (1958), Jean Rouch
A portrait of poor Nigerien migrants in Abidjan.

Chronicle of a Summer (1961), Jean Rouch, Edgar Morin
An exploration of French society in Paris and St Tropez.

Crisis: Behind a Presidential Commitment (1963), Robert Drew
Cinéma vérité exploring the University of Alabama's integration crisis.

Up (series, 1964–present), Michael Apted, Paul Almond
Follows the lives of fourteen British children from diverse cultural and
socio-economic backgrounds.

The War Game (1965), Peter Watkins
Fictional drama about a Soviet nuclear attack on Britain.

Titicut Follies (1967), Frederick Wiseman
Patient inmates suffer in a facility for the criminally insane.

The Sorrow and the Pity (1969), Marcel Ophüls
The Vichy government's collaboration with Nazi Germany during World
War II.

Phantom India (1969), Louis Malle
Malle documents his travels across India.

Salesman (1969), Albert Maysles, David Maysles, Charlotte Zwerin
Rivalries between four door-to-door Bible salesmen in small-town
America.

Gimme Shelter (1970), Albert Maysles, David Maysles, Charlotte Zwerin
The Rolling Stones at the tragic Altamont free concert.

World at War (1973), Jeremy Isaacs
Series chronicling World War II.

General Idi Amin Dada: A Self Portrait (1974), Barbet Schroeder
Auto-portrait of the infamous Ugandan dictator.

Grey Gardens (1975), Albert Maysles, Ellen Hovde, Muffie Meyer,
David Maysles
Mother and daughter reminisce on their decrepit Hamptons estate.

Cracked Actor (1975), Alan Yentob
David Bowie looks back on his Ziggy Stardust persona.

The Battle of Chile (1975), Patricio Guzmán
The 1973 military coup to overthrow Chile's government.

Welfare (1975), Frederick Wiseman
Profile of the welfare system.

The Memory of Justice (1976), Marcel Ophüls
War atrocities committed by the Nazis, the French in Algeria and
Americans in Vietnam.

Harlan County, USA (1976), Barbara Kopple
Labour strikes in rural Kentucky's coal-mining industry.

Decision: British Communism (1978), Roger Graef
British communism and democracy.

Town Bloody Hall (1979), D. A. Pennebaker, Chris Hegedus
Norman Mailer debates with four feminists.

The Orson Welles Story (1982), Alan Yentob
A look at his life and career in theatre, radio and film.

Sans Soleil (1982), Chris Marker
Experimental film on memory, technology and society.

Police (1982), Roger Graef
A year-long insight into the running of a British police department.

Shoah (1985), Claude Lanzmann
Interviews with Holocaust survivors, bystanders and perpetrators.

Sherman's March (1986), Ross McElwee
Autobiographical reflections on love, life and religion.

Eyes on the Prize (1987), Henry Hampton
Follows the American civil rights movement.

The Emperor's Naked Army Marches On (1987), Kazuo Hara
A Japanese World War II veteran searches for answers regarding the
other men of his unit.

The Thin Blue Line (1988), Errol Morris
A man is wrongfully convicted of murder by a corrupt justice system.

Paris Is Burning (1990), Jennie Livingston
New York's 1980s drag scene.

Hearts of Darkness: A Filmmaker's Apocalypse (1991), Werner Herzog
Behind the scenes of one of Hollywood's most acclaimed films.

Serbian Epics (1992), Paweł Pawlikowski
A fresh look at the Bosnian war.

The War Room (1993), D. A. Pennebaker, Chris Hegedus
Follows part of Bill Clinton's 1992 presidential campaign.

Crumb (1994), Terry Zwigoff
An intimate portrait of underground cartoonist Robert Crumb.

Hoop Dreams (1994), Steve James
Two boys from inner-city Chicago dream of playing professional basketball.

The Death of Yugoslavia (1995), Norma Percy
The fall of the Yugoslav state in the 1990s.

The Burger and the King (1995), James Marsh
Insight into Elvis Presley's favourite meals and love for food.

When We Were Kings (1996), Leon Gast
Delves into the 'Rumble in the Jungle' and its political context.

Nobody's Business (1996), Alan Berliner
An intimate look into personality and family.

Paradise Lost: The Child Murders at Robin Hood Hills (1996), Joe
Berlinger, Bruce Sinofsky
The trials of three teenage boys accused of murder.

Little Dieter Needs to Fly (1997), Werner Herzog
US pilot Dieter Dengler tells the story of his capture and escape during
the Vietnam War.

Wednesday (1997), Viktor Kossakovsky
Everyday life in St Petersburg.

McLibel (1997), Franny Armstrong, Ken Loach
The McDonald's Corporation's lawsuit against two members of Greenpeace.

Divorce Iranian Style (1998), Kim Longinotto
Three Iranian couples go through divorce in the Islamic republic.

One Day in September (1999), Kevin Macdonald
An extremist Palestinian group holds Israelis hostage at the Munich Olympics.

Gulag (1999), Angus MacQueen
The story of Stalinist labour camps.

A Cry from the Grave (1999), Leslie Woodhead
The story of the Srebrenica massacre of 1995.

The Gleaners and I (2000), Agnès Varda
The history of gleaning.

The Natural History of the Chicken (2000), Mark Lewis
A quirky, comprehensive look at poultry.

Southern Comfort (2001), Kate Davis
A transgender man spends his final days with his loved ones.

Bus 174 (2002), José Padilha
Socio-economic inequality in the context of a Brazilian hostage crisis.

Bowling for Columbine (2002), Michael Moore
The proliferation of guns and homicide in America.

My Architect (2003), Nathaniel Kahn
An estranged son's quest to understand his father through his architectural legacy.

Capturing the Friedmans (2003), Andrew Jarecki
A middle-class family whose father and son were charged with child molestation.

Aileen: The Life and Death of a Serial Killer (2003), Nick Broomfield, Joan Churchill
Follow-up piece to a documentary about a drifter convicted of killing six men.

Citizen King (2004), Orlando Bagwell, Noland Walker
Follows Martin Luther King through the turbulence of his final five years.

Guerrilla: The Taking of Patty Hearst (2004), Robert Stone
An American terrorist group kidnap and recruit a newspaper magnate's granddaughter.

Why We Fight (2005), Eugene Jarecki
The expansion of the American military industry following World War II.

Grizzly Man (2005), Werner Herzog
The life and death of bear enthusiast Timothy Treadwell.

Enron: The Smartest Guys in the Room (2005), Alex Gibney
The fall of Enron, a corporation known for its corruption scandals.

The English Surgeon (2007), Geoffrey Smith
British brain surgeon Henry Marsh travels to Ukraine to operate on poor patients for free.

Please Vote for Me (2007), Weijun Chen
Chinese third-graders learn about democracy as they elect their class monitor.

Taxi to the Dark Side (2007), Alex Gibney
Details the US's use of torture in the war on terror.

Waltz with Bashir (2008), Ari Folman
Animated documentary on the Sabra and Shatila massacre of 1982 in Beirut.

Man on Wire (2008), James Marsh
Philippe Petit performs acrobatics on a wire strung between the World Trade Center's Twin Towers.

Petition (2009), Zhao Liang
Documents the Chinese government's oppression of petitioners.

Enemies of the People (2009), Thet Sambath, Rob Lemkin
A decade-long quest for answers on the Cambodian genocide.

The Red Chapel (2009), Mads Brügger
Disguised as a vaudeville act, two comedians travel to North Korea to ridicule its oppressive regime.

The Arbor (2010), Clio Barnard
A mix of documentary and fiction telling the story of playwright Andrea Dunbar.

Project Nim (2011), James Marsh
A chimpanzee is raised like a human child by a family in New York's Upper West Side in the 1970s.

Knuckle (2011), Ian Palmer
Two feuding Irish families settle their conflict through bare-knuckle boxing.

Five Broken Cameras (2011), Emad Burnat, Guy Davidi
Palestinian Emad Burnat documents his village's resistance to the expansion of Israeli settlements.

Dreams of a Life (2011), Carol Morley
The life of Joyce Vincent, left in her home for three years following her death.

Stories We Tell (2012), Sarah Polley
Film-maker Sarah Polley investigates the truth behind her family history.

The Gatekeepers (2012), Dror Moreh
Six heads of the Israeli secret service discuss their successes and failures since the Six Day War.

Searching for Sugar Man (2012), Malik Bendjelloul
Two fans search for Sixto Rodriguez, a faded American musician who was a hit in 1970s South Africa.

Blackfish (2013), Gabriela Cowperthwaite
An examination of the deeply flawed oceanic theme park industry.

Muscle Shoals (2013), Greg 'Freddy' Camalier
A celebration of the legendary Alabama city that holds an iconic place in music history.

Brakeless (2014), Kyoko Miyake
Explores Japan's worst-ever train crash.

India's Daughter (2015), Leslee Udwin
Examines Indian society in the wake of a young woman's brutal gang rape and murder on a bus.

A Syrian Love Story (2015), Sean McAllister
The twenty-year love story of two Syrian revolutionaries who met in a prison cell.

The Show of Shows (2015), Benedikt Erlingsson
Using never-seen-before footage, the film looks back at circus acts and fairground attractions.

Cartel Land (2015), Matthew Heineman
The world of drug trafficking along the Mexico–US border.

Going Clear (2015), Alex Gibney
The abuses and bizarre practices of the Church of Scientology.

Bitter Lake (2015), Adam Curtis
The US and its role in the war in Afghanistan.

The Chinese Mayor (2015), Zhou Hao
A Chinese mayor adopts a radical approach to happily destroy a polluted city.

OJ: Made in America (2016), Ezra Edelman
American racial tensions in the context of O. J. Simpson's high-profile murder trial.

I Am Not Your Negro (2016), Raoul Peck
An analysis of race relations in America, based on an unfinished James Baldwin manuscript.

Exodus: Our Journey to Europe (2016), James Bluemel
A portrait of some of the million-plus people smuggled into Europe in 2015.

Bobby Sands: 66 Days (2016), Brendan J. Byrne
IRA volunteer Bobby Sands's hunger strike, which drew international attention in 1981.

Hospital (2017), BBC
Chronicles the NHS as it operates in turbulent times.

Last Men in Aleppo (2017), Firas Fayyad
The 'White Helmets' care for the wounded in the Syrian civil war.

The Patriot (2017), Daniel Sivan
A militant Zionist hacker declares a one-man war against anti-Semitism.

They Shall Not Grow Old (2018), Peter Jackson
Colourised archive synched with audio of Tommies fighting in World War I.

Sources

CHAPTER 1

18 'Vietnam drove a stake in the heart of this country', Ken Burns and Lynn Novick, *The Vietnam War*, prod. Florentine Films, WETA (2017)

19 'If the film seems like an epic of fiction', David Thomson, 'Merely an Empire', *London Review of Books*, 21 September 2017

20 'Documentaries are traditionally advocates', Ian Parker, 'Ken Burns's American Canon', *New Yorker*, 2 September 2017

21 'Only a stone would not have been terrified' ... 'the dead Marine zone', Ken Burns and Lynn Novick, *The Vietnam War*, prod. Florentine Films, WETA (2017)

30 'Memory fills the holes with things', Ari Folman and Bridgit Folman, *Waltz with Bashir*, prod. Film Gang, Les Films d'Ici, Razor Film Produktion (2008)

32 'Stories are what we tell to keep ourselves alive', Sarah Polley, *Stories We Tell*, prod. National Film Board of Canada (2012)

32 'Anything I want to say myself', Sarah Polley, 'Stories We Tell', blog.nfb.ca/blog/2012/08/29/stories-we-tell-a-post-by-sarah-polley

33 'It's seven hours too long', Noah Baumbach, *While We're Young*, prod. Scott Rudin Productions (2014)

39 'Yet why not say what happened?' Robert Lowell, 'Epilogue', *Day by Day* (Farrar, Straus and Giroux, 1977)

42 'Think about it', Nigel Andrews, 'Startling Truths Born of Artifice', *Financial Times*, 29 December 2010

CHAPTER 2

66 'Surgery's a blood sport', Geoffrey Smith, *The English Surgeon*, prod. Geoffrey Smith and Rachel Wexler (2007)

70 'You can't be both Che Guevara and a mother' ... 'Does it make you want to leave?' Sean McAllister, *Syrian Love Story*, prod. Sean McAllister and Elhum Shakerifar (2015)

CHAPTER 3

85 'The films were not an illusion', Mark Cousins and Kevin Macdonald, *Imagining Reality* (Faber & Faber, 2006), p. 4

89 'Our eyes see very little and very badly', Dziga Vertov, 'Provisional Instructions to Kino-Eye Groups', *Kino-Eye: The Writings of Dziga Vertov* (University of California Press, 1992)

91 'Caroline suddenly realised', Gore Vidal, *Hollywood* (Penguin Random House, 1989), p. 417

92 'A revolution is taking place', Walter Lippmann, *Public Opinion* (1922), Chapter XV

95 'der Englander', Leni Riefenstahl, *Olympia*, prod. Olympia-Film (1938)

96 'I don't need doubt', Hans Schnoots, *Living Dangerously: A Biography of Joris Ivens* (Amsterdam University Press, 1995), p. 72

99 'I cursed them now and then', ibid., p. 62

103 'Asleep in working Glasgow', W. H. Auden, from *Night Mail* documentary, prod. BFI (1936)

104 'Documentary represented a reaction', Jack C. Ellis, *John Grierson* (Southern Illinois University Press, 2000), pp. 82–3

105 'I am not going to pretend', Peter Morris, 'Rethinking Grierson: The Ideology of John Grierson', in T. O'Regan and B. Shoesmith (eds), *History on/and/in Film* (History & Film Association of Australia, 1987), pp. 20–30

105 'There was no question where one's duty lay', Mark Cousins and Kevin Macdonald, *Imagining Reality*, p. 96

106 'There's nothing like the camera for getting around', ibid., p. 97

109 'Are you going to have greed', Humphrey Jennings, *A Diary for Timothy*, prod. BFI (1945)

112 'Many of the film-makers', Denis Forman, *Persona Granada* (Andre Deutsch, 1997), p. 19

CHAPTER 4

117 'Startlingly different backgrounds' . . . 'Give me a child for the first seven years', Paul Almond and Michael Apted, *Up* series, prod. Granada (1964–present)

122 'If one looks deep and long into this picture', Emma Hanna, 'A Small Screen Alternative to Stone and Bronze: The *Great War* Series and British Television', *European Journal of Cultural Studies* (February 2007), p. 103

123 'I am sick to death of being told', ibid., p. 105

124 'as an officer and a general', *The Great War*, BBC TV, Imperial War Museum, Canadian Broadcasting Corporation, Australian Broadcasting Commission (1964)

127 'should have a realistic idea', James Chapman, 'The BBC and the Censorship of *The War Game*', *Journal of Contemporary History*, vol. 41, no. 1 (January 2006), pp. 75–94

127 '*The War Game* is the most important film', Jack G. Shaheen, '*The War Game* Revisited', *Journal of Popular Film*, vol. 1, no. 4 (1972), pp. 299–308

132 'The mid-sixties was, in my recollection', Robert Hughes, *Things I Didn't Know* (Harvill Secker, 2006), p. 323

135 There is more meaning', *Life on Earth*, BBC Natural History Unit, Warner Bros., Reiner Moritz Productions (1979)

137 'millions of British television viewers sat down', Peter Dale, personal communication

142 'Initially, the public will love seeing', Hannah Lazatin, 'Inside the Controversial Royal Family Documentary the Queen Hid from the World', *Town and Country*, 11 February 2018, www.townandcountry.ph/people/heritage/the-controversial-royal-family-documentary-a00184-20180211

CHAPTER 5

155 'It's what I dislike about so many documentaries', Philip French (ed.), *Malle on Malle* (Faber & Faber, 1993), p. 73

CHAPTER 6

170 'a millionaire, Catholic and Easterner', Robert Drew, *Primary*, prod. Robert Drew (1960)

174 'How could I answer that' . . . 'If I'm going to find out anything' . . . 'What is really the truth?' D. A. Pennebaker, *Don't Look Back*, prod. D. A. Pennebaker and C. Hegedus (1967)

175 'Bad news, bad news came to me where I sleep', 'Percy's Song', Bob Dylan (1963), in *Don't Look Back*, ibid.

176 'The world isn't that depressing', D. A. Pennebaker, personal communication

178 'For one reason and another', Vincent Canby, 'Screen: "Salesman," a Slice of America', *New York Times*, 18 April 1969

179 'Father's work' . . . 'I don't want to seem negative', Albert Maysles, David Maysles and Charlotte Zwerin, *Salesman*, prod. Maysles Films Inc. (1969)

182 'It's very hard to live nowadays', Albert Maysles, Ellen Hovde, Muffie Meyer and David Maysles, *Grey Gardens*, prod. Portrait Films (1975)

Sources

183 'I tell you, if there's anything worse', ibid.

186 'I have to constantly ask myself', Lola Peploe, 'Frederick Wiseman, The Art of Documentary No. 1', *Paris Review*, issue 226, fall 2018

186 'The film has to work for me on a literal level', Mary Hawthorne, 'The Exchange: Frederick Wiseman', *New Yorker*, 16 January 2011

189 'Shit isn't important', Frederick Wiseman, *Titicut Follies*, prod. Zipporah Films (1967)

191 'It's nice to be individualistic', Frederick Wiseman, *High School*, prod. Frederick Wiseman (1968)

195 'We're not, we're not giving', Frederick Wiseman, *Welfare*, prod. Frederick Wiseman (1975)

196 'in a war that had nothing to do with me' ... 'I'll wait. I've been waiting', ibid.

CHAPTER 7

204 'Before we despair at the calamities', Alain de Botton, *The News: A User's Manual* (Penguin, 2014), p. 44

207 'Talk sometimes dies when it's seen', Charles Wertenbaker, 'Edward R. Murrow: The World on His Back', *New Yorker*, 26 December 1953

213 'Part of its success was owed to', Denis Forman, *Persona Granada*, p. 169

215 'In those days of innocence', Nicholas Wright, *The Reporter* (Nick Hern Books, 2007), p. 7

221 'It opened me up as a person', Nick Broomfield, personal communication

222 'Documentaries felt like medicine', Michael Moore, *Here Comes Trouble: Stories from My Life* (Grand Central Publishing, 2011), p. 399

223 'Mr Smith, we just came down from Flint', Michael Moore, *Roger and Me*, prod. Dog Eat Dog Films (1989)

225 'shallow and facetious', Pauline Kael, 'Review of *Roger & Me*', *New Yorker*, 8 January 1990

225 'The film is so flat out phony', Christopher Hitchens, 'Unfairenheit 9/11: The Lies of Michael Moore', *Slate*, 21 June 2004

227 'every beaten-down stiff and forgotten worker', Michael Moore, *Michael Moore in Trumpland*, Dog Eat Dog Films (2016)

232 'I remember thinking at a very early stage', Torin Douglas, Sue Lloyd-Roberts obituary, *Guardian*, 14 October 2015

233 'I want to record world events', the Tim Hetherington Trust, www.timhetheringtontrust.org/

CHAPTER 8

237 'Tell him to come down to the Serbs', Leslie Woodhead, *A Cry from the Grave*, prod. Leslie Woodhead (1999)

237 'I was too late', Albert Camus, *The Fall* (Penguin Books, 1965), p. 52

239 'At that moment, you have no brains left', Leslie Woodhead, *A Cry from the Grave*, prod. Leslie Woodhead (1999)

243 'A dog run over by a car', Arthur Koestler, 'On Disbelieving Atrocities', *New York Times* magazine, January 1944

246 'In the spring of 1945', Sidney Bernstein, *German Concentration Camps Factual Survey*, prod. Psychological Warfare Division, SHAEF (2014)

248 'Who is going to warn us', Alain Resnais, *Night and Fog*, prod. Argos Films (1955)

249 'loved the veil that Simone cast', Claude Lanzmann, *The Patagonian Hare: A Memoir* (Gallimard, 2009, and Atlantic Books and Farrar, Straus and Giroux, 2009), p. 215

253 'told that Israeli audience watching', Jonathan Freedland, 'The Day Israel Saw *Shoah*', *Guardian*, 10 December 2015

257 'I can't. It's too horrible. Please', Claude Lanzmann, *Shoah*, prod. BBC, Historia, Les Films Aleph, Ministère de la Culture de la République Française, PBS (1985)

261 'We are all dead here', László Nemes, *Son of Saul*, prod. Hungarian National Film Fund, Laokoon Film Arts, Laokoon Filmgroup (2015)

CHAPTER 9

266 'I don't think you have to make a mark', Jennie Livingston, *Paris Is Burning*, prod. Academy Entertainment, Off White Productions (1990)

268 'my cross-dressing days' . . . 'Younger guys', Kate Davis, *Southern Comfort*, prod. Kate Davis (2001)

275 'Do you all wonder how I am living?' Steve James, *Hoop Dreams*, prod. Kartemquin Films (1994)

281 'I'm proud of what I did', Kevin Macdonald, *One Day in September*, prod. BBC Films, Passion Pictures (1999)

289 'Nothingness mattered to him', Nathaniel Kahn, *My Architect*, prod. Nathaniel Kahn and Susan Rose Behr (2003)

292 'Do you ever get bored?' Werner Herzog, *A Guide for the Perplexed, Conversations with Paul Cronin* (Faber and Faber, 2014), p. 13

293 'The art of lock picking', Werner Herzog, Rogue Film School, www.roguefilmschool.com

297 'If so much is invented', Ian Buruma, *Theater of Cruelty: Art, Film, and the Shadows of War* (NYRB Collections, 2014), p. 43

298 'Here I differ from Treadwell', Werner Herzog, *Grizzly Man*, prod. Discovery Docs, Real Big Production (2005)

300 'We never discussed should we be doing this', Robert Stone, *Guerrilla, the Taking of Patty Hearst*, prod. PBS (2004)

301 'I think there's a new enemy out there', Werner Herzog in conversation at Brandeis University, 2011, www.openculture.com/2011/06/errol_morris_and_werner_herzog_in_conversation

305 'Lesson #11: You can't change human nature', Errol Morris, *The Fog of War*, prod. Sony Pictures Classics (2004)

308 '"Documentary" is one of the fallacies', David Thomson, 'Donald Rumsfeld Is Finally Under Interrogation', *New Republic*, 11 October 2013

310 'We set the camera up', Katharine Viner, 'Adam Curtis: Have Computers Taken Away Our Power?' *Guardian*, 6 May 2011

313 'Increasingly . . . we live in a world', Adam Curtis, *Bitter Lake*, prod. BBC (2015)

CHAPTER 10

321 'Treat Africa as if it were one country', Binyavanga Wainaina, 'How to Write About Africa', *Granta*, 19 January 2006

329 'The rabbit goes underground', Dror Moreh, *The Gatekeepers*, prod. Estelle Fialon, Philippa Kowarsky and Dror Moreh (2012)

333 'When you're working in China', Edward Wong, 'Chinese Director's Path from Rebel to Insider', *New York Times*, 13 August 2011

CHAPTER 11

350 'Each one of us is a cause', Davis Guggenheim, *An Inconvenient Truth*, prod. Lawrence Bender Productions, Participant Productions (2006)

365 'Some people prefer to die', Feras Fayyad, *Last Men in Aleppo*, prod. Feras Fayyad, Kareem Abeed and Soeren Steen Jespersen (2017)

Index